Prisons in the United States

Recent Titles in the
CONTEMPORARY WORLD ISSUES
Series

Global Pandemic Threats: A Reference Handbook
Michael C. LeMay

Same-Sex Marriage: A Reference Handbook, second edition
David E. Newton

DNA Technology: A Reference Handbook, second edition
David E. Newton

Modern Sport Ethics: A Reference Handbook, second edition
Angela Lumpkin

Marijuana: A Reference Handbook, second edition
David E. Newton

Gun Control in the United States: A Reference Handbook, second edition
Gregg Lee Carter

The Right to Die: A Reference Handbook
Howard Ball

Student Debt: A Reference Handbook
William Elliott III and Melinda K. Lewis

Food Safety: A Reference Handbook, third edition
Nina E. Redman and Michele Morrone

Human Trafficking: A Reference Handbook
Alexis A. Aronowitz

Social Media: A Reference Handbook
Kelli S. Burns

Books in the **Contemporary World Issues** series address vital issues in today's society such as genetic engineering, pollution, and biodiversity. Written by professional writers, scholars, and nonacademic experts, these books are authoritative, clearly written, up-to-date, and objective. They provide a good starting point for research by high school and college students, scholars, and general readers as well as by legislators, businesspeople, activists, and others.

Each book, carefully organized and easy to use, contains an overview of the subject, a detailed chronology, biographical sketches, facts and data and/or documents and other primary source material, a forum of authoritative perspective essays, annotated lists of print and nonprint resources, and an index.

Readers of books in the Contemporary World Issues series will find the information they need in order to have a better understanding of the social, political, environmental, and economic issues facing the world today.

Prisons in the United States

A REFERENCE HANDBOOK

Cyndi Banks

An Imprint of ABC-CLIO, LLC
Santa Barbara, California • Denver, Colorado

Library of Congress Cataloging-in-Publication Data

Prisons in the United States

Library of Congress Cataloging-in-Publication Control Number: 2016053853

ISBN: 978-1-4408-4437-9
EISBN: 978-1-4408-4438-6

21 20 19 18 17   1 2 3 4 5

This book is also available as an eBook.

ABC-CLIO
An Imprint of ABC-CLIO, LLC

ABC-CLIO, LLC
130 Cremona Drive, P.O. Box 1911
Santa Barbara, California 93116–1911
www.abc-clio.com

This book is printed on acid-free paper ∞
Manufactured in the United States of America

The punishment of imprisonment is today a "taken-for-granted" element of the criminal justice system in the United States. However, as this book explains, at one time in our history, imprisonment in its modern form did not exist. Punishments were public affairs intended to shame and disgrace offenders, and depriving a person of liberty by imprisonment for an extended period was inconceivable. While prisons did exist, they were not used to incarcerate offenders for lengthy periods but to punish debtors and hold those awaiting trial in custody. Over time the nature of punishments in the West began to change, and in the United States, the transformative event was the birth of the penitentiary. The penitentiary was a distinctly American notion even though Europeans were the first to impose a term of imprisonment as a punishment. Following the creation of the penitentiary in the United States, Europeans visited to view its forbidding architecture and inspect its disciplinary regime based on silence, isolation, and forced labor. In all countries prisons and penitentiaries became the new instruments of punishment as public punishment replaced punishment in private and captivity supplanted freedom and liberty.

In Chapters 1 and 2, this book discusses prisons in the United States, their history, and the controversies and issues that challenge them today. The complexity of the historical account of the birth and development of the prison raises questions about why prisons came about in the United States. Did the

United States merely follow the logic of history, adopt existing European practice, and relocate punishments inside the walls of a prison, or were prisons in the United States created to control the "dangerous classes" of unruly populations because they were considered to be a threat to the power of elites? The historical account discusses these and other theories.

The original concept of incarceration claimed that isolation, hard labor, and a regime of silence would cause a prisoner to reflect on his or her sins and reach a redemptive state of mind; in modern times, this is the notion of rehabilitation. Questions persist about how to achieve rehabilitation and reduce recidivism. Is rehabilitation a viable project, or has it been completely supplanted by incapacitation (i.e., simply locking up offenders until their sentence is completed, or, if sentenced to life imprisonment without parole, imprisoning them until their death)? Prisons and incarceration will continue to raise important policy and ethical issues.

Several themes emerge from this book about U.S. prisons. First, until the 1970s, the prison population was relatively stable and not subject to any large increases or decreases. However, since then, as a result of a host of complex factors that included hardening public attitudes to crime and criminals, changes in criminal justice policies, and a punitive approach to punishment urged by political interests, the nation has experienced increasing incarceration rates that have given the United States the world's highest rate of incarceration.

Second, and congruent with the advent of punitive punishment policies, the notion of rehabilitating offenders has been eroded, if not completely supplanted, by theories of incapacitation and retribution. These theories hold that prisoners should receive lengthy sentences for their crimes and should be locked away without any substantive attempt to rehabilitate them. This approach satisfies the goal of exacting retribution for the offense committed and ensures that an offender will not re-offend for as long as he or she is incarcerated. Recently, a focus on the need for reentry programs toward the end of a sentence seems to have replaced the notion that rehabilitation is an ongoing process (beginning from entry into prison) that can also contribute to a successful reentry.

Third, following changes in the law resulting from punitive attitudes to offenders, prisons have reduced inmate amenities. Fewer amenities to keep prisoners occupied has meant fewer privileges that can be revoked for bad behavior. It has also produced a regime under which prisoners are largely idle throughout their sentences. It is unlikely that these conditions contribute to a successful reentry into the community at the conclusion of a sentence of imprisonment.

Fourth, history has repeated itself as the level of security known as maximum security has been augmented with a yet higher level of security—the super-maximum security prison or supermax. Supermax conditions stipulate virtually total isolation from human interaction over many years of incarceration. The supermax project recalls the strict isolation and silence of the early penitentiary. Only recently have these practices been questioned for their adverse psychological effects.

A final theme is the gradual professionalism of prison systems as daily decision making and the exercise of powers over inmates became regulated by complex rules that rendered prison systems bureaucracies to be managed. Professionalism was intended to replace arbitrary administrative decision making and eliminate staff-on-inmate violence and other abuses of power. Evidence suggests, however, that some prison systems continue to operate harsh and punitive regimes that lack accountability. In private prisons, constructed and managed to meet the unceasing need for more prison beds, reports have revealed a significant lack of professionalism. There is now a growing realization that the model of a private prison operating for profit is flawed both morally and organizationally.

The modern prison is a legacy of the prisons and penitentiaries that faced their own time-bound challenges. Prison reforms responded to those past challenges by measures such as improving prison conditions, eliminating rules that required inmates to be silent always, and ceasing the practice of whipping inmates for disciplinary infractions. However, correctional systems then faced a new set of challenges. These are discussed in Chapter 2, and many relate to problems caused by prison overcrowding and harsh prison conditions, especially those experienced in supermax segregation, as well as issues associated with inmates' physical and mental health. Correctional officers argue that the stress they suffer from the prison environment has been exacerbated by overcrowding and a deficit of staff and resources.

Chapter 3 presents perspectives on prisons that offer a range of views about aspects of incarceration. Other chapters provide appropriate and valuable reference materials that add context to the overall discussion, including a chronology of events, a resource inventory, and a glossary of terms. Overall, therefore, this book comprehensively addresses the topic of prisons in the United States and provides an indispensable resource for students and others. Those who wish to undertake a deeper study of prisons will find this text a useful starting point and guide.

Prisons in the United States

U.S. correctional systems are commonly divided both organizationally and functionally into two categories: corrections that take the form of *institutions* and corrections that are regarded as *community corrections*. The former includes jails and prisons (termed "correctional facilities") and other detention facilities, such as those holding persons detained for immigration violations. The community corrections category represents a wide range of non-custodial punishments, including probation, parole, home detention, electronic monitoring, community service, and forms of residential treatment programs such as those for drug abuse (Gillespie 2004: 17). This text, being a reference book on prisons in the United States, does not engage in any substantive discussion of jails, juvenile institutions, and other detention facilities, or with community corrections.

A prison may be either a *state* or *federal* facility. The 2005 Census of State and Federal Correctional Facilities (Stephan 2008) reveals that on December 30, 2005, there were 1,719 state correctional facilities and 102 federal facilities, an increase of 9 percent in the number of state facilities and 21 percent in the number of federal facilities since 2000.

The *federal corrections system* is operated by the Federal Bureau of Prisons, which was established in 1930, and is part

---

A view of the penitentiary complex and central guard tower of Eastern State Penitentiary in Philadelphia, Pennsylvania. Eastern State was a part of the Pennsylvania system, where inmates spent the majority of their sentences in solitary confinement. (Library of Congress)

of the Department of Justice. Federal prisoners are persons convicted of federal crimes. *State corrections systems* are operated by the states usually under a commissioner of corrections appointed by the governor. Inmates in state prisons are persons convicted of offenses against state criminal laws.

Prisons have two goals: *custody* and *treatment*. Correctional administrators and officers generally give more effect to custody than to treatment. Custody means the legal and physical control of inmates, and treatment relates to the conditions that are associated with a person's criminality.

Generally, there are three *levels of security applied to prisons*: minimum, medium, and maximum, but within maximum security prisons are separate facilities known as super-maximum or "supermax" prisons or units, however described. On December 30, 2005 (the most recent data available), there were 372 maximum security facilities, 480 medium security facilities, and 969 minimum security facilities (Stephan 2008: 2).

Generally, criminal punishment is justified as serving one or more of four purposes: *rehabilitation, deterrence, retribution*, or *incapacitation*. Current data on imprisonment shows that the dominant purpose is incapacitation. However, the historical account of imprisonment shows that at different times other purposes have been paramount.

History of the Prison

The dominant narrative of the history of the prison in the United States begins with traditional physical and shaming punishments in the colonial period and the creation of jails and local prisons, followed by the birth of the reformist penitentiary and its decline, then by the creation of male and female reformatories and finally by the modern professionalized prison system. These changes, as well as gender and incarceration and the racial dynamics associated with imprisonment, will be explored and contextualized according to ideologies, beliefs, and assumptions of the times and the social, economic, and cultural settings.

The institution of the prison as a place of imprisonment emerged through a complex historical process. At one time, the prevailing narrative of penal history was of one steady improvement and transformation instigated by benevolent reformers. However, in the 1970s revisionist historians deconstructed that narrative and reoriented the study of penality toward issues of punishment and social control, the social and economic context of change, and the study of associated carceral institutions like workhouses and asylums (Spierenberg 2007: 1). For example, David Rothman, in his study of the development of the prison (1990), shows how in the United States the movement to incarcerate offenders was linked to the use of workhouses and asylums. In England, Europe, and the United States, poverty also became closely associated with deviance and therefore with forms of social control that included imprisonment and hard labor. These studies link penal systems to wider social relations and show the importance of understanding prisons in the social and historical context.

French social theorist and philosopher Michel Foucault published a number of works that have influenced the study of the prison, the foremost of which is *Discipline and Punish* published in English in 1977. Foucault contends that ideas or discourses about discipline and punishment functioned to ensure the effective management of citizens within society. Foucault views public punishments like hanging, drawing, and quartering as the state publicly eradicating the body and soul of the criminal with the aim of demonstrating the power of the king. He argues that in a second historical stage there emerged techniques of discipline that produced citizens who were obedient to the state. These techniques included incarceration—the punishment of the criminal behind closed doors. Therefore, Foucault argues, punishment and the law came to focus less on the body and more on the mind of the criminal. Foucault's ideas about public punishments, the creation of the prison, and the disciplining of citizens are reflected in the history of imprisonment and the prison in the United States.

Traditional Punishments: Colonial Period

In this early period, the range of punishments did not include incarceration. The social environment was largely rural and comprised small communities that could easily be policed by community leaders and that were suspicious of newcomers, strangers, and vagrants. In Massachusetts, for example, in 1765, only 15 of the more than 200 towns had populations of more than 2,500 persons (Rothman 1990: 12). In enforcing local social control, vagabonds and the poor faced the threat of the workhouse, the house of correction, and the almshouse (Rothman 1990: 29).

Incarceration was used primarily to punish debtors and hold persons awaiting trial in custody. There was no incentive to add incarceration to the established physical punishments and no tradition of confining persons as a form of punishment (Kahan 2012: 10; Rothman 1990: 53). Moreover, it was possible to simply banish many deviants from the community rather than imprison them (Rothman 1990: 53).

The colonial mind-set regarded persons as having been born in sin and perceived criminal tendencies as unchangeable. Punishment was therefore designed to remove criminals from society by banishing or hanging them, or by punishing them physically as retribution for their criminality (Kann 2005: 43). There was no conception of reforming and rehabilitating criminals. Publicly performed physical punishments included whipping; physical mutilation through branding, burning, and removal of the ears; and dragging an offender through the streets while tied to a wagon. Shame and humiliation were enforced by placing offenders in the stocks. Punishments either inflicted pain or humiliated the offender or both (Kann 2005: 118), and the death penalty was readily imposed (Rothman 1990: 51).

Jails, Prisons, and Penal Reform

In the early modern period, there was a strong tradition within the Christian faith of charitable giving to the poor. Over time, however, attitudes changed, and the poor began to be categorized as either "deserving" or "undeserving." As early as 1500, the undeserving poor had come to be regarded as a threat to the stability of society (Spierenberg 2007: 19), and in Europe and in England the earliest prisons were established from the second half of the sixteenth century as a response to concern about idleness among the population, especially in relation to jobless vagrants who roamed the country begging. It was believed that these forms of idleness could be counteracted by forcing vagrants to work. The notion of imprisoning them and requiring them to perform labor emerged out of these beliefs (Spierenberg 2007: 12).

Some penologists contend that incarceration developed as a form of social control in Europe and England as the feudal system transitioned to a capitalist society characterized by groups of jobless vagrants roaming the country (Kann 2005: 26; Melossi and Pavarini 1981: 6). Therefore, for example, in his seminal study of incarceration in America, David Rothman argues that "incarceration became first and foremost a method for controlling the deviant and dependent population" (1990: 240).

The concept of deprivation of liberty for an extended period also has roots in the institution of the monastery and the convent. While in theory persons were free to join and leave these institutions, in reality freedom to leave was restricted and those who left without permission might be apprehended and placed in a monastic cell, and, in effect, imprisoned, as punishment. Monastic imprisonment was therefore the first mode of incarceration (Spierenberg 2007: 14). The solitude of monastic life also gave the person an opportunity to reflect and mediate on his or her sins, and this central factor of isolation reappears in the later regime of the penitentiary (Melossi and Pavarini 1981: 5).

In England, the Bridewell, located just outside the London city walls, was the place of confinement of the undeserving poor, both male and female, from about 1550. Jobless and idle persons, beggars, vagrants, and prostitutes were confined there and required to perform forced labor under a strict, disciplined regime of systematic punishment during periods of extended incarceration (Spierenberg 2007: 8). The Bridewell provided the United States with a model for the prison and later for the penitentiary (McGowen 1995: 75).

Birth of the Prison in the United States

In 1790 the U.S. population was less than 4 million, and no town had more than 50,000 inhabitants. Most of the population lived in the rural areas, but by 1820 the rural population had doubled and the urban population tripled (Melossi and Pavarini 1981: 108). The rapid post-revolution change from rural to urban life increased personal mobility, and the demobilization of soldiers caused community leaders to fear an increase in crime brought about by social change (Hirsch 1992: 54).

Boston, New York, Philadelphia, and other cities attracted white vagrants, free blacks, and newly arrived immigrants. These groups were feared because of their potential for criminality (Kann 2005: 21), with immigrants in particular being closely associated with crime (Kann 2005: 73). Freed blacks were believed to be disposed toward criminality because their basic needs were no longer met by the slave masters (Kann 2005: 75). In response, community leaders asserted the value of the Protestant work ethic and, to ensure social control, passed anti-vagrancy laws that empowered magistrates to incarcerate the poor, especially the nonresident poor, in workhouses, poor houses, and almshouses where they were required to labor and learn skills that would keep them out of poverty (Kann 2005: 32). Hard labor was regarded as an appropriate sanction for crimes, especially property crime committed by vagrants, because it punished idleness (Hirsch 1992: 43).

Prisons of the time were indistinguishable from ordinary residences and modeled on the home environment. Inmates lived collectively in large rooms and ate in a common eating area. They could move about freely, and the environment was casual and undisciplined. Unruly inmates were whipped, placed in chains, or isolated in a single room on a reduced diet.

Jails

Jails, like workhouses, were used as places of temporary confinement for a wide category of persons. Jails were distinguished from prisons because the latter involved a more systematic process of incarceration associated with a penal regime that included forced labor (Kann 2005: 123). Jails resembled ordinary residences, were insecure, and suffered from frequent escapes (Rothman 1990: 55).

Over time, community leaders began to regard jails as a cause of crime because deviants, pretrial detainees, and debtors were collected together enabling criminal techniques to be passed on to young men by experienced criminals. In addition, visitors to jails provided contraband to those detained and helped them to plot escapes (Kann 2005: 124). New York City jail was described by reformer Thomas Eddy as a place where minor offenders, vagrants, and those awaiting trial lived in a state of inactivity and intoxication in filthy conditions (Kann 2005: 57). The adverse perception of jails from the 1780s onward prompted some states to revise their penal codes and replace jails with penitentiaries (Kann 2005: 126).

Penal Reform

Between 1776 and 1845 Americans zealously promoted penal reform, including the reform of punishments (Hirsch 1992: 47; Kahan 2012: 11). American reformers were influenced by, and communicated with, European reformers such as Jeremy Bentham and John Howard (Kahan 2012: 2) although for nationalistic reasons they may have been unwilling to acknowledge their inspiration (Hirsch 1992: 31, 49).

Englishman John Howard (1726–1790) surveyed English and European jails and exposed the appalling conditions of prisoners. His publication in 1777 of *The State of Prisons in*

England and Wales led to the enactment of the English Penitentiary Act of 1779, which included provisions for solitary confinement and prison labor and instructions aimed at reforming
criminals. Prisoners were to be isolated during the night, but
congregate work was permitted during the day (Ignatieff 1978:
93). Howard's recommendations for inmates to be isolated in
separate cells and classified according to the nature of their
crime were adopted by nineteenth- and twentieth-century
penal reformers in England, Europe, and the United States
(Kahan 2012: 7).

Italian penal reformer Cesare Beccaria (1738–1794) completed his *Dei Delitti e Delle Pene* (*On Crimes and Punishments*)
in 1764, and an English translation appeared in 1778. His
work influenced U.S. reformers, and he was cited in support
of ideas about separate confinement. He argued that capital
punishment should be abolished because of its arbitrary nature
(Hirsch 1992: 21).

The first generation of U.S. penal reformers including Benjamin Rush, William Bradford, William White, and Caleb
Lownes (Kahan 2012: 12) attributed criminality to social factors and to men's failure to control their natural feelings and
emotions. They argued that if adverse social factors and men's
passions could be controlled, this would reduce criminality
(Kann 2005: 43, 49). Rush stressed the value of labor as a virtuous habit that would counter urges to criminality and bring
about rehabilitation. He favored isolating persons to prevent
moral contamination and thought that silence, labor, and solitude would inevitably bring about moral reform (Kann 2005:
95). Rush wanted to keep the actual length of a sentence secret
from the inmate so as to increase its terror (Kann 2005: 104).
He and other reformers of the 1780s "were the first to argue
that criminals actually had a capacity for remorse, which could
be awakened by carefully legitimated and scientifically inflicted
pain" (Ignatieff 1978: 73).

Rush ignored female inmates because he did not regard them
as capable of threatening public order. Rush's thinking set the

trend for future reformers who became almost entirely fixated on the problem of managing male offenders (Kann 2005: 106). Rush's disregard of the prevalence of black inmates in Philadelphia prisons probably indicated his belief that they could not be reformed (Kann 2005: 107).

Reformist states changed their criminal codes to abolish or restrict the death penalty and replace it with incarceration. The Newgate Prison in New York and the New Jersey Penitentiary were opened in 1797, and Virginia and Kentucky opened prisons in 1800. In 1790, the Walnut Street Jail in Philadelphia was transformed from a jail into the nation's first penitentiary (Kahan 2008: 15). By the 1830s the American penitentiary had become a celebrated institution worldwide (Rothman 1990: 62, 81).

From the 1790s therefore, public officials and reformers agreed that punishments should be performed away from public gaze and within the confines of the prison (Kann 2005: 121). Punishing in private meant that the traditional punishments like whipping could now be performed behind the prison walls. This made them more acceptable to the public, who could justifiably claim no knowledge of them. In addition, prison staff could punish inmates as they wished (Kann 2005: 216).

In order to reinforce the notion that a penitentiary was a place of terror, the design and architecture of prisons during the period of the penitentiary were intended to impress the population and display incarceration as a terrifying experience. They would be a "visible symbol of state power" (Colvin 1997: 47). Therefore, during this period the nature of incarceration, as a punishment, was expressed through the institutional design.

The Birth and Decline of the Penitentiary

While Rothman argues that the invention of the penitentiary was a distinctly American concept, other scholars such as Ignatieff, Hirsch, and Spierenberg argue that the penitentiary has its origins in developments in Europe and England as early as the sixteenth century. As Hirsch (1992: 27) points out, when the first emigrants to the United States left England, workhouses were an established feature of English social control, and the settlers carried with them the ideology of using incarceration to combat idleness. Accordingly, for Hirsch (1992: 113), "The Jacksonians reared the penitentiary, they did not conceive it."

As discussed, prison reformers had agreed that traditional punishments should be replaced by long-term incarceration in penitentiaries where rehabilitative regimes involving hard labor and solitary confinement would bring about individual reform. As Rothman (1990: 105) explains it, "The doctrines of separation, obedience, and labor became the trinity around which officials organized the penitentiary."

Solitary Confinement

The notion that solitary confinement possessed transformative power was widely believed by eighteenth-century reformers, including John Howard (Semple 1993: 80). Howard revised his view about the efficacy of isolation after he had visited English jails and found that inmates had been kept in isolation for more than a year. He concluded that isolation should be limited and carefully regulated, describing absolute solitude as "more than human nature can bear" (quoted in Semple 1993: 89).

Generally, U.S. reformers claimed that solitary confinement was redemptive because when inmates heard no human voices, they were able to hear their own consciences, be penitent, and achieve rehabilitation (Kann 2005: 129). One reformer wanted the penitentiary environment to feel like "the stillness of the tomb" (Kann 2005: 136). Several states legislated for solitary confinement to be half to one-twelfth of the total prison sentence. While most states believed that inmates should be isolated only during the night with silence being enforced during the day, some favored solitary confinement for the entire length of the sentence (Kann 2005: 141). In practice, the outcome of extended periods of isolation was problematic. For example, in 1821, New York officials placed eight offenders in indefinite isolation and silence with no work and with a Bible as the only distraction. After 18 months, several had committed suicide, and others had become insane.

Rehabilitation

Reformers agreed that rehabilitation required a prolonged period of incarceration. A Massachusetts commission claimed that sentences of less than three years would be insufficient, and reformer Thomas Eddy thought that there should be a minimum period of four or five years (Kann 2005: 135). All agreed that rehabilitation must involve total institutional control of an inmate's life, appearance, and environment because this would isolate an inmate from forms of vice and enable adequate self-reflection.

Auburn and Pennsylvania Systems

Two contrasting regimes are associated with the penitentiary regime in the United States: the Auburn system and the Pennsylvania system. The *Auburn system* placed inmates in isolation overnight but allowed congregate work during the day. Inmates were to remain silent at all times. Frenchmen Tocqueville and Beaumont visited Auburn Prison in 1831 and commented that "nothing is heard in the whole prison but the steps of those who march, or sounds proceeding from the workshops" and following the return of inmates to their cells "the silence within these vast walls . . . is that of death" (quoted in Rothman 1990: 97). The regime was introduced at the Auburn Prison, New York, in 1816 but was most closely associated with Sing Sing Prison that opened in 1828 (Kahan 2008: 36). The essence of the Auburn system was the factory-like production of goods for sale by the inmates (Melossi and Pavarini 1981: 60, 129). Therefore, for example, the directors of the Massachusetts State Prison required that prisoners "move and act like machines" (quoted in Hindus 1980: 166).

Under the competing *Pennsylvania system* that persisted between the 1820s and 1860s, inmates were to spend their entire sentence in isolation but could earn the privilege of working in their cells (Kann 2005: 144). Charles Dickens visited the Eastern State Penitentiary in Pennsylvania in 1842 and described solitary confinement as "slow and daily tampering with the mysteries of the brain [and] measurably worse than any torture of the body" (quoted in Kann 2005: 181). Dickens termed the isolation regime "unnatural solitude" that was "fraught, beyond dispute, with such a host of evils" (quoted in Kahan 2012: 33).

In reality, the total isolation mandated by the Pennsylvania scheme never existed. For example, in the Eastern State Penitentiary the prison warden was required by law to visit every prisoner once a day, inmates were allowed to visit with friends and relatives who were also incarcerated there, and the first wardens permitted inmates to work outside their cells. Between 1855 and 1860, 13 percent of inmates were classified as "domestics" and performed duties outside their cells (Kahan 2012: 33). Therefore, the Pennsylvania system never actually isolated inmates from all human contact but regulated their environment so as to ensure they came into contact only with what were judged to be beneficial influences (Kahan 2012: 32).

The relative merits of each system were intensely debated, and foreign reports of each system prompted retorts in the United States by those whose chosen system was critiqued (Rothman 1990: 81). Advocates of the Pennsylvania system asserted that it removed an inmate from all forms of contamination, that labor in a cell following a period of idleness in solitary confinement would encourage regularity and discipline, that guards needed little or no training because they had so little contact with prisoners, and that men in isolation would have almost no opportunity to violate prison regulations. The Auburn supporters argued that their scheme was more practical and that keeping men in isolation for lengthy periods was unnatural and likely to cause insanity (Rothman 1990: 86, 87).

The Pennsylvania system was criticized for its cost, and largely for this reason most states opted to follow the Auburn system of congregate work and inmate separation (Hindus 1980: 220). Visitors from overseas favored the Pennsylvania system but did not put it into practice in their countries because of the cost of constructing the required cellular buildings (Melossi and Pavarini 1981: 61).

Forced Labor

Forced labor was a key rehabilitating element of the penitentiary regime, but it was also touted as a source of state revenue. Several systems of labor were employed. Early on, under the *public account system* of labor, inmates made goods that were sold by the prison authorities on the open market and that competed with non-inmate production. All profits under this system belonged to the state. The inmates received no pay for their labor, and the prison was able to market goods at very competitive prices (Melossi and Pavarini 1981: 133). The workingmen of the states complained from the very beginning that this cheap forced labor threatened their livelihoods (Kahan 2012: 37, 38; Melossi and Pavarini 1981: 141).

The *contract system* was the most widely adopted labor system in the North and involved inmates working inside the prison for a private contractor who paid the prison a fixed price for every prisoner employed, supervised inmates, and ran the prison workshops. Over time, the public account system was displaced by the contract system because the production under the former was of inferior quality to that obtained under the contract model (Melossi and Pavarini 1981: 135, 136).

Under the *convict leasing system* widely used in the South after the end of the Civil War, inmates were hired out to a contractor for a fixed period and amount and the contractor maintained and disciplined them. Convict leasing was essential to the economic reconstruction of the South following the Civil War. Convicts labored in plantations, coal mines, and cotton mills in conditions that closely resembled slavery. The convict lease system came to an end largely because of objections to it by labor and business, but it endured until profitable alternatives had been developed such as state farms and plantations where convicts could be worked to the benefit of the state rather than for private enterprise (Farrell 2005: 177). Convict leasing ceased to be in operation in any state by 1923, and by 1940 the system of private contracts had almost disappeared from prison systems.

Discipline and Surveillance

The first penitentiary administrators believed that institutional disciplining through whipping should be replaced by the authority of wardens and guards who would act toward inmates as "caring but stern father figures." In reality, this meant that wardens and guards had almost unlimited authority over inmates and were not accountable for their actions (Kann 2005: 151, 165).

Rothman suggests that the penitentiary followed a military model because inmates moved within the prison in a military march that took the form of the lockstep (a march that involved making shuffling steps with one hand on the shoulder of the next man in line and all heads facing the guard in order to ensure silence), and the daily schedule of the inmates was organized like a military machine. The cells also took on a military character containing only a set of basic objects, and uniformed guards performed like military sentries (1990: 106). The military model was also found in prison design, with some being shaped like monumental fortresses with thick walls to inspire the respect of citizens (1990: 107).

By the 1820s and 1830s notions of disciplinary benevolence had generally been rejected. For example, in 1815 the Massachusetts State Penitentiary adopted a rule that discipline "should be as severe as the law of humanity will by any means tolerate" (Kann 2005: 156). State administrations punished rule violations with solitary confinement (often in total darkness), reduced rations, whipping, loss of access to the exercise area, placement in the stocks, and being required to wear chains and strait jackets (Kann 2005: 157). At Eastern State Penitentiary, inmates who refused to work received only bread and water rations or were placed in a totally darkened cell for a number of days (Kahan 2012: 57).

A regime that privileged discipline necessitated extensive and intense surveillance. Therefore, in the Auburn system the cells were placed so that they could be inspected without the inmate seeing the guard, and in the Pennsylvania system each cell had an iron door with a small aperture through which meals would be passed to the inmate, who was not able to see the guard. In some prisons guards even wore soft shoes during the night so they could move silently between cells (Kann 2005: 153).

The ultimate mode of inmate surveillance was revealed in the model of the Panopticon. In 1791, English penologist Jeremy Bentham (1748–1832) formulated and published a proposal for the ideal prison, which he called the Panopticon. It functioned not only as a prison where inmates would be controlled and kept under constant surveillance but also generally as a means for the state to exercise control over large numbers of disorderly persons. Bentham famously described it as "a mill for grinding rogues honest, and idle men industrious" (quoted in Semple 1993: 107).

The architectural design of the Panopticon enabled all inmates to be kept under continuous surveillance and proved to be influential in prison management and design. The Panopticon was to be a circular building with cells placed along its circumference. The guard would occupy the center of the building and have an unobstructed view of all the cells. Inmates would never see the guard because the guard area would be made impenetrable by placing blinds over the windows and small lamps outside each window. Inmates would never know whether they were under surveillance at any given time (Davies 2005: 664). The U.S. Stateville Penitentiary in Joliet, Illinois, built between 1916 and 1924 (Davies 2005: 665), opened with four Panopticon-style units, three of which were demolished in the 1980s. The remaining unit appears to be the only operational Panopticon worldwide (Thomas 2005: 73).

Bentham's ideas about the discipline, management, and control of prisoners greatly influenced the regimes adopted in U.S. penitentiaries (Kahan 2012: 9). French philosopher Michel Foucault identifies the Panopticon as a key element in his penal history. Michael Ignatieff sees the Panopticon as an outcome of reforms that originated in the work of Beccaria and Howard and describes it as "the most haunting symbol of the disciplinary enthusiasms of the age" (1978: 109).

Penitentiaries and Racial Dynamics in the South

Before the Civil War almost all prison and jail inmates in the South were white, but during the remainder of the nineteenth century, 90 percent of inmates were black (Colvin 1997: 220). Generally, states tried to keep blacks out of penitentiaries because it was thought they would contaminate the white inmates. In Virginia prisons, blacks were considered to be more unruly than whites (Kann 2005: 205).

Reformers gave little thought to how blacks might be treated in Southern penitentiaries due to a widespread belief that they were undisciplined, had hereditary criminal traits, and were more corrupted than whites (Kann 2005: 202). In South Carolina, for example, it was inconceivable that middle-class values could be taught to former slaves and therefore "rehabilitation was as impossible, unnecessary, and undesirable" (Hindus 1980: xxvii).

Convict leasing enabled Southern states to avoid building new prisons to accommodate blacks sentenced under the Black Codes. Prisoners in chain gangs and in convict lease camps endured severe conditions. They slept side by side in rolling iron cages, shackled together on narrow wooden slabs. Their toilet was a single bucket, and they washed in a single tub of dirty water. In Alabama, prisoners leased to mining companies were hung from makeshift crucifixes, stretched on wooden racks, and placed in coffin-sized sweatboxes for many hours (Colvin 1997: 246). The conditions ensured a very high death rate; for example, in 1868 and 1869, 17 percent and 18 percent of Alabama convicts died, respectively, and in 1870 the death rate was 41 percent. In 1883, a doctor estimated that in Alabama most convicts died within three years (Colvin 1997: 247).

Women in Penitentiaries

Women who committed serious felonies served their sentences in penitentiaries, but sentences for crimes most often committed by women—minor street crimes and crimes against chastity or decency that applied only to women—were usually served in jails (Freedman 1984: 11). In 1850 women comprised only 3.6 percent of all inmates in 34 state and county prisons. Women offenders were generally poor, immigrants, or black and were regarded as "fallen women" who could not be rehabilitated and as "the refuse of society" (Kann 2005: 17, 82).

As early as 1791, at the Walnut Street Jail, women previously accommodated with men were separated and housed in their own apartment where they spun cotton and carded wool (Colvin 1997: 135). However, generally, women were initially treated as part of the inmate population and, apart from being accommodated together in large rooms or cells, were not segregated from males. Later, they were located in separate facilities that were usually adjacent to or attached to the male section of the prison, and ultimately, they were removed to completely separate facilities within the prison perimeter. Women were generally neglected and lacked protection from male guards, but they were considered competent to perform domestic duties within the prison (Rafter 1985: 10, 12). In the Massachusetts State Prison, women were locked in a single room, and in the New York State Prison at Auburn, 20–30 women, some serving sentences as long as 14 years, were accommodated in a one-room attic above the kitchen where they were left to fend for themselves (Kann 2005: 194). In Missouri, women inmates were hired out to private interests as domestic servants, returning to the prison every night where they were locked in their cells.

Prior to 1895 black women were disproportionately represented in prisons in the Northeast and Midwest, but in the South, few went to prison because slaves were subject to the private, informal punishment of their masters and only freed blacks suffered public punishment. Following the end of the Civil War, Southern prisons were filled with black prisoners; therefore, for example, between 1860 and1887 black women comprised 70 percent of women committed to the Tennessee Penitentiary, and this increased to over 90 percent by 1900 (Rafter 1985: 132). Jim Crow laws, differential treatment for blacks and whites in justice systems, black women's lack of alternatives to imprisonment, and the desire to profit from inmate labor all contributed to the disproportionate incarceration of black women (Rafter 1985: 135).

Englishwoman Elizabeth Fry (1780–1845) significantly influenced the reform of women's prisons in the United States (Zedner 1995: 298). News of Fry's reforming work in England reached the United States in 1823 and motivated Quaker women to make regular visits to the Arch Street Prison in Philadelphia. Middle- and upper-middle-class women began campaigning to improve prison conditions. In 1825 Fry published a compendium of how prisons should be run, arguing that for women, cleanliness, plain clothing and warm organized surroundings together with labor, education, and daily religious observance constituted an ideal regime (Zedner 1995: 301).

The first entirely separate prison for women in the United States was the Mount Pleasant Female Prison located in Ossining, New York, established in 1835. From 1844 through 1847 Mount Pleasant superintendent Eliza Farnham introduced activities such as teaching and music and a system of rewards and privileges that foreshadowed the later development of the women's reformatory. Farnham modified the total silence rule by allowing inmates "to talk in a low tone to each other half an hour every afternoon, providing that they had conformed to the rule of silence during the remainder of the day" (Rafter 1985: 18). However, the traditional design features of the prison persisted, and Framingham and Indiana women's prisons were massive stone structures with rows of rooms located in wings (Freedman 1984: 70).

Further, six women's prisons were opened between 1870 and 1935. Often, establishing a women's prison required no more than renaming an already-constructed institution that was deemed no longer suitable for men (Rafter 1985: 92).

The Decline of the Penitentiary

By 1815 increased overcrowding had brought disorder to the penitentiaries. Those in Philadelphia and New York often held twice their designed capacity (Colvin 1997: 67). Pardons to relieve overcrowding were granted largely to the elite who had the wealth, influence, or friends to secure them and were considered to be undermining the penitentiary regime by facilitating mild punishments for serious offenses (Kann 2005: 189).

During the 1820s, reformers began to question the likelihood of inmate rehabilitation. Reformer Thomas Eddy believed that hardened criminals who showed no contrition would not be rehabilitated, and others thought repeat offenders and former black slaves were intractable (Kann 2005: 173). Also, there were concerns that the highly disciplined penitentiary regime did not diminish recidivism. The shock that an inmate suffered after being put back into a world where he or she had freedom to act but had no structure to regulate his or her life meant he or she would likely reoffend (Kann 2005: 189). The solution to incorrigible inmates who could not be redeemed was to abandon efforts at redemption and simply incapacitate them (Hirsch 1992: 108).

Inmates viewed reformers' claims about rehabilitation as mere rhetoric. As one former inmate of Vermont's Windsor Penitentiary expressed it, "That prison is called penitentiary. As properly might Hell be called heaven. . . . Not the reformation of the convicts is sought . . . and they are treated just as an intelligent but heartless slaveholder would treat his Negroes—made to work as long as they can earn their living and then cursed with freedom that they may die on their own expense" (quoted in Kann 2005: 176, 178). Convicts complained about the cruel treatment they received and claimed it caused them to seek revenge and reinforced their criminality (Kann 2005: 227).

Reformers also began to doubt the value of keeping inmates in isolation, believing that this encouraged only sinful acts and schemes for future unlawfulness (Kann 2005: 175). Solitary confinement, especially for prolonged periods, was criticized for its inhumanity, and some regarded corporal punishment as more humane than isolation (Kann 2005: 181).

The transformative power of hard labor was judged to have failed. Gradually, labor began to be associated more with revenue for the prisons and less with rehabilitation as inmates were required to work both longer and harder (Kann 2005: 175). Individualized treatment was largely ignored due to lack of time and resources. Penal reform groups like the Boston Prison Discipline Society regarded prison guards as bullies, who provoked inmates to commit rule violations so they could inflict punishments, and noted that wardens who tried to be humane were regarded as too lenient and were replaced.

In addition, by the late 1860s, conditions in American penitentiaries had significantly deteriorated because of overcrowding brought about by improvements in the detection, capture, and prosecution of criminals and the establishment of municipal police forces. For example, in Philadelphia between 1880 and 1894 criminal convictions grew by almost 40 percent and sentences increased in length so that by 1901 there had been a 16 percent increase in sentences longer than 12 years as compared to the years before the Civil War (Kahan 2012: 56).

In 1867 a landmark report by reformers Enoch Wines and Theodore Dwight, commissioned by the New York Prison Association, investigated the state of rehabilitation in American prisons and criticized states for their ill-maintained buildings and facilities, poor living conditions, inhumane punishments, and lack of staff professionalism. They estimated that at least one-third of all inmates were not sleeping in individual cells (Rothman 1990: 242). They concluded that prisons did not regard the reformation of inmates as a primary objective and called for numerous changes, some of which were derived from prison experiments conducted in 1840 in Norfolk Island, Australia, by Alexander Machonochie and by developments in 1854 in Ireland by Sir Walter Crofton. These initiatives had emphasized earned incentives for good conduct and systems of grading that moved inmates on an ascending scale through to a more relaxed prison environment and experience (Rotman 1995: 154).

Elmira Reformatory and the Men's Reformatory Movement, 1876–1920

The 1867 report by Enoch Wines and Theodore Dwight recommended rehabilitation as the ultimate goal of incarceration. A new type of custodial institution, the "adult reformatory," was proposed, which would separate serious and habitual offenders from minor offenders. Wines convinced other reformers that convening an international conference to discuss penal issues might result in endorsement of the proposed reforms, and in 1870 over 250 delegates convened in Cincinnati at the Congress of Penitentiary and Reformatory Discipline and formulated a declaration (Pisciotta 1994: 12).

The declaration stated, "Reformation is a work of time; and a benevolent regard to the good of the criminal himself, as well as to the protection of society, requires that his sentence be long enough for reformatory processes to take effect" (quoted in Rothman 2012: 32, 33). It called for nurturing inmates' self-respect, indeterminate sentencing, release to be determined according to the degree of rehabilitation, a system of rewards where inmates could ascend through a number of grades until they had earned the right to a "ticket of leave" (called parole), and an individualized approach to treatment (Rothman 2012: 50). The Congress also declared that there should be separate prisons for women and that women should be employed in reformed prison systems (Rafter 1985: 29).

The terms of the 1870 declaration were translated into practice at the Elmira Reformatory which opened in New York in 1876 and which marked the start of a different model for American penology (Rotman 1995: 155). Indeterminate sentencing and parole were key elements of the Elmira project. The new mode of sentencing involved a judge fixing the minimum and maximum terms of a sentence, rendering its length indeterminate. Inmates no longer knew when their sentence would end because a parole board would determine the inmate's actual release date (Rothman 2012: 44).

While major stakeholders in criminal justice welcomed the change to indeterminate sentencing, for example, prison wardens believed that inmates now had an incentive—the granting of parole—to conduct themselves satisfactorily (Rothman 2012: 74), many prisoners despised the new sentencing practice because it robbed them of the certainty of knowing their release date and because they resented wardens, guards, and a parole board having so much power over their lives (Rothman 2012: 80).

Zebulon Brockway and Elmira

Zebulon Brockway, the first superintendent of Elmira, held that position from 1876 for the next 20 years (Rothman 2012: 33). With a background in prison administration, he was regarded as a professional prison administrator (Kahan 2012: 62). Brockway viewed his mission at Elmira as instilling the Protestant ethic in youthful offenders and training them to be economically productive so they would be transformed into "Christian gentlemen" who had accepted responsibility for their criminality (Pisciotta 1994: 18).

Elmira was to accept first-time offenders aged between 16 and 30 years who had received indeterminate sentences. An inmate's actual release date was determined by the reformatory managers but could not exceed the maximum sentence imposed. Individual diagnosis and personalized treatment were the cornerstones of the Elmira project. After an interview with Brockway in which he identified the cause of the inmate's deviance, an inmate was assigned a cell and appropriate education and training courses (Pisciotta 1994: 19). Under a complex grading system, an inmate could, by fulfilling work and education assignments and by committing no disciplinary violations, earn a maximum number of marks each month. He could then ascend to a higher grade and ultimately to grade one when he could be released. Infractions could mean being demoted to a lower grade. Higher grades meant better accommodation with more facilities, the right to send and receive letters, better uniforms, and the right to speak to others during meals (Rothman 2012: 34). Inmates who were out of control would be placed in solitary confinement or given hard labor and, where no improvement was discerned, transferred to the state prison. Elmira received public praise and came to represent the reform ideal. By the late 1890s Elmira operated with 1,296 cells but almost 1,500 inmates.

Inmates worked from 7:30 a.m. through 4:30 p.m. in an iron foundry, in shoe and broom factories, and on a small farm and then attended classes from 7:00 p.m. through 8.30 p.m. where they were educated in reading, writing, arithmetic, history, geography, and composition (Kahan 2012: 63). In 1888, legislation prohibited inmate labor schemes, and Brockway initiated a military program, with inmates organized into regiments and companies, drilling daily between five and eight hours. Brockway used recreation as part of treatment, and by the late 1880s baseball, basketball, track and field, and football were all being played (Pisciotta 1994: 24).

From about 1882, Brockway began a public relations and marketing campaign with the aim of disseminating the Elmira model to the penal community. Brockway gave visitors guided tours of the facility (Pisciotta 1994: 25). Elmira became the most important institution in the country despite the fact that by the 1890s it held more than twice its capacity of inmates, of whom at least one-third were recidivists and not the first-time offenders it was designed for (Rotman 1995: 156). The reason was the introduction of the penalty of probation, which, as an alternative sanction to the reformatory, effectively ended the supply of youthful offenders to Elmira.

Discipline at Elmira

In 1894 an investigation into charges that Brockway had imposed brutal and excessive punishments found that Brockway had personally administered whipping (twice a week on average) with a leather strap nearly one-quarter of an inch thick and that solitary confinement was used regularly, with the inmate shacked by his hands or feet to the cell door. Brockway termed the use of the strap as "spanking," which he considered to be "simple, altogether harmless physical shock" (Pisciotta 1994: 36). Inmates were placed in solitary confinement for lengthy periods on bread and water—a punishment Brockway termed a "rest cure" (Blomberg and Lucken 2000: 76). Severe punishment and not rewards and education as promised had become the dominant mode of maintaining order (Rotman 1995: 156).

The investigation also revealed gross mismanagement and understaffing and that treatment programs were failing to achieve their objectives. The charges of "brutal, excessive, degrading and unusual punishment of the inmates" were found proved (Pisciotta 1994: 35), and the report stated that "the brutality practiced at the reformatory has no parallel in any modern penal institution in our country" (Pisciotta 1994: 42).

Management at Elmira

The inquiry also exposed Brockway's poor management techniques, which included appointing 60 inmate monitors who acted as correctional officers and whose decisions on disciplinary issues, marks, promotions, and classifications were found to have been arbitrary and unfair (Pisciotta 1994: 43). Parole was essentially under Brockway's control because the reformatory managers, meeting as a parole board, made release decisions that generally followed the recommendations of Superintendent Brockway (Pisciotta 1994: 48). The investigation also revealed that Brockway viewed "colored boys" as inferior both psychologically and morally and therefore were less likely to be reformed than whites (Pisciotta 1994: 51). In July 1900 Brockway was forced to resign after managers appointed by Governor Theodore Roosevelt conducted a thorough evaluation of all aspects of Elmira.

Eugenics at Elmira

During the Progressive period, in line with the new science of eugenics that tested inmates for mental capacity, psychological tests conducted at Elmira designated many inmates as "mental defectives" and therefore biologically inferior and incapable of reform. In 1908 the physician at Elmira reviewed 8,000 commitments and concluded that 37 percent were "mental defectives," either congenitally or acquired due to poverty, slums, and the "temptations of America's decadent big cities" and recommended that they be transferred to custodial care (Pisciotta 1994: 113). In 1917 the superintendent at Elmira called for sterilization of inferior inmates (Pisciotta 1994: 117).

Other Reformatories

By 1900 almost all state prisons had adopted some of the elements of the Elmira Reformatory system (Kahan 2008: 63). Prisons could easily be reconfigured to become reformatories; for example, Iowa, Massachusetts, and Kentucky, which operated the Auburn system, simply renamed their state prisons "reformatories" (Rotman 1995: 156). In reformatories that opened between 1889 and 1899 states modified the Elmira model to reflect state needs and interests. For example, the Michigan State House of Corrections and Reformatory, opened in 1877, was a combined prison and reformatory that accepted felons and minor offenders without any age limitations and where sentences were determinate and where first-time young offenders were mixed with career criminals (Pisciotta 1994: 83). In Colorado, the reformatory operated as a penal work camp where inmates were subjected to very harsh discipline (Pisciotta 1994: 89). Adopting alternative reformatory models weakened the identity and purpose of the adult reformatory. The opening of the Wisconsin Reformatory in 1898 marked the end of the formative stage of the adult reformatory movement (Pisciotta 1994: 91).

All adult reformatories for males that opened between 1876 and 1920 received black inmates, but only three accepted females: those in Minnesota, Iowa, and Kentucky (Pisciotta 1994: 143). Racism and sexism in reformatories reflected the values of the time; therefore, for example, the superintendent of the Minnesota Reformatory relied on racist and sexist stereotypes when writing in inmate case files, noting that black inmates were untrustworthy, lazy, and immoral; that female inmates were inherently weaker than men and were therefore viewed as victims of bad men and social circumstances; and that Native American inmates were simple, like children, and prone to drinking "firewater" (Pisciotta 1994: 144, 145).

By 1920 the reformatory movement had ended. The reasons for its decline were succinctly catalogued by the director of education of the Washington State Reformatory, who visited a number of facilities in 1914 and 1915, as unqualified superintendents, incompetent guards, ineffective treatment programs, guard and inmate subcultures that undermined reform, and a dominant focus on security and control of troublesome inmates rather than on reform (Pisciotta 1994: 143).

The Women's Reformatory Movement

From the 1870s women reformers contested the notion that fallen women were incapable of reform. They argued that women needed a new form of treatment that differed from that offered to men. Reformers claimed that healthy surroundings within and outside the prison would aid in restoring natural womanhood and that training would restore the female qualities of piety, purity, domesticity, and submissiveness that they themselves valued (Freedman 1984: 53, 54). They wanted fallen women to be socialized to middle-class qualities and values. For example, women's reformatory superintendent Ellen Cheney Johnson favored "softening" influences such as flowers, farm animals, and music on women inmates that would reawaken "the germs of goodness in the heart" (quoted in Freedman 1984: 55). These ideas were promoted by the reformatory movement and embodied in the new female reformatories.

However, the liberalization of punishment that women's reformatories advocated also delivered a "net-widening" effect because many young women offenders who, like male offenders, would have been sent to local jails or not imprisoned at all were now subject to extended punishment (Rafter 1985: 35, 36). Women's reformatories therefore created differing standards for men and women offenders that punished women more severely than men based on the reformers' perspective that women needed special care and protection (Rafter 1985: 36).

The growth of the women's reformatory movement was a protracted one, and from its inception in about 1870 through 1900, only four institutions were created. During the next 30 years or so the pace quickened and, the ideal reformatory plan having been articulated, 17 state institutions were opened. By 1935 the reformatory movement came to an end.

The writings of Englishwoman Mary Carpenter were influential in the reformatory movement in the United States. In her 1864 book, *Our Convicts*, Carpenter argued that women should be incarcerated together in a separate facility where a merit system would regulate access to treatment and privileges and where female staff would provide cultural and intellectual support and male guards would be excluded. These ideas prompted Quakers Charles and Rhoda Coffin to establish the

Indiana Reformatory Institution for Women, which opened in Indianapolis in 1873 and was the first completely independent women's prison and the first to be operated by entirely female staff (Rafter 1985: 30).

The "House of Shelter" established in Detroit in 1868 as an adjunct to the Detroit House of Correction is described as America's first women's reformatory because it applied a number of techniques that later characterized the women's reformatory (Freedman 1984: 50). The shelter's matron, Emma Hall, formed a society of 30 women living as a family and instituted a merit system. Hall gave education a prominent role in the institution and introduced the notion of training women to lead a "true good womanly life" through regular assemblies of the institution's "family" dressed in their best clothing to converse, do needlework, and listen to visiting speakers with the aim of creating an environment that would match that of "refined society" (Rafter 1985: 27). The shelter closed in 1874 (Rafter 1985: 28).

Twenty female reformatories were set up between 1870 and 1935, mostly in rural areas and on vast acreages. For example, the Western House of Refuge at Albion was sited on 100 acres and the Massachusetts Reformatory Prison for Women at Framingham on 30 acres. Framingham, located 22 miles west of Boston, opened in 1874 as the first women's reformatory in the nation (Freedman 1984: 52). The reformatories set up in the 1870s and 1880s set the standard that would continue into the next century.

Reformatory Inmates

Some states sent felons to reformatories to serve long sentences of up to life, while others admitted women convicted only of misdemeanors or accepted women convicted of both misdemeanors and felonies. The inmates were often white, young, American-born working-class women, who were morals offenders and therefore qualified as fallen women in need to aid (Freedman 1984: 82). Morals or public order offenses included vagrancy, drunkenness, and conduct considered immoral, such as flirting, attending dance halls, or being involved in sexual relationships (Rafter 1985: 159, 160).

Except for the Bedford Hills Reformatory, New York, where Superintendent Katherine Bement Davis refused to segregate black and white women, reformatories with a significant black population were segregated (Rafter 1985: 153). The New Jersey State Reformatory for Women, opened in 1913, accommodated black women in Stowe Cottage, "the colored cottage" specifically designed for them, which was located some distance from other buildings and operated "almost like a separate institution" having its own school and a black officer (Rafter 1985: 152).

Reformatory Design

The northeastern reformatories gradually adopted the cottage plan design, comprising a number of cottages, each accommodating about 20 women, surrounding a central administration facility that was intended to represent family life. The first reformatory for women to utilize an exclusively cottage design was the New Jersey State Reformatory for Women at Clinton, opened in 1913. While this design might suggest that conditions were less restrictive than those in a traditional prison, in fact, intense and intrusive surveillance was exercised over inmates because of the minimum levels of security. Ironically, then, the open cottage model actually fostered greater restrictions on movement and activity generally (Dodge 2005: 196).

An alternative to the cottage plan was the design at Framingham, built at an early period in the transition from prison to reformatory, consisting of a central building with 300 cells and two dormitories of 50 beds each of 50–90 square feet with iron bedsteads and white sheets. Inmates could decorate their rooms and have unbarred windows, and the size of the room occupied by an inmate was determined by a merit system (Freedman 1984: 69; Rafter 1985: 34).

In reality, the notion that family life could be represented in a reformatory was illusory because inmates were graded on their performance and subject to discipline and to the management of matrons. Research into reformatory files has shown that the matrons and inmates constantly negotiated power relations in the operations of the cottages (Dodge 2005: 197).

Reforming Women through Domestic Training

Reformatory managers attempted to convey a message that their aim was reformation and not punishment. Framingham informed new inmates that the institution would be "a starting point in their existence . . . a time for reflection, an opportunity for new principles to be formed," and at the Hudson Reformatory, managers advised that it was not a prison "but an educational institution."

Domestic training became the central element in the reformatory project. Therefore, for example, at Indiana by the 1890s, annual reports extolled the virtues of domestic training, claiming that "a love for women's work should be carefully instilled into the minds of the girls" (Freedman 1984: 91). Overall, there existed a tension between the goal of training women to adopt the traditional feminine virtues and teaching them self-sufficiency because teaching domestic skills failed to equip the women to be economically self-sufficient (Freedman 1984: 105).

At Framingham, during the superintendence of Ellen Cheney Johnson, an indenture program operated under which inmates on parole served as domestic servants in nearby private homes (Freedman 1984: 92). They could be returned to prison if they did not perform satisfactorily, and in 1880 running away from service was made a criminal offense. Parolees were permitted to keep the wages paid by their employers, which were only slightly lower than the rates paid to most domestics (Freedman 1984: 93). Employers were authorized to open and read all mail received by the parolees and were expected to monitor their morals (Rafter 1985: 165). This program provided trained, cheap domestic aid to middle-class women from the 1860s through 1914 when there was a shortage of domestic servants as women came to prefer wage-earning factory jobs that offered higher wages and shorter working hours (Colvin 1997: 170).

Reformatory Discipline

Despite the reformatory emphasis on kindness and forgiveness, discipline and control remained strict and absolute. As Rafter (1985: xxii) explains, "The entire regimen was designed to induce a childlike submissiveness." At Indiana, the superintendent banned tobacco smoking, which she considered an "unwomanly vice," and allowed only religious newspapers into the reformatory. At Framingham, Ellen Cheney Johnson disapproved of unsupervised conversation among inmates, and her successor Frances Morton reduced inmate recreational time, which she regarded as "evil and detrimental to discipline," and insisted that women use the time sewing (Freedman 1984: 97).

To some extent, reformatory discipline was modeled on that of the prison. At its most severe it comprised solitary confinement and a diet of bread and water for an inmate who was disrespectful, talked during meals, or tried to escape. Superintendents believed that isolation was a more humane mode of punishment than straitjackets, handcuffs, gags, hair cropping, or whipping, which were still used in state prisons (Freedman 1984: 99). At Framingham, the harshest punishment of committing to a basement cell and a diet of bread and water was imposed on women who assaulted officers, destroyed property, or threatened other women. Indiana and Albion both used corporal punishment to enforce discipline (Freedman 1984: 99).

The Decline of the Women's Reformatory

A decline in the ideals and practice of the women's reformatory began early in the twentieth century as the inmate population was radically transformed by the arrival of numerous prostitutes, drunks, and drug abusers, who did not garner the sympathy shown to less "hardened" women. Bedford Hills was forced to accept incoming inmates who did not match the profile that had been envisaged—it was intended to house women aged 16–30, convicted of only minor offenses—because probation and parole had appropriated the population intended for the reformatory.

Between 1890 and 1910, the activist women reformers who had campaigned for improved conditions for incarcerated women and designed the reformatory died, along with the missionary spirit that had driven the reforms of that time (Freedman 1984: 109). In addition, reformatories were actually established in only seven states, mostly in the Northeast and Midwest, and as late as 1976 15 states had no reformatories and continued to accommodate women inmates in part of men's prisons.

By the 1930s most reformatories resembled traditional women's prisons in their regimes of discipline, paucity of treatment programs, and inability to recruit qualified staff. Numerous rules were applied, including what inmates could wear, how to fold their clothes, and how they should sit when in the dining room. All activities were closely monitored and recorded, including friendships that were regarded as excessively intimate and therefore not properly "wholesome" (Dodge 2005: 198).

Gradually, the cottages were supplanted by dormitories and cell blocks, which were far more cost-effective facilities. The cottage plan was hugely expensive, requiring a number of discrete cottages, each with its own cooking and dining facilities and staff, as well as separate buildings for administration, teaching, staff accommodation, and a farm (Rafter 1985: 77).

Post-Penitentiary Developments, 1865–1940

By the end of the Civil War, rather than being places for reformation, penitentiaries had become places for warehousing and brutalizing prisoners (Kahan 2012: 56). That convicts could be recast into model citizens despite experiencing an inflexible regime that suppressed their will and cooperation was now recognized as a futile project. Nevertheless, penitentiaries continued to enjoy the support of the public, prison officials, and political leaders. One disincentive to change was that the cost of maintaining prisons was modest. Most prisons hired out convicts as labor, and the state therefore had a guaranteed income to offset maintenance and running costs (Rothman 2012: 27).

Inmates suffered brutal punishments, such as hanging them by their thumbs or requiring them to wear an iron cap comprising an iron band supporting a cage around the head weighing between 6 and 8 pounds (Rothman 2012: 18). In New York one punishment was 40 or 50 blows with a paddle, made of two thicknesses of shoe leather, applied to the bare buttocks of an inmate stretched across a frame (Rothman 2012: 19). Public reaction to these conditions was muted because many inmates were immigrants; for example, in 1890 some 60 percent of the penitentiary population in the state of Illinois comprised mostly foreign-born or second-generation German and Irish with little education. The substandard penal conditions were deemed suitable for deviant members of alien groups (Rothman 2012: 24).

Individual Deviance and the Medical Model: Progressive Period, 1900–1920

The Progressive Era was marked by a move away from the notion that the power of religion and hard labor could correct offenders and to a correctional approach based on science. Reformers now believed that justice and fairness required that each offender be assessed individually in a medical-like process of diagnosis that would uncover the proximate causes of individual deviance (Rothman 2012: 57). The new approach focused on the "mental life" of an offender as psychologists and psychiatrists set out to examine "bad habits of mind" and "mental imagery" as causative factors in criminality (Rothman 2012: 55). However, these professionals offered little that was specifically therapeutic to correct diagnosed psychological problems. They generally recommended vocational training and schooling as treatment (Rothman 2012: 125). Education, vocational training, and especially combating illiteracy, therefore became the main forms of training and treatment but were generally lacking in quality (2012: 126, 135).

From about 1910, following new practices and procedures, incoming inmates were isolated between two and four weeks during which time they took tests and were interviewed as part of the process of diagnosing their deviance. Psychologists and psychiatrists began to take staff appointments in prisons, and by 1926, 67 institutions employed psychiatrists and 45 employed psychologists (Rotman 1995: 159). However, those institutions that employed only a few medical and psychological professionals faced the impossible task of interviewing and classifying every new inmate in a total intake of between 500 and 700 a year, giving progress reports on as many as 1,500 inmates over a year, and making recommendations of the issue of the appropriate release date. The impact of these new services was therefore very limited (Rothman 2012: 134). Unfortunately, as had occurred with previous penal innovations, additional resources were not provided to the extent desired and reform goals were not met (Kahan 2012: 89).

The focus on individualized treatment and the importance of individual social circumstances brought about systems of probation, which was adopted between 1900 and 1920, although its antecedents go back to the 1850s. By 1915, 33 states had probation systems (Rothman 2012: 44).

From 1900, as prison populations increased, prison mangers were urged to expand parole so as to avoid having to construct new prisons, and by 1918 many states enabled parole to be granted for a broad range of prisoners, including habitual criminals and those convicted of murder. In California, for example, the percentage of prisoners released on parole increased from 7 percent in 1907 to 35 percent in 1914 (Blomberg and Lucken 2000: 111). Little time was spent assessing parole applications, and typically, the entire process was completed in only a few minutes (Rothman 2012: 164). In New York a full-time board that operated after 1930 decided 80–160 cases a day, and the Pennsylvania board spent, on average, six minutes reviewing and adjudicating each application (Rothman 2012: 165).

By the 1920s, over 80 percent of offenders sentenced to imprisonment were on parole (Pratt 2009: 19). Parole supervision following the grant of parole was often nonexistent. In California, where parole commenced in 1893, 10 years elapsed before an adequate supervision system was developed (Blomberg and Lucken 2000: 110).

Prison Discipline

Despite Progressive reforms, "prisons were places of pervasive brutality" (Rothman 2012: 152). Numerous prison rules rendered an inmate liable to punishment at any time, and prison rule books included prohibitions on "fighting, grimacing, hands in pockets, hands or face not clean, hair not combed . . . impertinence to visitors, insolence to officers, . . . laughing and fooling, loud talking in cell, not out of bed promptly . . . profanity, quarreling, refusal to obey, . . . spitting on the floor" (quoted in Rothman 2012: 149). Guards were forbidden to talk with inmates except to issue instructions. Disciplinary action lacked even a minimal standard of fairness and justice until the 1920s, and while some prisons did create independent boards to hear discipline violations, in many the truth of the charge was decided by the warden, deputy warden, or captain (Rothman 2012: 151).

Punishment for infractions of discipline rules included withdrawing privileges and reducing "good time." Where tougher punishment was thought necessary (whipping having been prohibited by the 1930s in most systems, although it continued to be sanctioned in Delaware prisons until 1954), solitary confinement was the chosen punishment. This could be isolation in a regular cell receiving normal food rations or solitary confinement proper, termed "the hole," "the pit," or "the cage," comprising a bare concrete cell without lighting or ventilation with a ration of bread and water only provided. Wardens might confine an inmate for six days, release the inmate for one day, and then return him or her to solitary confinement for a further six days, and so on until many months were spent there (Rothman 2012: 152).

These practices reflected the thinking that prison authorities ought to be free to run a prison as they saw fit, an attitude that continued right up to the mid-1960s (Rothman 2012: 156). For the state concerned, if its prisons were operated securely and attracted no adverse publicity, wardens were free to administer state prisons as they wished (Rothman 2012: 157).

The Big House

In 1929 a declaration by the newly created Federal Bureau of Prisons that rehabilitation was the principal objective of incarceration put a new focus on treatment for rehabilitation (Rotman 1995: 169). The outcome was the so-called Big House, an institution administered by professional penologists with the objective of retraining inmates to reenter society by re-creating that society in microcosm within the penal institution. Big Houses were large-capacity prisons holding on average 2,500 inmates, such as Sing Sing, San Quentin in California, and Stateville in Illinois. By 1929 two of these facilities held over 4,000 inmates each and another four more than 3,000 (Rotman 1995: 163).

The Big Houses failed to implement the stated objectives. Instead, inmates were controlled by strict routines and rigid schedules and endured isolation that denied any individual initiative that would prepare them to resume social life (Rotman 1995: 165). Nevertheless, the Big House was an advance on the harsh conditions that prevailed in the penitentiaries. For example, tobacco use by inmates was introduced, corporal punishment was abolished as was the lockstep (abolished in Sing Sing in 1900), and inmates were given the freedom to move around the prison yard (in Sing Sing from about 1912). However, the silent system remained in force for most prison activities (Johnson 1996: 71). The Big House environment has been characterized as "boredom bred by an endlessly monotonous routine" (Johnson 1996: 72).

Big Houses endured until about 1940 (Johnson 1996: 74). Their demise is associated with increased staff professionalism, as qualified prison administrators began to enter the prison systems from the 1930s, and with the rise of prisoner litigation that restricted authoritarian control over inmates and recognized and articulated inmate's rights. Nevertheless, the impact of these changes varied from state to state; therefore, for example, in Texas, prisons were able to sustain the environment of the Big House even until the 1980s (Johnson 1996: 140).

Women's Reformatories

From 1900 through the 1930s a new generation of women reformers appeared, who were not committed to the propagation of female domesticity or to the conversion of fallen women and lacked the religious backgrounds of their predecessors. Many were highly educated in the social sciences, law, medicine, and social work and saw themselves as "social engineers" who would apply the principles and thinking of their disciplines to the study of incarcerated women. New reformatories established in this period and in the following years were concentrated in the Northeast and Midwest, and only three were created in the South, in Arkansas, North Carolina, and Virginia, and one in the West, in California in 1933 (Rafter 1985: 55).

Two issues in Progressive thinking impacted female offenders: eugenics, and prostitution and "promiscuous women" (Rafter 1985: 54). The eugenics movement viewed crime, vagrancy, and prostitution as the outcome of mental deficiency and feeble-mindedness that rendered criminals incapable of controlling criminal urges and was traceable to faulty heredity.

The new science of mental testing would identify defective delinquents so they could be segregated and prevented from breeding more of their kind (Rafter 1985: 54). Women's prisons and reformatories became sites for the investigation of these notions.

At the Bedford Hills Reformatory, which opened in 1901, Superintendent Kathleen Bement Davis studied the records of former inmates between 1901 and 1909, as well as of more than 600 prostitutes. The results appeared to show that 15 percent were feeble-minded and that "degenerate strains" were present in the heredity of 20 percent of the cases examined (Freedman 1984: 117). Davis set up a Bureau of Social Hygiene staffed by up to 20 women social scientists who conducted mental and clinical tests on incoming prisoners. The bureau was to determine the appropriate sentence, provide a diagnosis for a treatment plan, and collect data on the causes of crime and prostitution (Freedman 1984: 118). In 1916 Bedford Hills opened a Psychopathic Hospital for delinquent women who were considered to be "a menace to society" (Rafter 1985: 72, 73). Women who were identified as mentally defective were to be segregated in asylums instead of being allowed, as the New York attorney general put it, "to add to the population of defective and criminally inclined persons" (quoted in Colvin 1997: 179).

The social purity movement raised concern about prostitution, arguing that society ought to be protected from the immoral woman, and encouraged the establishment of reformatories for fallen women. World War I raised fears about soldiers being infected with venereal disease, and reformatories started admitting women who had contracted those diseases and needed to be confined until treated and cured (Rafter 1985: 54). Women's reformatories were seen as an appropriate means of protecting society from "those who scatter disease through every community" (Rafter 1985: 58).

Kathleen Bement Davis and Jessie Donaldson Hodder, the superintendent of the Massachusetts women's prison, focused on improving classification and diversifying and improving nontraditional training. At Bedford Hills, despite teaching a diversity of nontraditional skills that would enable the women to "earn an honest livelihood," including stenography and typing (Freedman 1984: 133) in practice, women found it challenging to secure nondomestic work. At the Massachusetts prison, Hodder succeeded in 1911 in having the name changed from "prison" to the Massachusetts Reformatory for Women. Her objective was to transform the facility into an "Industrial Training Institute for Women" (Freedman 1984: 136), but beyond a few new programs domestic training continued to be the predominant training activity (Freedman 1984: 136). A 1927 survey of prisons found that training for employable skills in women's reformatories was "wholly inadequate"; however, its recommendations applied gender stereotypes to exclude training for the kinds of work the authors deemed unsuitable for women. Therefore, for example, they wrote that "printing is a man's industry." Inevitably, work that was considered suitable included household work, sewing, and laundering (Freedman 1984: 149).

By now the original reformatory design—a small inmate population having a close relationship with staff so as to resemble the family unit—had been overwhelmed by overcrowding that brought tensions and disciplinary problems (Rafter 1985: 79). In 1915 a state investigation of Bedford Hills confirmed that the classification system was unable to function properly because of overcrowding. It revealed mismanagement, abusive punishments, and racial and sexual tensions. The investigators claimed that Davis's policy of integrating races in the cottages had encouraged sexual attachments between blacks and whites (Freedman 1984: 140). The report identified the high proportion of "feeble-minded" inmates as a major constraint to performance and insisted that some inmates be transferred to state institutions for the mentally defective (Rafter 1985: 80).

By the 1930s states had begun to close women's units in prisons and transfer convicted felons housed there to reformatories so that "the women's reformatory ceased to exist in all but name"

(Rafter 1985: 81). Filling reformatories with felons either diluted or pushed out the minor offenders, who were once again sentenced to local jails as in the pre-reformatory days. The financial impact of the Great Depression of the 1930s and the 1929 stock market crash meant that states could no longer afford to fund reformatories in their original form. After 60 years of operation, the women's reformatory no longer existed (Rafter 1985: 82).

The 1940s

The new postwar corrective institutions were characterized by liberalized discipline practices and less brutality. Soledad Prison, for example, displayed fences and guard towers instead of high walls. Cell blocks had dayrooms and windows, and there were well-equipped libraries and gyms. A broad range of vocational and educational programs as well as group counseling were offered (Rotman 1995: 170). Recreational privileges and amenities included movie screenings and liberal mail and visitation procedures. While inmates still had little to occupy their time, the environment lost some of the oppression of the Big Houses (Johnson 1996: 75).

By the end of World War II, inmate classification systems were administered by teams of psychologists, caseworkers, psychiatrists, sociologists, and vocational counselors, who collectively created an inmate's case history. Based on the data collected, prisoners were assigned to a particular type of prison, where a rehabilitation plan would be drawn up and progress was reviewed regularly. In practice, however, rehabilitation as a core objective was always subordinated to security. The viability of the therapeutic approach was questioned and discredited. The indeterminate sentencing model was also challenged when it was implemented arbitrarily, in a discriminatory manner, and resulted in longer sentences (Rotman 1995: 171). In this period and into the 1950s there were only minor changes in prison administration until federal funds began to flow into penal systems in the 1960s.

Developments in Corrections: The 1950s to Date

The 1950s: Unrest and Riots

During the 1950s prisons in New Jersey, Michigan, Ohio, Illinois, California, and in other states experienced riots that commonly included events such as hostage taking, destruction of property, and looting. In less serious events inmates conducted sit-down strikes or self-mutilated (Rotman 1995: 168). Between 1950 and 1953 there were more than 50 prison riots (Blomberg and Lucken 2000: 118). In 1953 the American Prison Association stated the causes of the riots as lack of funding to prisons, official indifference to prison issues, lack of qualified personnel, idleness among inmates, lack of leadership, prison overcrowding, imprudent sentencing practices, and politicization of management. The absence of truly rehabilitative measures would lead to a greater emphasis on therapeutic programs in the next decades (Rotman 1995: 165).

In 1954, the American Prison Association revisited the ideal of rehabilitation by changing its name to the American Correctional Association and proposing that prisons be designated "correctional institutions."

The 1960s: Rehabilitation and Prisoner Litigation

In this period reforms again advanced the ideal of rehabilitation. Under the policy maxim "more is better" penal systems expanded on the assumption that this would increase their capacity to provide individualized treatment (Blomberg and Lucken 2000: 99). The drive toward therapeutic methods of rehabilitation was impeded by a lack of practical implementation and therefore by the absence of actual successful outcomes. Individualized treatment plans were designed by a team of professionals who developed life histories for each incoming inmate and then determined the appropriate therapeutic regime: therapeutic, academic, or vocational. The inmate's progress would be continuously reviewed for any required changes in treatment, and the preferred mode of treatment was group counseling (Blomberg and Lucken 2000: 108). In practice however, classification teams were not always deployed, and counseling became a method of control rather than treatment because counseling leaders tended to be correctional officers who possessed no qualifications to treat therapeutically. Similarly, in academic programs, teachers were substandard and textbooks were outdated (Blomberg and Lucken 2000: 113).

Inmate populations and the costs of incarceration expanded enormously. In the period 1880–1960 the imprisonment rate per 100,000 persons for federal prisons almost doubled, and between 1902 and 1960 the costs of state penal systems increased from $14 million to $1.51 billion (Blomberg and Lucken 2000: 114).

In 1966 when the state of the nation's prisons was surveyed for the President's Commission on Law Enforcement and Administration of Justice, the commission report concluded that life in prison was "barren and futile . . . [and]unspeakably brutal and degrading" and "the poorest possible preparation for their successful reentry into society" (quoted in Rotman 1995: 173).

Prisoner Rights

Under the "hands-off" doctrine, with some exceptions, the courts took the approach that prison administration would be disrupted if it interfered in prison issues, that interfering would violate the separation of powers doctrine, and that judges did not possess the capacity to exercise oversight of prisons. Therefore, before the agitation for inmate's rights, inmates had almost no rights while incarcerated. Supreme Court decisions blocked their access to the federal courts, and state courts such as the Virginia Supreme Court had ruled that as a "slave of the state" a prisoner had only the rights given by the state (Pollock 2004: 149).

Action to secure inmate rights through the courts evolved gradually, starting with the riots of the 1950s followed by black inmates organizing under Muslim leaders as the Nation of Islam. Crackdowns on black leaders of this movement prompted strikes and lawsuits. Finally, the rights movement became politicized through the Black Panthers, who were most effective in the California prison system between 1968 and 1971. Ultimately, inmates of all races became a united force in solidarity against prison administrations (Blomberg and Lucken 2000: 139).

By the early 1960s the Supreme Court was supporting prisoners' claims under the writ of habeas corpus and the Civil Rights Act for enforcement of freedom of religion, including the right to obtain copies of the Koran and to hold religious services (Rotman 1995: 173). Courts adjudicated a range of inmate issues, including enforcement of standards of health care, due process requirements in disciplinary cases, prohibition of segregation under the equal protection right, the guarantee against cruel and unusual punishment, and restrictions on mail.

The Eighth Amendment prohibition against *cruel and unusual punishment* attracted numerous claims. Courts decided that claimants must show that the punishment alleged was both cruel *and* unusual and that correctional officers, as part of their official duties, engaged in the "serious deprivation of a human need." The claimant must also show that the correctional officers involved in the punishment had a "culpable state of mind" when depriving an inmate of a human need and prove that they acted with "deliberate indifference" in relation to the deprivation. This means showing that the officer was aware that the inmate would face a serious risk of substantial harm but failed to act on that knowledge (Carleton 2005: 279). In *Wilson v. Seiter* 1991, the Court held that placing two inmates in a single cell did not automatically violate the Eight Amendment (Carleton 2005: 280).

In claims concerning the *use of force* within the prison, the reasonableness of the force used must be assessed on a case-by-case basis. Therefore, elements such as the level of force used, the staff's reasonable perception of injury, and the means used to resist an assault can be examined. In the riot at Attica Prison in 1971, the court agreed that unreasonable force had been used because injured inmates were beaten with sticks even though on stretchers, and others were stripped and forced to run naked through lines of guards armed with clubs and struck during that process (Blomberg and Lucken 2000: 146).

The Supreme Court decided in *Hudson v. Palmer* in 1984 that cells could be searched at any time to ensure security but that deliberate harassment unrelated to security concerns was not authorized. Where inmate property was lost or destroyed through a cell search, inmates had no recourse (*Bell v. Wolfish* 1979).

The issue of prison *overcrowding* led the courts to develop limits on prison capacity, and in a number of states, all or parts of their prison systems have operated under court control or special masters were appointed to act as the agent of the court in ensuring its orders were implemented (Morris 1995: 219).

By 1984, 33 states had at least one major prison operating under court order, including 8 states where the entire system was under court supervision (Haney 2006: 272). Inmate litigation radically affected the administration of prisons in that it forced improved professionalism, better health care, due process, and the overall accountability of prison administrations. Improvements in classification systems, work programs, and education were later challenged by the overcrowding that began in the 1980s. Judicial activism in prisons is said by one former high-level prison administrator to have "dragged many prisons and entire correctional systems into the twentieth century" (Riveland 1999: 173, 183).

Women Prisoner Litigation

The landmark decisions resulting from litigation by women prisoners have established that

- women inmates have a right to a range and quality of programs that is substantially equivalent to that available to men, but nevertheless based on the needs of female inmates (*Glover v. Johnson* 1979);

- women inmates are entitled to reasonable parity with men in vocational programming and in the provision of vocational facilities as well as to assignment to wage-paying work within a facility (*Barefield v. Leach* 1974);

- women inmates' conditions were inadequate where pregnant prisoners were not receiving adequate diets and prenatal education, were denied access to toilets and showers, and were shackled in leg irons in late pregnancy (*West v. Manson* 1983);

- male inmates' privacy rights were not violated where the observation of male nude inmates by female officers was "infrequent and casual" and pat down searches were also valid provided they were done professionally (*Grummett v. Rushen* 1985);

- random searches of clothed women by male officers that involved officers totally flattening the breasts of women being searched were ruled offensive in the extreme and prohibited (officers were required to run their hands over the entire body "squeezing and kneading her breasts, probing her crotch by pressing the flat of the hand against the genitals, and squeezing and kneading seams in her crotch area)." The Court differentiated searches by female officers of male inmates on the basis that women were disproportionately victims of rape and sexual assault and that men rarely experienced those acts (*Jordan v. Gardener* 1993).

The 1970s: Diversion Out of the Formal Correctional System

From the late 1960s through the 1970s the maxim that "more is better" was superseded by a policy that proclaimed "less is best." Policy makers viewed correctional systems as having failed to deter crime and as having labeled and stigmatized offenders in ways that perpetuated their criminality. The new policy approach was to replace treatment in the formal corrections system with informal modes of treatment. Now, offenders would be corrected in the community by "community correction" (Blomberg and Lucken 2000: 153).

For prisons this meant reserving imprisonment for violent offenders and diverting other offenders into community-based corrections through appropriate diversion schemes. The aim was to build ties between the offender and the community so as to reintegrate an offender into community life, restore family ties, and obtain employment and education (Stone 2005: 715). Ultimately, the policy failed, and diversion programs were most often applied to juveniles who would not ordinarily have been captured by the penal systems. The overall effect was to widen the net of the justice systems (Blomberg and Lucken 2000: 160). Other impediments to success were the Attica Prison riot in 1971, the Nixon administration's shift to victims' rights and crime control, and the "nothing works" claim in a study by academic Robert Martinson and others in 1974 (Stone 2005: 717) that assessed 231 evaluations of rehabilitation and treatment programs over the period 1945–1967 and claimed to show that in terms of rehabilitation, with few exceptions, nothing works. While Martinson later retracted these views, the study was influential in penal policy planning and resonated when there were riots in prisons and when corrections in the community had been deemed a failure (Blomberg and Lucken 2000: 166).

The nothing works critique of rehabilitation resulted in a full-scale assault on the ideal of rehabilitation. Political pressure resulted in the abandonment of indeterminate sentencing, which was opposed by liberals who were concerned about abuse of rights and discrimination by parole boards and by conservatives who believed that this form of sentencing meant lenient sentences, especially when such sentences were linked to early release through parole (Pratt 2009: 21). Rehabilitation, as an ideal of corrections policy, was supplanted by theories of retribution and incapacitation. While in 1968 73 percent of Americans thought rehabilitation should be the main objective of imprisonment, three decades later support for rehabilitation stood at only 26 percent, with almost 60 percent believing that the primary objective of imprisonment was "to punish and put away" offenders (Pratt 2009: 24, 54).

States legislated sentencing guidelines that removed the discretion of judges in calculating an appropriate sentence and severely restricted the factors that a judge could take into account to mitigate a sentence. The guidelines generally mandated increased sentences. Truth in sentencing laws restricted the time off for good behavior in prison, and in many states, life sentences were commonly imposed without any right to seek parole (Morris 1995: 217, 218).

Gender and Differential Treatment

During the 1970s, the notion that treatment should differ based on gender was replaced by a perspective favoring equality, but this standard was later also judged problematic because it generally meant that the male standard was applied to women prisoners regardless of their discrete needs and issues (Rafter 1990: 202). Over time it became generally recognized that where women have special needs they should be treated differently than men but not so that the differential treatment works to their disadvantage (Morash and Schram 2002: 64).

The 1980s to the 1990s: Retribution, Deterrence, and Incapacitation

In 1981 President Ronald Reagan declared a *war on crime* (Blomberg and Lucken 2000: 173). It was claimed that crime could be controlled with enough punishment and enough incarceration (Blomberg and Lucken 2000: 174). The outcome was that between 1980 and 1996, state and federal imprisonment rates increased by over 200 percent (Blumstein and Beck 1999: 17). The war on crime severely punished drug offenders, abolished parole, introduced mandatory minimum penalties for drug and violent offenders, and developed "three strikes and you're out" provisions that in many states introduced long sentences for habitual offenders. The war on crime and the subsequent war on drugs massively increased the incarceration rate, brought on a prison-building boom, privatized some prisons, and caused severe overcrowding. Prisons were now restored as frontline actors in crime control and would remain so.

Despite there being no increase in the rate of crime, from 1970 to 1980 the inmate population in U.S. prisons doubled, and from 1981 to 1995 it doubled again, leading to a crisis of overcrowding at both federal and state levels (Morris 1995: 211). Between 1980 and 1992 the number of persons incarcerated in state and federal prisons and jails rose from 333,000 to 883,000, an increase of 168 percent.

Racial disparities throughout justice systems radically altered the composition of the inmate population. Whereas in 1982, 1 in 49 black males aged 20–29 years was incarcerated—a ratio eight times that of whites, by 1989 one-quarter of black males in that age range were under correctional supervision in some form. By 1993 blacks comprised 44 percent of the state and federal prison population while comprising only 12 percent of the U.S. population, whereas whites made up 74 percent of the overall national population but only 36 percent of the state and federal prison population. This racial disparity was attributed largely to the war on drugs (Blomberg and Lucken 2000: 181).

Gender Issues

Women who are mothers suffer disadvantage in prisons because even with decentralization their families are unable to visit where a prison is located in an isolated area and there is no reliable transportation. One study in 1993 found that over half of children never visited their imprisoned mothers, less than 10 percent visited once or more a week, and just under 17 percent visited once a month (Morash and Schram 2002: 80). Only New York provides nurseries enabling newborns to stay with their mothers for a limited period. Most states have no legislation at all relating to the issue of mothers and their children in prisons (Morash and Schram 2002: 83).

Once imprisoned a mother may lose her parental rights if she is judged by her criminality to have abandoned and neglected a child, is found unfit because of the nature and circumstances of the offense she has committed, or fails to maintain contact with a child following her incarceration (Morash and Schram 2002: 88). Women inmates try to demonstrate fitness as a mother through arranging visitation to show that relations with children are being maintained, by enrolling in parenting skills classes, and by planning for reunification with children (Enos 2001: 84–89).

The 1990s and Beyond: Mass Incarceration

By this time corrections had become the fastest-growing budget item in state budgets. Despite this, the policies that had massively increased the rate of incarceration were supplemented by yet more punitive policies intended to incapacitate habitual criminals (Blumstein and Beck 1999: 19). The focus necessarily shifted from treatment to the efficient management of a massive permanent inmate population (Caplow and Simon 1999: 98).

Due to policies focused on retribution and incapacitation, the U.S. justice system now imprisons more persons for longer periods than any other country. Data on prisoners in 2014 shows the following:

- On December 31, 2014, the number of prisoners held by state and federal corrections systems was 1,561,500, resulting in a rate of imprisonment of 612 per 100,000 U.S. residents, the highest in the world. Of this total, 112,961 were females.

- By race, in 2014, 6 percent of all black males aged between 30 and 39 years were in prison compared to 2 percent of Hispanics and 1 percent of white males in that age group.

- The states with the largest male prison population were Texas (151,717), California (129,706), and Florida (95,567).

- The states with the largest female prison population were Texas (14,326), Florida (7,303), and California (6,382).

- The states with the highest imprisonment rates were Louisiana (1,072), Texas (792), and Mississippi (788).

- The states with the lowest imprisonment rates were Alaska (78), Maine (189), and Rhode Island (223).

As will be discussed in Chapter 2, political initiatives are now aiming to ameliorate some of the effects of these punitive policies. They include releasing nonviolent offenders and treatment programs that prepare inmates for life outside prison so they do not recidivate. Nevertheless, without radical change, policies that promote retribution and incapacitation will continue to dominate the nation's corrections systems.

References

Blomberg, Thomas G. and Lucken, Karol. 2000. *American Penology: A History of Control*. New York: Aldine de Gruyter.

Blumstein, Alfred and Beck, Allen J. 1999. Population Growth in U.S. Prisons 1980–1996, in Tonry, Michael and Petersilia, Joan, eds. *Prisons: A Review of Research*. Chicago: University of Chicago Press, pp. 17–62.

Caplow, Theodore and Simon, Jonathan. 1999. Understanding Prison Policy and Population Trends, in Tonry, Michael and Petersilia, Joan, eds. *Prisons: A Review of Research*. Chicago: University of Chicago Press, pp. 63–120.

Carleton, Francis. 2005. Eighth Amendment, in Bosworth, Mary, ed. *Encyclopedia of Prisons and Correctional Facilities*, Volume 1. Thousand Oaks, CA: Sage Publications, pp. 278–280.

Colvin, Mark. 1997. *Penitentiaries, Reformatories, and Chain Gangs: Social Theory and the History of Punishment in Nineteenth Century America*. New York: St. Martin's Press.

Davies, Kim. 2005. Panopticon, in Bosworth, Mary ed. *Encyclopedia of Prisons and Correctional Facilities*, Volume 2. Thousand Oaks, CA: Sage Publications, pp. 663–666.

Dodge, L. Mara. 2005. Cottage System, in Bosworth, Mary, ed. *Encyclopedia of Prisons and Correctional Facilities*, Volume 1. Thousand Oaks, CA: Sage Publications, pp. 195–198.

Enos, Sandra. 2001. *Mothering from the Inside: Parenting in a Women's Prison*. New York: State University of New York Press.

Farrell, William. 2005. Convict Lease System, in Bosworth, Mary, ed. *Encyclopedia of Prisons and Correctional Facilities*, Volume 1. Thousand Oaks, CA: Sage Publications, pp. 175–177.

Freedman, Estelle B. 1984. *Their Sisters' Keepers: Women's Prison Reform in America, 1830–1930*. Ann Arbor: University of Michigan Press.

Gillespie, Wayne. 2004. The Context of Imprisonment, in Stanko, Stephen, Gillespie, Wayne, and Crews, Gordon A., eds. *Living in Prison: A History of the Correctional System with an Insider's View*. Westport, CT: Greenwood Press, pp. 63–88.

Haney, Craig. 2006. *Reforming Punishment: Psychological Limits to the Pains of Imprisonment*. Washington, DC: American Psychological Association.

Hindus, Michael Stephen. 1980. *Prison and Plantation: Crime, Justice and Authority in Massachusetts and South Carolina, 1767–1878*. Chapel Hill: University of North Carolina Press.

Hirsch, Adam Jay. 1992. *The Rise of the Penitentiary: Prisons and Punishment in Early America*. New Haven, CT: Yale University Press.

Ignatieff, Michael. 1978. *A Just Measure of Pain: The Penitentiary in the Industrial Revolution 1750–1850*. London: Penguin Books.

Johnson, Robert. 1996. *Hard Time: Understanding and Reforming the Prison*. Belmont, CA: Wadsworth Publishing.

Kahan, Paul. 2008. *Eastern State Penitentiary: A History*. Charleston, SC: History Press.

Kahan, Paul. 2012. *Seminary of Virtue: The Ideology and Practice of Inmate Reform at Eastern State Penitentiary, 1829–1971*. New York: Peter Lang.

Kann, Mark E. 2005. *Punishment, Prisons and Patriarchy: Liberty and Power in the Early Republic*. New York: New York University Press.

McGowen, Randall. 1995. The Well-Ordered Prison: England 1780–1865, in Morris, Norval and Rothman, David J., eds. *The Oxford History of the Prison: The Practice of Punishment in Western Society*. Oxford: Oxford University Press, pp. 71–99.

Melossi, Dario and Pavarini, Massimo. 1981. *The Prison and the Factory: Origins of the Penitentiary System*. New Jersey: Barnes and Noble.

Morash, Merry and Schram, Pamela J. 2002. *The Prison Experience: Special Issues of Women in Prison*. Prospect Heights, IL: Waveland Press.

Morris, Norval. 1995. The Contemporary Prison: 1965–Present, in Morris, Norval and Rothman, David J., eds. *The Oxford History of the Prison: The Practice of Punishment in Western Society*. Oxford: Oxford University Press, pp. 202–234.

Pisciotta, Alexander W. 1994. *Benevolent Repression: Social Control and the American Reformatory—Prison Movement*. New York: New York University Press.

Pollock, Jocelyn M. 2004. *Prisons and Prison Life: Costs and Consequences*. New York: Oxford University Press.

Pratt, Travis C. 2009. *Addicted to Incarceration: Corrections Policy and the Politics of Misinformation in the United States*. Thousand Oaks, CA: Sage Publications.

Rafter, Nicole Hahn. 1990. *Partial Justice: Women, Prisons, and Social Control* (2nd ed.). Newark, NJ: Transaction Publishers.

Rafter, Nichole Hahn. 1985. *Partial Justice: Women in State Prisons 1800–1935*. Boston, MA: Northeastern University Press.

Riveland, Chase. 1999. Prison Management Trends, in Tonry, Michael and Petersilia, Joan, eds. *Prisons: A Review of Research*. Chicago: University of Chicago Press, pp. 163–204.

Rothman, David J. 1990. *The Discovery of the Asylum: Social Order and Disorder in the New Republic*. New York: Aldine de Gruyter.

Rothman, David J. 2012. *Conscience and Convenience: The Asylum and Its Alternatives in Progressive America*. New Brunswick, NJ. Transaction Publishers.

Rotman, Edgardo. 1995. The Failure of Reform: United States, 1865–1965, in Morris, Norval and Rothman, David J., eds. *The Oxford History of the Prison: The Practice of Punishment in Western Society*. Oxford: Oxford University Press, pp. 151–177.

Semple, Janet. 1993. *Bentham's Prison: A Study of the Panopticon Penitentiary*. Oxford: Clarendon Press.

Spierenberg, Pieter. 2007. *The Prison Experience: Disciplinary Institutions and Their Inmates in Early Modern Europe*. Amsterdam. Amsterdam University Press.

Stephan, James J. 2008. *Census of State and Correctional Facilities 2005*. Washington, DC: Department of Justice, Office of Justice Programs, Bureau of Statistics.

Stone, Josh. 2005. President's Commission on Law Enforcement and Administration of Justice, in Bosworth, Mary, ed. *Encyclopedia of Prisons and Correctional Facilities*, Volume 2. Thousand Oaks, CA: Sage Publications, pp. 715–717.

Thomas, Jim. 2005. Bentham, Jeremy, in Bosworth, Mary, ed. *Encyclopedia of Prisons and Correctional Facilities*, Volume 1. Thousand Oaks, CA: Sage Publications, pp. 71–73.

Zedner, Lucia. 1995. Wayward Sisters: The Prison for Women, in Morris, Norval and Rothman, David J., eds. *The Oxford History of the Prison: The Practice of Punishment in Western Society*. Oxford: Oxford University Press, pp. 295–324.

Many of the issues and controversies affecting prisons reflect the divergence of opinion concerning the rationale for imprisonment. Some argue that the purpose of incarceration is retribution and that inmates should suffer a degree of discomfort while in prison to differentiate them from "law-abiding" citizens. Others contend that human dignity requires no lesser treatment be accorded inmates because they are incarcerated *as* punishment and not *for* punishment. Some question even the existence of the punishment of incarceration, and others point to the outcomes of the mass imprisonment policies that have been followed since the 1980s, contending that they have resulted in the "warehousing" of prisoners, disregarded rehabilitation, and have failed to properly address the human and financial costs of a policy of incapacitation.

Contemporary structural and operational challenges to corrections systems are largely an outcome of federal and state criminal justice policy making. Since the 1970s these policies have increased inmate populations beyond capacity, caused gross overcrowding, and necessitated the construction of more prisons. Correctional administrators have been unable to advance a corrections agenda that detracts from "tough on crime" policies, and as a result, there has been no substantive

---

A U.S. veteran with post-traumatic stress sits in a segregated holding pen at the Cook County Jail after he was arrested on a narcotics charge in Chicago in 2014. At Cook County, one in five detainees is locked up because of mental health problems. (AP Photo/Charles Rex Arbogast)

change in penal policies since the 1970s. The task of prison administrators therefore remains one of implementing penal policies and managing difficult inmate populations with inadequate resources.

This discussion of problems, controversies, and solutions commences with an explanation of the contemporary pains of imprisonment which remain the source of multiple issues facing corrections administrators today both operationally and structurally.

The "Pains of Imprisonment" and Recidivism

In 1958 Gresham Sykes published *The Society of Captives*, a sociological study of the inmate social system at the New Jersey State Maximum Security Prison. His focus was the mental and psychological impact of the prison environment on inmates. Sykes argued that the psychological challenges to inmates could equate to physical pain and termed these frustrations the "pains of imprisonment." He identified a set of deprivations—of liberty, of autonomy, of goods and services, of heterosexual relationships and the loss of security—and examined how inmates coped with these deprivations. According to prison psychologist Haney (2006: 169), "Little has changed inside contemporary American prisons" since Sykes identified the pains of imprisonment, and "harsh punishment not only is widespread but has become the *raison d'etre* of American corrections" (Haney 2006: xiv). Moderating forms of punishment, he argues, does not dishonor victims, nor does justice for victims require that the pains of imprisonment be unconstrained (2006: 17). Studies that continue to identify the pains or psychological consequences of incarceration represent a counter-narrative to the principle of less eligibility.

Constant media depictions of inmates as "brutal, hardened criminals" and public and political discourses employing dehumanizing language to cast offenders as dangerous, violent, and less than human have inhibited an analysis of the "pains of imprisonment" and its long-term consequences. The demise of rehabilitative programming with its replacement with a discourse of incapacitation and public safety has legitimated attacks on inmates that cast them as outside society and unworthy of even minimal consideration (Haney 2006: 169). Public support for the principle of less eligibility has reinforced these notions.

Beginning in the mid-1970s, the objective of inmate rehabilitation was replaced by politically driven policies of retribution and incapacitation. The effectiveness of the new "get tough" approach to crime control and punishment was questionable. For example, recidivism rates did not improve; one study found that of 100,000 prisoners released in 1983, 62.5 percent were rearrested within three years (Haney 2006: 71). In U.S. prison systems, fewer than 20 percent of inmates are kept in minimum security facilities where tension and stress levels can be expected to be moderated. The mass of inmates are therefore subjected to the pains of imprisonment in the interests of maintaining security (Haney 2006: 187). What are the psychological pains associated with confinement in prison?

Psychological Impact of Incarceration

While early psychological studies showed that inmates tended to adapt over time to the pains of imprisonment and concluded that the effects of prison were largely minimal, more recent empirical studies have found a significant correlation between physiological and psychological responses to stress and overcrowded facilities, between misconduct and overcrowding, between overcrowding and post-release recidivism, and between inmate disruptions and high inmate turnover (Haney 2006: 168). They indicate that long-term imprisonment results in increases in "hostility and social introversion" and that inmates' coping abilities undergo what is termed "a behavioral deep-freeze" that stores their pre-prison behaviors that led to conviction and incarceration until they are released (Haney 2006: 168).

Overall, the effects of imprisonment ("prisonization") depend on how it is experienced by an individual (under differing levels of security) and on his or her psychosocial background (Liebling and Maruna 2005: 11). It follows therefore that prison is not "a uniform experience" and that "damage may be immediate or cumulative" whether the period of confinement is continuous and lengthy or a series of repeated shorter terms (Liebling and Maruna 2005: 12).

Psychological Dimension of Prisonization

According to Haney (2006: 176–179, 202), the psychological dimension of prisonization includes the following elements:

- Inmates must surrender control over all aspects of their daily life: the prison routine determines all actions from waking to sleeping, and inmates are infantilized by this process.

- Inmates come to depend on prison officials to make choices for them and on the prison structure and routines to structure their lives. Prior dependence on an institutional structure means that some may be unable to cope when they are forced to live in an unstructured environment.

- Inmates are denied basic rights to privacy: almost 40 percent of inmates in the United States are placed in maximum-security prisons which are typically large and use multiple control mechanisms to regulate behavior. Over time, inmates lose the capacity for self-control because they come to rely on the routine and constant surveillance to control their behavior.

- Living conditions are much diminished from those in the outside world. Inmates generally occupy small cramped cells often in deteriorating old buildings—one-quarter of inmates in 2000 were housed in facilities more than 50 years old. Most are required to share their cell with another inmate whom they do not choose to live with and with whom they must constantly negotiate the minutiae of life. They will sometimes be locked down with their cell mate for months, with only brief periods out of the cell for showers and exercise.

- Overcrowded prisons promote hypertension, produce high stress levels, and lead to a greater incidence of complaints of illness and a higher rate of disciplinary infractions. The sheer number of social interactions required in overcrowded conditions itself creates high levels of uncertainty and personal instability in a dangerous environment where mistakes in interacting with others can prove fatal.

- In addition to adhering to a multitude of formal rules (e.g., in California, Title 15 is a manual of 189 pages of prison rules and regulations provided to inmates, many of whom will be functionally illiterate [Irwin and Owen 2005: 99]), inmates must observe the informal norms that are part of the inmate culture.

- Inmates are commonly denied gainful work or are able to obtain only very poorly compensated work, which does not equip them with skills they can use on release. Furloughs and work release programs are in decline (Johnson 2005: 257).

- Inmates are often idle, and psychological evidence indicates that chronic idleness produces frustration and negative behaviors, such as violence and destructive activity.

- In the majority of states, inmates are denied conjugal visits and are drawn into sexual relationships and contacts where substitute experiences may be found. Visits no longer constitute entitlements but are classed as privileges that can be withheld without explanation. Compassionate leaves, once commonplace, are increasingly rare (Johnson 2005: 257).

To this dimension can be added what Irwin and Owen (2005: 107) refer to as "degradation ceremonies," meaning the process of being handled from the moment a prisoner enters a prison or jail, including regular strip searches, and the contempt and hostility exhibited by criminal justice professionals. These practices are gendered because they include rules about clothing and styles of dress that in California, for example, mean that women are dressed as men, being required to wear the same clothing as men, comprising blue denim pants, a baseball cap, t-shirts, and state-issued shoes (2005: 108). Criminologist Michael Tonry (2004: 20) argues that prison administrators ought to avoid imposing "petty and stigmatizing indignities," such as requiring that uniforms be worn, regulating styles of haircut, censoring reading and media material and access to the Internet, and restricting visits and writing of letters to editors and reporters. By comparison, in Europe many prisons are less restrictive and allow prisoners to wear street clothes and have regular furloughs out of the prisons.

Prisonization has been exacerbated by lengthy sentences, with the outcome that adaptations to the prison environment are no longer short term and capable of being easily jettisoned on release. For example, between 1986 and 1997 the average time actually served by inmates in the federal system increased from 15 months to 29 months and for drug offenders from 20 months to 43 months. By 1997, about 70 percent of all persons committed to a federal facility in that year could expect to be serving five years or longer before release. In the states, by 2002, offenders were receiving on average a sentence of 4.5 years, and a number of states now have between 15 percent and 20 percent of inmates serving life sentences. These facts suggest that prisonization "evolves from being merely a set of short-term adaptations to an actual long term strategy of living" (Haney 2006: 181).

Adaptation to Prison

Many inmates find the initial period of imprisonment the hardest, and those entering prison with preexisting disorders may experience acute psychiatric symptoms. Subsequently, many adapt, and symptoms may subside or persist. When inmates reveal psychological symptoms, including clinical depression, paranoia, and psychosis, few will receive treatment. In the worst cases, inmates react to the stress of the environment by suicide (Haney 2006: 185). Ironically, inmates who successfully adapt will experience the greatest challenges in transitioning from confinement to freedom (Haney 2006: 170).

One long-term inmate's perspective is that prison must provide six basic functions: recreation, property, mail, phones, laundry, and food. For inmates, the efficient operation of these functions is fundamental to prison life. As he expresses it, "The thing about the six basic functions is that you experience them all the time, you need them every day. If there are problems every day with these six functions, then frustration quickly builds up among the prisoners" and "problems in basic services are the most dangerous problems for a prison to have" (Carceral 2006: 30, 31).

Inmate Coping Strategies

Inmate accounts reveal how they must always be alert to the dangers of prison and hypervigilant to ensure their personal safety. One study of a maximum-security prison in Tennessee found that fear shaped the lives of numerous inmates, causing them to avoid high-risk areas and to remain in their cells. More than one-quarter kept a "shank" or other weapon for self-defense and adopted behavioral strategies that projected a tough persona that conveyed the potential for violence. One prison administrator described the environment as "a barely controlled jungle where the aggressive and the strong will exploit the weak, and the weak are dreadfully aware of it" (quoted in Haney 2006: 173).

Inmates adopt a "prison mask" to hide emotions and identity, and some shun open communication to the extent that they withdraw from social interactions and retreat into themselves, trusting no one and leading lives of isolation (Haney 2006: 173). Prisonization means that many inmates will find the transition to normal life hugely challenging because the responses learned in prison such as mistrust, the prison mask, and a tendency to react to minor provocations, while acceptable in the prison, are problematic in the outside world. Thus, former inmates may be seen as withdrawn, guarded, unfeeling, suspicious, and capable of overreactions (Haney 2006: 179, 180).

The idleness that most inmates experience often develops a lethargy or tiredness that is reinforced by the monotony of the daily prison routine and contrasts sharply with the rapid rhythms of life outside. The absence of opportunities for exercising initiative coupled with dependence on the structures and procedures of the prison can result in depression, especially in long-term inmates who exhibit "a flatness of response which resembles slow, automatic behavior of a very limited kind, and he is humorless and lethargic" (Haney 2006: 174).

The significance of the "pains of imprisonment" lies in its association with the problem of recidivism. When inmates are released and forced to engage with the world outside the prison, prisonization will influence the likelihood of recidivism. Recent efforts to improve so-called reentry programs that are designed to prepare an inmate for release into free society have recognized the importance of minimizing recidivism, but much remains to be done.

Recidivism

This term describes the return to criminality of an offender following his or her conviction and punishment for a criminal offense. There are a number of theories about why convicted persons recidivate, including:

- Incorrigibility: this theory argues that some persons cannot change their criminal ways and will not be deterred from further offending whatever sanction is imposed.
- Failed sanction: it is claimed that recidivism is the outcome of an inappropriate punishment that failed to operate as a deterrent; for example, the punishment was too lenient or too harsh.
- Failed reintegration: when offenders are unable to adjust from a highly structured prison life to the outside world

where social changes always occur, they may return to criminality. Here, recidivism is associated with the lack of preparation for a return to society, for example, because there were no reentry programs in the prison, and with the nonexistence or the ineffectiveness of support measures. For example, in 1997, in California, of 142,000 persons released from prison, only 5 percent had completed a reentry program before release (Haney 2006: 337).

- Failed programs: this relates to the adequacy and effectiveness of programming in prison and the willingness of offenders to fully participate in such programs. Low levels of participation or poor or inappropriate programming may contribute to recidivism.

- Peer pressure and social constraints: social stimuli outside the prison such as peer pressure may cause on offender to return to criminality.

- Economic stress: in many cases released offenders will be unable to obtain employment because of bars to the employment of felons, or will be ineligible for public housing or other benefits that will provide support and prevent recidivism.

- Mental health issues: offenders with mental illness may recidivate even where programming was adequate because their mental condition remains unchanged following release (Cole 2005: 823–824).

Measuring Recidivism

In the United States recidivism has been estimated at between 40 percent and 80 percent of those released, but estimates are problematic because different techniques are employed to measure recidivism. One method looks at rearrest data, another examines reconviction rates, and a third method examines data on resentencing (Cole 2005: 824). Studies have revealed general trends in recidivism, which show that on balance recidivism usually occurs within the first year of release and almost all recidivism occurs within three years of release, property offenses are most likely to be recidivism offenses, violent offenders are least likely to recidivate, young offenders are most likely to recidivate; men are more likely than women to recidivate, and African Americans and Latinos are more likely to recidivate than whites in every crime category largely due to socioeconomic factors (Cole 2005: 825). In addition, one study found that offenders who have been released from prison are responsible for up to 11 percent of homicides, 10 percent of robberies, and 12 percent of burglaries (Pratt 2009: 83).

Prison and Amenities: Principle of Less Eligibility

The notion of less eligibility under which life in prison would intentionally be experienced as less attractive than life outside first took hold informally during the first decades of the development of the prison. Even as late as 1855 prison inspectors felt obliged to publicly refute the notion that some tried to enter prison because life was easier there than outside (Hindus 1980: 167).

Reducing and Banning Amenities

More recently, the less eligibility argument has caused states to follow the lead of the federal system under the No Frills Prison Act 1996 and reduce or ban inmate facilities such as weightlifting equipment, televisions, coffeepots, and hot plates in the cells of federal prisoners. It also prohibits computers, electronic instruments, certain movies rated above PG, possessing pornography, and unmonitored phone calls (Lenz 2002). State action has included the following:

- In 1994 the Wisconsin governor ordered all free weights removed from prisons and then ordered a ban on movies and pornography.
- In Georgia, 150 tons of weightlifting equipment was ordered removed from prisons. Ohio, South Carolina,

Arizona, Mississippi, and California followed suit (Parenti 1999: 175).

- In January 1995, Mississippi banned private televisions and prohibited inmates who refused to work or attend education programs from using weightlifting equipment (Finn 1996: 36).
- In Arizona, the Department of Corrections reduced the property and clothing that an inmate could keep inside a cell, the number of items for sale in the commissary, the number of types of movies and television programs prisoners could watch, and the frequency of telephone calls (Finn 1996: 36).

Until the 1990s telephoning charges to call family members from prison were similar to those charged outside prisons. However, subsequently, prison telephone systems have been contracted out to private enterprise and have become a $1.2 billion a year industry, with companies setting telephone rates and fees far in excess of those charged to private customers. Following complaints, the Federal Communications Commission (FCC) found that phone companies pay hundreds of millions of dollars ($460 million in 2013) in concession fees to state and local correctional systems for exclusive contracts to control the telephone services in prisons. According to the FCC, the fees fund a range of prison costs from inmate welfare to salaries or are simply remitted to the state concerned. All proposals to eliminate the fees have been fiercely opposed by prison and jail officials. In one case, a company fee for using its prison phone service included a charge for processing the bill and another charge if the bill was paid over the telephone (Williams 2015).

Perspectives on Amenities

Prison administrators generally favor permitting inmates some amenities to keep them occupied. Officers are able to withdraw amenities to sanction misconduct, but providing few amenities renders a system of rewards less effective (Lenz 2002: 506).

The general public appears to have a different view to prison professionals about amenities because most studies of public perceptions about prison life have found that respondents perceive prison life to be "too easy and comfortable for inmates, and many people resent inmates' access to amenities, like TV and exercise equipment" (Wozniak 2014: 306). One national survey conducted in 2001 found that 10 percent believed that prison life was too harsh, 35 percent believed it was about right, and 42 percent believed it was not harsh enough (Wozniak 2014: 307). A similar survey conducted in 2014 also suggested that a plurality of Americans countrywide (46%) wanted prisons to be harsher. These surveys suggest that political leaders will be reluctant to support improvements in prison conditions (Wozniak 2014: 318).

Proponents of the less eligibility rule argue that the prison experience should be harsh in order to reflect proper concern for crime victims and to act as a deterrent to future criminality. However, there are no studies that support this proposition. Concern for crime victims creates a "status competition" between offenders and their victims and prompts political arguments about whether there should be greater concern about the welfare of criminals or about crime victims. Making this argument the basis for justice policy leads to the conclusion that providing any amenities to inmates amounts to slighting crime victims (Zimring and Hawkins 2004: 164).

The No Frills Prison Act 1996 exemplifies this status competition by providing that inmates serving a sentence for a crime that caused serious bodily injury to a victim are denied television viewing and are limited to one hour a day for sports and exercise (Zimring and Hawkins 2004: 165). Some argue that states save costs by cutting amenities; however, the 31 states that allow inmates televisions in their cells do not pay for them (prisoners or their relatives pay for them), and cablevision is paid for out of profits from the prison commissary, vending machines, and long-distance telephone charges (Finn 1996: 6–7).

Some proponents of the less eligibility rule contend that medical care should also be regarded as a luxury to properly reflect the punitive character of incarceration. Others believe that there should be equivalent care regardless of whether or not the patient is incarcerated and that providing lesser care would be a violation of medical ethics and inflict pain and suffering (Welch 2005: 58).

College Courses in Prisons

Research has shown that college education programs assist in rehabilitating inmates, improve their job prospects following release, and reduce recidivism. The first prison-based college program began in 1953, but because of funding constraints, only 12 such programs were operational by 1965. In that year, however, Congress enacted legislation giving inmates the right to apply for federal financial aid for college programs through Pell grants. The result was that by 1973 there were 182 college programs in operation, and by 1982 the number had increased to 350 in 45 states covering about 27,000 inmates. Inmates were subject to the same criteria as others when applying for Pell grants, and only one-tenth of 1 percent of the annual budget for Pell grants was spent on inmates (Mentor 2005: 142). Nevertheless, permitting inmates to undertake a college education while incarcerated remained controversial. In 1994 Congress eliminated Pell grants for inmates. The stated rationale was that federal money was being given to inmates at the expense of law-abiding students. The effect was devastating, and by 1997 only eight such programs remained (Mentor 2005: 142).

Moral Perspectives

Philosopher Richard Lippke (2007: 3) argues that "harsh and restrictive prison conditions, combined with the disrespectful or abusive treatment of inmates, sends the message that offenders are contemptible, little more than dangerous wild animals to be severely chastised and restrained." Lippke contends that prison conditions should be at or near what he terms "minimum conditions of confinement" as contrasted with "extreme conditions of confinement," which he identifies as those prevailing in many supermax prisons (2007: 5).

Minimum conditions in his view comprise inherent restrictions such as limits on freedom of movement, freedom of association, and privacy. As to amenities, Lippke agrees that the level of these should always be "relatively low" but that inmates could be permitted to purchase items that would improve their quality of life (Lippke 2007: 107). Extreme conditions of confinement include living in overcrowded conditions, enforced idleness, exposure to violence, bad food, inadequate medical care, and, in extreme cases, solitary confinement (2007: 109).

The Supreme Court in *Turner v. Safley* has adopted the position that inmate rights can legitimately be restricted as long as the restrictions are reasonably related to the state's pursuit of legitimate penal aims. In practice, the Courts have deferred to the judgment of prison administrations on the issue of reasonableness (2007: 140).

Conjugal Visits

Conjugal or family visits are a privilege afforded to inmates in the low-risk category in only a few states. Visits may have been permitted informally, such as in Mississippi, early in the development of the prison as a means of promoting labor productivity. Later, around 1940, makeshift houses were constructed at Parchman Prison, Mississippi, for all incarcerated males regardless of race. Official status was granted to the informal practice of permitting conjugal visits in 1965, and in 1972 the program was extended to female inmates. Inmates were not required to request participation in the program. By 1974 the program allowed an inmate's family to spend up to three days and two nights in apartments within the prison grounds constructed especially for this program. At that time then, a typical inmate family could expect to have a conjugal visit every two weeks and a three-day visit every other month. In 1987, following the opening of the Central Mississippi Correctional Facility for

Women, married female inmates were given equal privileges with men, including conjugal visits. Condoms were provided to those in the program (Hensley et al. 2002: 145, 146).

Other conjugal programs are the following:

- California introduced a conjugal visits program at one facility in 1968. Today, 32 of the 33 male and female state prisons operate the program, which emphasizes family stability rather than sexual release. Maximum-security inmates may not participate, and condoms must be provided by spouses (2002: 147).

- New York commenced a program in 1976 at seven facilities, with visits taking place in mobile homes at the prisons. Condoms are provided by the corrections department.

- In Washington, a program began in 1980 in a women's prison and was subsequently extended to 11 of the 12 state prisons using mobile homes, with the corrections department providing contraceptives.

- In 1983 New Mexico introduced a similar program in four state prisons, with inmates being provided condoms. Prisoners having records of violence must meet strict eligibility criteria to enter the program (Hensley et al. 2002: 147, 148).

Conjugal visits are justified on the basis that maintaining normal conjugal life assists in inmate management, prevents sexual attacks, and promotes lower rates of recidivism. Supporters also claim that enabling an inmate to maintain regular contact with his or her children, and with even a truncated form of family life, negates some of the psychological impacts of imprisonment. One study in Mississippi found that inmates who did not participate in the conjugal visit program in that state were more likely to show violent behavior than those who participated. Most inmates who participated, and most who did not, agreed that the program reduced violence and tension (Hensley et al. 2002: 10).

Opponents say visits favor only married persons, that visits are a source of pleasure to inmates and therefore morally inappropriate, and that they may result in the birth of children who may suffer lack of parental support when one spouse is incarcerated (Welch 2005: 152, 153). Others claim that visits facilitate the smuggling of contraband and generate negative attitudes in those inmates who are not permitted to participate. Some research indicates that a majority of inmates in Mississippi, both participants and nonparticipants, believed that the program reduced the incidence of sexual behaviors in prisons (Hensley et al. 2002: 155).

As part of the move to get tough on offenders, conjugal visits have been categorized as a privilege that can be withdrawn. In 1995, California prohibited visits for sex offenders, lifers, and inmates with disciplinary records on the basis that inmates ought not to seem as if they have greater rights than victims and that it must be made clear that prison was a place for punishment (Parenti 1999: 175).

Rising Correctional Costs

Between 1978 and 2000 correctional costs nationwide increased from $5 billion to almost $40 billion, and during the 1990s the costs of new prison construction averaged almost $2 billion each year (Culp 2005: 163). Despite new construction, prisons remained over capacity, so, for example, by 1997 the federal system was operating at 119 percent of capacity and the average state at 115 percent of capacity. California, Pennsylvania, and Virginia were operating at 150 percent, and at one point California reached its highest rate of 206 percent. In nearly all states, increased prison expenditure was financed in part by cutting higher education appropriations, so from 1987 to 1995 state governments spent 30 percent more on prisons and higher education spending fell by 18 percent. During the period 1987–1997 state increases in prison populations ranged from a low of 25 percent in Maine to a high of 180 percent in Colorado (Caplow and Simon 1999: 74, 75).

Beginning from about 2007 there has been a gradual acknowledgment at the political and policy levels that the costs of incarceration are now excessive, especially since there has been no dramatic reduction in crime despite the policy of incapacitation. Nevertheless, "prisons remain central to the agenda of public protection" (Clear 2015: 358). Therefore, any suggestion that the policy of mass incarceration is about to end is overly optimistic. For one reason, prison populations and penal policies differ state to state, and therefore, strategies to counter mass incarceration will have to be created state by state (Clear 2015: 360).

A recent approach to corrections costs is for states to attempt to recover costs from inmates. For example, in Illinois, former inmates convicted of the most serious crimes are being sued by the state to secure a lump-sum payment toward the costs of their incarceration. Even offenders who completed only short sentences for less serious offenses are liable to be sued if they are fortunate enough to receive a windfall such as an inheritance or the proceeds of a legal claim. In one case, a former inmate who served a 15-month sentence for a drug offense was ordered to pay $20,000, and the money was appropriated from a $31,690 settlement he received following his mother's death (Walters 2015).

Mentally Ill Prisoners

During the 1960s and 1970s a policy of "transintitutionalization" resulted in the closure of many state hospitals for the mentally ill and the displacement of patients into the community. It was envisaged they would be treated locally by non-stigmatizing community health centers that would dispense drugs and monitor them. The effect of this policy was to decrease the number of beds in public and private mental hospitals from 451,000 in 1965 to 177,000 by 1985. While in 1955 there were 560,000 hospitalized mental patients, by 1999 this had fallen to less than 80,000 (Kupers 1999: xvi).

During the same period the overall prison population doubled from about 200,000 to about 400,000.

In most cases, local communities did not create the planned treatment facilities for the mentally ill under the Community Health Centers Act 1963 because the states failed to provide funds (Kupers 1999: 12). This failure caused the justice system to become the repository of many mentally ill persons, who were not dangerous enough to be committed to the remaining mental health hospitals. It is argued therefore that prisons and jails have become the new mental hospitals (Kendall 2005: 787) and that mental hospitals and prisons exchange populations according to the relative allocation of resources (Blomberg and Lucken 2000: 200).

Screening inmates to determine mental health needs occurs systematically only in the federal prison system. In 2001 a survey of over 1,500 state and private prisons found that one-quarter conducted no screening at all (Haney 2006: 251). While the number of mentally ill prisoners is not accurately known, estimates for 2000 suggest that 16.3 percent of state prisoners are mentally ill, with 6.4 percent to 8 percent of that percentage suffering from severe mental disorders such as schizophrenia and major depression (Finn 2005c: 239). A 2000 report by the American Psychiatric Association on psychiatric services in prisons and jails indicated that about 20 percent of inmates had serious mental disorders and that up to 5 percent were psychotic. There is a professional consensus that substantial numbers of inmates have mental health issues and do not receive adequate care (Kendall 2005: 788). One psychiatrist estimates that the prevalence of mental illness among inmates is at least five times that prevailing among the general free population (Kupers 1999: 11).

Evidence suggests that prisons over-rely on drug therapy and especially on antipsychotic drugs that alter moods to treat mental illness. In 2000 a survey reported that about 10 percent of inmates were being issued with psychotropic drugs. Other studies have indicated that female inmates are more likely to receive this kind of medication than males (Kendall 2005: 789). Dispensing such drugs to control symptomatic behavior without any actual therapy that treats the underlying anxieties and conflicts is liable to lead to adverse side effects in the long term (Pollock 2004: 127). As Kupers (1999: xvi) expresses it, "Many of the most severely disturbed prisoners are simply knocked out with strong antipsychotic medications and warehoused in their cells." Therefore, other than brief periods of hospitalization for the most disturbed, ordinarily treatment in prison is limited to prescribed medications following a brief appointment with a psychiatrist (Kupers 1999: 9).

Special problems associated with the mentally ill in jails and prisons include unwillingness to exit their cells because they find them safe and secure places, destruction of property, and self-mutilation. Mentally ill inmates often have a history of violence and are viewed as likely to be dangerous. Staff may fail to recognize that an inmate's behavior, such as wanting to remain isolated in a cell, violating rules, or participating in disruptions, is due, wholly or in part, to mental illness. Instead, they may view such behaviors as manipulation (Kupers 1999: 109). For example, Conover, writing of his experience as a correctional officer, states that a mentally ill person is known as a "bug" by both officers and inmates at Sing Sing Prison and that "mostly, you just learned to live with the bugs." Officers believed many inmates played "a bug game" in order to get themselves sent to the psychiatric unit or hospital where "you had more room to yourself, and there were more staff looking after you" (2001: 139). According to Conover, the main objective of the psychiatric hospital at Sing Sing was to manage the inmates with medication ("bug juice") so they could quickly return to the general population.

Research has shown that mentally ill inmates take longer to adapt to prison routine, experience greater difficulty learning prison rules and regulations, and, as a consequence, accumulate more rule violations than an average inmate (Haney 2006: 258). They are more likely to be segregated for violations of discipline in conditions that exacerbate their unstable mental condition (Kupers 1999: 29; Pollock 2004: 125). Prison officers generally do not regard rule violations as a sign of mental illness, but once labeled a troublemaker, a mentally ill inmate is liable to be subjected to further punishment, including isolation.

The mentally ill are more likely to be violent offenders (53% as against 46% of other inmates), and about 75 percent are likely to be repeat offenders. Overcrowding can also affect the mentally ill because research has shown that it is associated with increased levels of violence and psychiatric disturbances (Kupers 1999: 47).

Among women prisoners, depression and bipolar disorder have been found at higher rates than for women in the general population. A high proportion of women in prison who are mentally ill report prior physical and sexual abuse, and at much higher rates than do male prisoners (78% for women and 30% for men) (Morash and Schram 2002: 146).

Elderly Prisoners

Managing and caring for elderly inmates has become a major challenge for corrections systems. There are three main categories of elderly prisoners:

- Those who are elderly when their first offense is committed, usually an offense involving violence
- Those who habitually offend and are imprisoned when they have become elderly
- Those who become elderly while imprisoned due to serving a long sentence; for example, in the large number of states that have repealed provisions for parole, made parole extremely difficult to gain, or passed life sentences without parole, elderly inmate populations will inevitably increase.

The past three decades have shown a dramatic growth in the number of elderly inmates, who now represent the fastest-growing element of the inmate population. Between 1981 and 1991 the number of inmates aged more than 55 years increased by 50 percent. The dominant issue associated with elderly inmates is health care, but others include the design of prisons that are not conducive to elders who become increasing immobile, and providing the kind of accommodation that best fits elderly needs for low noise levels and reduced interpersonal conflict. In 2000, only 21 state correctional systems provided special accommodation in the form of special units or dedicated housing for the elderly.

The cost of accommodating an elderly or infirm inmate is about $60,000 a year in a unit that functions both as a prison and as a nursing home. In 1999 U.S. prisons accommodated more than 43,000 inmates over the age of 55 years, representing an increase of 50 percent since 1996. Therefore, while presenting little or no threat to public safety, elderly inmates will continue to require additional resources from already-tight correctional budgets (Welch 2005: 72).

Prison Violence

Violence in male prisons, and to a much lesser extent in female prisons, has been categorized as interpersonal violence, collective violence, and intrapersonal violence. *Interpersonal violence* describes violence occurring in the daily routine of the prison, such as violence between inmates or between inmates and staff. This type of violence, while significant, does not disrupt the prison routine. *Collective violence*, however, adversely impacts the smooth functioning of the prison. The American Correctional Association has identified three types of collective prison violence: an incident, a disturbance, and a riot. A riot occurs when a significant number of inmates control a major portion of a facility for a considerable period. A disturbance is a lesser incident than a riot because fewer inmates are involved and the prison administration retains control of the entire facility despite the disturbance. An incident is a lesser occurrence than a disturbance, it involves only a few inmates, and no part of the facility is taken over (Carrabine 2005: 853). *Intrapersonal violence* describes acts of violence that an inmate performs upon himself or herself, such as self-mutilation and attempts at suicide (Finn 2005b: 995).

During his training as a corrections officer in New York State, Conover (2001: 52) was informed by instructors that the warning signs of a potential disturbance included inmates stockpiling food in cells, unusually quiet cell blocks, inmates dressing in bulky clothes (often with magazines or newspapers underneath their clothing) to deflect knife attacks, and, in warm weather, inmates trying to remain locked in their cells so that they would not have to mix with the general population.

Violence may also be *instrumental*, that is, aimed at achieving a specific goal, such as incidents where some inmates threaten or physically assault others to gain power or increase their status, or *expressive*, that is, the kind of violence that is impulsive and irrational in the sense that no specific goal is sought. Because prisons are often overcrowded, lack privacy, and contain numerous idle inmates, even minor irritations can bring about incidents of expressive violence. Instrumental and expressive violence are not mutually exclusive, and both are often experienced in incidents (Welch 2011: 289, 290).

Collective Violence

It is estimated that more than 1,300 riots have occurred in U.S. prisons in the twentieth century, most often in maximum-security prisons, larger prisons, and older prisons where there is often minimal inmate and officer contact. Riots have been classified as

- traditional riots associated with escape attempts during the period 1865–1913;
- riots against conditions in prisons that challenged those in power;

- consciousness-raising riots from the mid-1960s to the mid-1970s that were intended to promote political objectives; and
- post-rehabilitation riots based on self-interest and of a predatory nature following the collapse of rehabilitation. This category includes the riots at Attica and New Mexico in 1971 and 1980, respectively (Carrabine 2005: 854).

It has been suggested that riots occur because breakdowns in administrative control challenge the legitimacy of imprisonment in the eyes of the imprisoned. This suggests that there are conditions under which those who are confined will reject the authority of the custodians because they see their actions as illegitimate (Carrabine 2005: 857).

Apart from riots, group violence may be perpetrated by prison gangs and individual members of those gangs. Prison gangs are commonly termed "inmate disruptive groups" or "security threat groups" (Finn 2005b: 998). Much present-day violence is linked to gangs, and gang members are typically more involved in assaults on staff and inmates than non-gang members (Mays and Winfree 2005: 209).

Interpersonal Violence

This violence may take the form of inmate-on-staff violence, staff-on-inmate violence, or inmate-on-inmate violence. In 1995, inmates assaulted more than 14,165 state and federal prison staff, and 14 of the assaults proved to be fatal. The number of assaults increased to 16,152 in 1999 when 33 officers died on duty. In Texas alone, there were 6,001 attacks on guards between 1995 and 1999 (Pollock 2004: 232).

In 1995 there were 3,311 inmate deaths in all prison systems, state and federal. Of this, 83 were reported as being inmate-on-inmate homicides and the remainder was attributed to unknown causes. There were about 26,000 inmate-on-inmate assaults, with an overall rate of 28.4 per 1,000 for state prisons and 12.4 for federal institutions. Data for 1999 shows an increase in assaults to about 31,000. In an analysis of 694 assaults on guards in New York State, it was found that much of the violence was unplanned, with 25 percent categorized as having no explanation. Violent retaliation in response to guard directions or orders made up 13 percent of the total (Pollock 2004: 233).

Staff-on-inmate violence has a long history, and until quite recently, physically brutal methods were used to control inmates. In 1994 a study of discipline in maximum-security prisons between 1945 and 1990 found that 62.1 percent of responding inmates reported having seen officers assaulting inmates, with the two most frequent justifications being inmates verbally abusing staff and inmates not following staff orders (Pollock 2004: 235). Instances of such assaults continue to be reported in the media from time to time. In a 1996 report, Human Rights Watch documented sexual assaults on female inmates by male staff in five states, including acts of rape, sexual assault, sexual abuse, verbal abuse, and sexual harassment. Younger, first-time offenders and mentally ill inmates were found to be most susceptible to this kind of violence (Finn 2005b: 997).

Authorized staff-on-inmate violence occurs when special response teams—the prison version of police Special Weapons and Tactics units—are called out to control incidents or to conduct cell extractions where inmates refuse to exit their cells after being ordered to do so. According to Conover (2001: 134) who observed a cell extraction at Sing Sing Prison, following the successful completion of the procedure, the cell-extraction team "were sweaty and charged-up, like victorious football players." Conover, himself at guard at the prison, observes that "prison work filled you with pent-up aggression" and the successful extraction "was a thrilling release, our team coming out on top."

Conover comments that the potential for violence and actual violence was a continuing cause of stress for both guards and inmates, but violence was not a constant. Nevertheless, he believes that "due to the constant tension of prison life and the general lack of catharsis, violence and the potential for violence, became a thrill" (2001: 275). This he attributes to the existence of numerous unresolved angry interactions. He quotes one guard, who was involved in chasing inmates who attacked some officers: "It was the first time in five years that I've been involved in a major incident. . . . And I loved it! I wanted to hit somebody!" (2001: 276).

Building on this account, Conover makes the general point that officers at times "feel like strangling an inmate, that inmates taunt us, strike us, humiliate us in ways civilians could never imagine, and that through it all the guard is supposed to do nothing but stand there and take it" (2001: 282). Similarly, Michael Santos, who received a 45-year sentence for drug offenses, observes that in the federal prison system "I knew I was living in a community where others felt comfortable or at ease with Armageddon and looked to altercations as a welcome break to the daily monotony of penitentiary structure" (Santos 2004: 101).

It is claimed that official estimates grossly underestimate the level of physical violence and victimization in prisons, so, for example, violence between inmates goes unreported when there is a threat of retaliation for "snitching." Similarly, staff-on-inmate violence may be underreported because of the possibility that staff will retaliate against inmates. A 1998 survey of 581 inmates drawn from three prisons in Ohio found that about 1 in every 10 inmates reported a physical assault in the preceding six months, and 1 in every 5 reported being a victim of theft in that same period. When all the crimes reported were aggregated, including physical assault, theft, property damage, and robbery, the outcome revealed that one in two inmates surveyed reported having been a crime victim in the previous six months. Another survey of 500 male inmates in Tennessee prisons found that one-quarter of all inmates surveyed reported carrying weapons, such as a shank, for personal protection. Others deliberately avoided areas susceptible to victimization, such as the showers, the yard, and blind spots, by remaining in their cells (Wolff et al. 2009: 112).

Research concerning *inmate-on-inmate* violence in women's prisons has shown that violence and racial tension are uncommon. Organized gang-type conflict is extremely rare. One study found that women inmates made much less use of weapons than male inmates and were more likely to use an object that was close at hand as a weapon rather than manufacturing one (Pollock 2010: 178). However, fights do occur between women inmates. Inmate Erin George, serving a life sentence in a maximum-security facility in California, notes that a "sure sign of a fight in the offing" was when two inmates "both smeared their faces heavily with the hair grease" (sold in the prison commissary) so that punches thrown were less likely to make a serious impact.

In this facility, however, "double-banking" an inmate, meaning several inmates ganging upon a single victim, was disapproved as a sign of cowardice. "Blanket parties" also take place where a sleeping inmate is covered with a blanket and then assaulted. Fights are usually about "boos" (girlfriends) or about allegations that property has been stolen (2010: 55). At the Central California Women's Facility (CCWF), the largest women's prison in the country, fighting was the result of quarrels between "lovers," drug and contraband deals that were unsuccessful, insults that exceeded those normally experienced, and, rarely, assaults on strangers or acquaintances (Owen 1998: 187).

Male inmate-on-inmate violence is common in most prisons and is often attributed to inadequate supervision because of overcrowding or to lack of correctional staff. In addition, inmate assaults are more likely to occur in prisons where the prison architecture facilitates acts outside the scrutiny of guards. Prison-made weapons include strap-on shanks (knives) and weapons comprising a nail inserted into a plastic handle (e.g., plastic eating utensil). Cloth is often used to wrap a shank around the wrist so that the weapon cannot be taken away during an attack (Welch 2011: 304). Inmate Santos (2004: 107) attributes violence in part to the underground prison economy that delivers the goods inmates believe will minimize the pains of incarceration.

Prison Gangs

Scholars once argued that there existed a single inmate subculture to which all inmates subscribed. However, this notion has been supplanted by studies that show the existence of numerous discrete subcultures constituted by gangs. For example, at Stateville Prison, Jacobs argues that the existence of four super-gangs had a "profound impact on the inmate social system" because the norms of the inmate subculture had weakened, and gang members identified with their organization rather than giving allegiance to a single set of inmate norms. In that prison, while the inmate code rejected stealing from other inmates, gang members did not regard stealing from non-gang members as a violation of inmate norms (Jacobs 1977: 157).

Gangs are a dominant force within prison systems, and one gang investigator has described their control as follows: "What people don't realize is that almost everything that happens in a prison setting has some sort of gang involvement, whether it be extortion, intimidation, trafficking narcotics. There's nothing that goes on that at least one gang member is not involved with . . . nothing" (quoted in Skarbek 2014: 9).

A prison gang has been explained as

an organization which operates within the prison system as a self-perpetuating criminally oriented entity, consisting of a select group of inmates who have established an organized chain of command and are governed by an established code of conduct. The prison gang will usually operate in secrecy and has as its goal to conduct gang activities by controlling their prison environment through intimidation and violence directed toward non-members. (Lyman 1989: 48)

Penologists agree that the world of the U.S. male prison is dominated by gangs, including the Aryan Brotherhood (started at San Quentin Prison in 1967, a white supremacist group), the Mexican Mafia (*La Eme*, started in California in the 1950s and the first California gang), the Black Guerilla Family (emerged at San Quentin in 1966 and formed with a political agenda), *La Nuestra Familia* ("Our Family" formed in Soledad Prison in the 1960s by Hispanics from northern California to gain protection from the Mexican Mafia), the Texas Syndicate (emerged in 1958 in California prisons because other gangs were harassing native Texans, composed largely of Texan Mexican Americans), the *Mexikanemi* (also known as the Texas Mexican Mafia, established in 1984 and the largest gang in the Texas prison system), the Crips and the Bloods (Los Angeles street gangs), and the Latin Kings and others which are commonly differentiated by race (Fleisher and Decker 2009: 164; Gillespie 2004: 80, 81).

According to Shelden (2005: 359), prison gangs were first noted to exist in Washington in 1950 and California in 1957. In 1969 they appeared in Illinois. By 1985 gangs were active in 49 states, with an estimated 114 gangs and 13,000 members, and by 1992 it was estimated that gang membership had increased to about 46,000 members. About 70 percent of all gang members are found in prisons in Texas and California, and a recent estimate puts the number of members at about 308,000 (Skarbek 2014: 9). Prison gangs spread by the inter-prison transfer of gang members or by the arrest and imprisonment of a gang member who attempts to reproduce in the prison environment the gang organization to which he or she belonged before imprisonment. Known gang members often suffer administrative restrictions on work, recreation, and housing (Shelden 2005: 360).

Psychologists argue that inmates join gangs for protection in the face of a common threat. Gangs also represent a response to social disorganization in that they construct order within a world of disorder. The growth of prison gangs can therefore be viewed as a consequence of prison conditions and as a response to the need to establish a stable identity and gain a source of security (Haney 2006: 219). In one survey of 37 prisons, 91 percent of respondents stated their dominant reason for joining gangs was fear of other inmates. In addition, gangs were favored because they facilitated access to contraband and provided status and a sense of belonging (Skarbek 2014: 97).

At Stateville Prison one gang function was as "a buffer against poverty." Gang members collected cigarettes from members and stored them for those in need. Gang membership conferred a sense of belonging and "an air of importance." Membership allowed inmates "to feel like a man," and the gang was seen to be a family and worthy of dying for (Jacobs 1977: 153).

One theory of gang formation (Skarbek 2014) suggests that gangs form to provide a form of institutional governance that enables the supply of goods and services to inmates where no comparable official institution exists within a prison to perform this task. As Skarbek notes (2014: 59), while an individual prison drug dealer faces numerous challenges such as deterring theft by other inmates and ensuring the quality of contraband drugs, prisons gangs have a "comparative advantage in self-enforcing exchange in the underground economy." Gangs are effective because other inmates know they are prepared to use violence to protect their assets, including collecting payment for drugs sold on credit.

Gangs contribute to prison order by controlling common areas of the prison and the prison yard, where illicit transactions occur, and by resolving inmate disputes when "shot-callers" settle disputes over showing disrespect, drugs, and property theft (Skarbek 2014: 83). Violence unsanctioned by gangs is considered a serious violation of the gang order because it can result in lockdowns, which effectively prevent inmate trading in contraband (2014: 86). When gangs agree to sanction inmate-on-inmate violence to settle a dispute, they will order inmates to fight in a cell to limit disruption (2014: 87).

Gangs commonly express their organization, rules, and structure in the form of written constitutions or in unwritten form as a commonly understood code of conduct. Gang constitutions usually demand a lifetime commitment to the gang, and when a gang member exits a gang while still incarcerated, this can result in an automatic death sentence. For example, the Texas Aryan Brotherhood declares that "those Brothers chosen for the Organization are life term members: death being the only termination of membership" (quoted in Skarbek 2014: 116). For this reason, exited gang members are often moved to protective custody and then go through a debriefing process with prison officials to share their detailed knowledge of the gang and its operations. Inmates who put their lives at risk in this manner also run the risk of having their families targeted (Skarbek 2014: 113).

Some constitutions, such as that of a Hispanic prison gang in Texas, require that a recruit's sponsor put to death a recruit who reneges on the gang, and others expressly prohibit gang members from being "a homosexual, an informant, or a coward" (Skarbek 2014: 114, 117). Members exit gangs for a number of reasons, including losing interest in gang activities, refusing to carry on a death sentence imposed on a non-gang inmate, and disagreement with the gang leadership (Fleisher and Decker 2009: 162).

The 1999 gang survey found a correlation between disturbances caused by gangs and the degree of security of the prison, with a greater number of disturbances involving gangs being reported in maximum-security prisons. In 1999, only 10 percent of minimum-security prisons reported such disturbances compared to 59 percent of medium-security and 64.7 percent of maximum-security prisons (Shelden 2005: 361). One long-term inmate claims that while gangs are responsible for much prison violence, any violence that cannot otherwise be explained is attributed to gang action so that gangs function to excuse proper investigation of violent incidents (Carceral 2006: 113).

Race is a key factor in constituting gangs. A 1999 survey found that 87 percent of prison disturbances related to conflicts involving race. Surveys have found several gangs composed of a specific racial group exist in prison systems, so, for example, in the Florida system, six major gangs were identified with the racial composition of Puerto Rican, white, black, and three Mexican American gangs.

Even inmates who are not affiliated with a gang are expected to align with their racial group, namely "blacks, whites, Hispanics from Southern California, Hispanics from Northern California, Paias (Columbians), American Indians, and Asians." Inmates affiliated by race are expected to comply with demands made by the gang's appointed shot-callers who operate their businesses, and when violence erupts, an inmate is obliged to defend his own race (Skarbek 2014: 79). Aligning on racial lines facilitates identification of friends and enemies, and because racial characteristics cannot change, the ability to move from group to group to gain an advantage is very constrained. As Skarbek puts it (2014: 101), "Gangs do not form to promote racism: race facilitates criminal governance."

Michael Santos, an inmate who received a sentence of 45-years imprisonment for a nonviolent drug offense, says that in the federal system prison gangs should be differentiated from "crews." A crew is an informal alliance without any established leader and with no mutual obligations. Crews exist because "in the penitentiary, strength comes through alliances," and vulnerability as an individual inmate can be countered by being part of any informal grouping (Santos 2004: 92).

Today, gangs are involved in bringing drugs into prisons and distributing cocaine and heroin. Drugs are smuggled in by visitors, who pass them mouth to mouth to inmates in balloons or condoms while kissing during visits. In addition, gang members outside the prison will throw drugs, perhaps inside a tennis ball, over the wall or fence of the prison or will use slingshots to propel the drugs. Correctional officers may also be recruited by gangs, sometimes by making threats against their families or by voluntary acts (Ross and Richards 2002: 132).

How do prison administrators respond to gangs? One approach is to "look the other way" when gangs act against one another because this maintains a degree of order within the prison. Other approaches include improving race relations, eliminating weight training, and monitoring telephone calls and mail. The most common strategies are separating gang members, using informers to obtain intelligence on gang activities, segregating gang members, and isolating gang leaders (Shelden 2005: 362). Other more questionable practices are said to include guards encouraging racial violence in order to divide and rule and prevent inmates from joining together to attack guards (Pollock 2004: 107). In California, the Department of Corrections tries to identify hard-core gang members and place them in segregation or tries to discourage membership by showing new inmates a video about "gang diversion" and running programs such as Cage Your Rage.

A survey of 148 correctional institutions in 48 states asking what strategies were used to control gangs found the most common responses focused on disrupting gang communications, with the second major strategy being limiting gang members' movements and interactions. As Skarbek (2014: 160) notes, in California, such strategies have failed because about two-thirds of the nearly 6,000 inmates in restrictive housing are gang members or are affiliated to gangs. Skarbek suggests that improving official governance in prisons would be a better strategy because this would reduce inmate demands for governance by gangs, so, for example, improving the means of protecting inmates' property and persons by using more video surveillance and making some contraband items legal could erode gang power (2014: 162).

Psychologists argue that prison systems that view gang membership as punishable deviance merely ensure the continued existence of the gang and enhance its power because suppression intensifies the need to belong. This view has found support in a National Institute of Corrections study of the causes of increased gang activity which implicated the poor environment of the prison, including the general lack of programs, constant idleness, restrictive visiting policies, and overcrowded, run-down, and unsafe facilities (Haney 2006: 220).

Juveniles in Adult Prisons

Juveniles convicted of crimes in adult courts may be sentenced to adult prisons for terms that can include life imprisonment without parole. They cannot receive the death sentence in adult court as decided by the case of *Roper v. Simmons* 2005. In 1998, 7 percent of all juvenile admissions into custody were referred directly to the adult criminal court, and the average prison sentence for a juvenile convicted as an adult was about 9 years and for violent offenses about 11 years (Shelden 2005: 1023). The rationale commonly offered for punishing youth with incarceration in adult prisons is that it operates as a deterrent.

In 2008 3,650 juveniles under 18 years of age, comprising 3,531 males and 119 females, were held in state prisons (West and Sabol 2009). There has been a significant increase over time in the juvenile population of adult prisons, so, for example, in 2000, the standing population of inmates younger than 18 years held in state prisons was 70 percent greater than that in 1985 (Sickmund 2004: 20).

Adult prisons are generally much larger and more formidable than juvenile facilities, and officers in the former tend to be focused on security and custody, whereas more attention is given to treatment in juvenile facilities. One juvenile described his placement in prison as akin to being in a foreign country (Eisikovits and Baizerman 1982: 9). Juveniles in prison undergo formative development into adults while incarcerated, involving psychological, physical, and emotional changes. While the effect of incarceration on this developmental process is unknown, it clearly poses serious challenges (Leigey and others 2009: 117). The consequences of conviction and imprisonment as an adult can severely impact juveniles and are much more significant than those applying after juvenile court proceedings. They can include loss of the right to vote, to enlist in the military, and to possess firearms, and disqualification from receiving several sources of federal aid. Given that juveniles who finish their terms in adult prison are likely to be younger, these consequences may impact juveniles in a different and more damaging way than adults (Leigey et al. 2009: 126).

Generally, there are four means of accommodating juveniles in adult prisons:

- They are placed in administrative segregation until they reach 18 years.
- They are confined in a separate facility within the prison accommodating only prisoners under 18 years.
- They are accommodated with others under 18 years in units that also hold adults.
- They are integrated into the general inmate population as if they were adults (Levinson and Greene 1999: 61).

The federal prison system accommodates juveniles sentenced as adults in juvenile facilities and not in prisons because federal law mandates that juveniles and adults are separated (Leigey et al. 2009: 116).

Research has shown that male juveniles in adult prisons are exposed to much greater risk of harm than youth in juvenile facilities (Austin et al. 2000: 7). For example, one study of youth in an adult prison (Eisikovits and Baizerman 1982: 5) found that the youth's daily concern was their survival among an adult population. They had to know the inmate culture and "fit in," but survival also meant coping with their low status compared to life on the streets where they had been stronger and tougher, or were leaders of gangs. In prison, they were faced with a population far stronger and tougher and constituted a marginalized population. To cope, youth in adult prisons relied on their "street smarts" or on membership of a gang or ethnic group for protection. They might also try to maintain a low profile, but this was problematic because their youth made them stand out (Eisikovits and Baizerman 1982: 15).

There is little research on female juveniles in adult female prisons. One study reported that female juveniles feared being physically or sexually assaulted by adult inmates and also by other juveniles, but they did not report any instances of victimization. In one female prison, staff believed that juvenile females would benefit from being mentored by adult inmates from whom they could learn survival skills, but youth reported that their interactions with adults taught them new criminal skills (Leigey et al. 2009: 121).

One study found that being a juvenile in an adult prison "was a painful and denigrating experience that they pointed to as reason or justification for becoming more angry, embittered, cynical and defeated, and/or skilled at committing crime" (Bishop and Frazier 2000: 259). The effect of imprisoning juveniles as adults may therefore be to criminalize them further.

Placing juveniles in adult prisons is problematic for correctional administrators, who must make special arrangements for this special population. It is likely, however, that states and the federal government will continue to provide for juveniles to be punished in this manner because doing so promotes the notion that very severe punishments should be imposed on youth who commit crimes of violence or who are chronic offenders (Kupchik 2006: 109).

The Corrections Industrial Complex

The involvement of the private sector in punishment has been termed a "corrections commercial complex" or "corrections industrial complex" in which all parties involved in punishment decision making, including legislators, lobbyists, private enterprise, and corrections professionals, work collectively for their own benefit with minimum public oversight. Companies now supply goods and services to prisons and operate prisons and jails as well as supplying various technologies that support correctional services.

The corrections commercial complex represents a formidable presence that can influence government at the state and federal levels to ensure that the corrections sector continues to thrive. It is argued that the participants in this complex have a vested interest in states maintaining large inmate populations and that they profit from a policy of incapacitation. It is expected therefore that this complex will lobby legislators against changes in the law that could diminish inmate populations and ultimately reduce the number of prisons throughout the states. One example of the growth of prison services of this nature is the advertising in journals that serve the correctional services: *Corrections Today* is the foremost corrections trade publication, and the amount of advertising it carried tripled in the 1980s. Companies that advertise in it and in *The American Jail* include those offering health care programs, fence security with technological upgrades, stainless steel "Penal Ware" for prison fixtures, cell construction, blankets, and forms of transport described as "Prison on Wheels" (Shelden 2005: 726). Another service that relies on a large inmate population is that provided by "bed brokers," who, for a fee, will locate jail or prison beds for prisons that are overcrowded (Shelden 2005: 728).

The commercial and political aspects of corrections described here raise serious questions about the viability of corrections reform, especially where proposed reforms involve reducing prison populations and even closing some prisons.

Private Prisons

Private prisons have been explained as "prisons or other institutions of confinement (jails, immigration and nationalization service facilities, detention centers, and secured juvenile justice facilities) operated and managed by private corporations for profit" (Shichor 1995: 2).

Having private enterprise operate prisons is not a novel idea. For example, during the 1800s Louisiana's first state prison was privately operated, as were the Auburn and Sing Sing prisons in New York State. While a few facilities for juvenile offenders were privately operated during the 1970s, adult prisons remained within the public sector until 1985 when Kentucky contracted with the Corrections Corporation of America for the company to run a state prison (Kunkel and Capps 2005: 768).

Since the 1980s a rising demand for prison accommodation due to vastly increased incarceration rates has resulted in states looking to private enterprise to provide prison beds. In addition, the prevailing free market economic thinking of the Reagan years of the 1980s encouraged the privatization of government services based on the argument that the private sector was more efficient and cost effective (Welch 2011: 511). By 1998 there were 158 private prisons contracting for inmates (Culp 2005: 163). By 2000, 31 states and the federal system were housing more than 87,000 inmates in private facilities, which by that time held 5.8 percent of state prisoners and 10.7 percent of federal inmates (Welch 2011: 512). On December 31, 2014, 131,261 inmates were held in private prisons, making up 8.4 percent of the total inmate population in the country, and about 40,000 of those prisoners were serving sentences for federal crimes comprising 19 percent of federal prisoners (Carson 2015: 14). The federal system has made significant use of private prisons since 1997.

Most private prisons are of the minimum- and medium-security type, and their capacity gradually increased from typically 500 inmates to 1,500 or more now (Kunkel and Capps 2005: 768). Privatization of prisons reached its zenith in 1997 when a private company proposed to Tennessee that it take over the state's entire prison system, a proposal that was ultimately rejected (Blomberg and Lucken 2000: 221). Other factors tending toward the increased use of private prisons have been the unwillingness of voters during the late 1980s and early 1900s to support tax increases or bond initiatives for new prison construction, and court orders to reduce prison over-crowding. For example, in 1993, 40 state prison systems were under court order to reduce their population density (Kunkel and Capps 2005: 769). The trend toward privatization has been leveling off, and since 2000 no state has contracted for new private prisons, and some have reduced their involvement with the industry.

Opponents of prison privatization argue that the concern to maximize profits will lead a corporation to lobby for harsher punishments in order to ensure that as many prison beds are filled for as long as possible. Corporations in the corrections business have developed sophisticated lobbying strategies that can influence policy making on corrections (Blomberg and Lucken 2000: 222). Opponents claim that corrections officers in private facilities enjoy less favorable terms and conditions of employment than officers in state prisons and that using lower-paid and less well-trained staff can affect security and morale. It is also claimed that private prisons have an interest in obstructing, or at least not supporting, parole applications because it is in their interest to keep an inmate incarcerated as long as possible. They might do this by encouraging staff to write adverse conduct reports on an inmate applying to the parole board. A fundamental objection is the lack of transparency concerning privatization contracts and the influence of the private corporations over politicians, corrections bureaucrats, and legislatures (Kunkel and Capps 2005: 771).

Advocates of privatization contend that private enterprise will save money by constructing prisons at a cheaper price than the state and that the state is burdened with bureaucratic procedures when it comes to contracting that increase costs and delay projects. They claim that efficiencies can be enforced under privatization by terminating contracts for poor performance (Kunkel and Capps 2005: 771). The private corporations argue that they have a greater incentive than public prisons to treat inmates fairly because if they do not, their reputation will be harmed and they will not win any further state contracts.

As to the supposed efficiency of private prisons and their capacity to save costs, reports and research have found that there is little difference between public and private facilities in these respects. In 1996 the General Accounting Office of the United States found that after analyzing five states and comparing their public and private prison costs, there was no support for the claim that privatization saves taxpayers' money. On the most optimistic view, a 1 percent cost saving could be identified in some instances (Kunkel and Capps 2005: 772). Similarly, a 2001 report from the Department of Justice found that savings from privatization averaged only about 1 percent, mainly attributable to lower labor costs (Gottschalk 2015: 70).

State use of private prisons varies widely, with about half of the states having no or only a few inmates housed privately, and about one-third having 10 percent or more of inmates accommodated in private prisons. Privately operated prisons are concentrated in the South and Southwest where 7–9 percent of inmates are accommodated in private prisons, compared to 2–3 percent in the Northeast and Midwest (Gottschalk 2015: 67).

The pragmatic, rational arguments that stress the supposed economic benefit of contracting out the function of imprisonment have largely dominated the privatization debate, but the moral and ethical issues associated with prison privatization remain salient. A key argument is whether the administration of state-ordered punishment should be conducted by non-state entities. Historically, punishment has always been regarded as a function of the state because this eliminates or minimizes the influence of private interests in the criminal justice process and ensures that all persons receive equal treatment according to the law. In 1986, the American Bar Association objected to the notion of private prisons, arguing that "incarceration is an inherent function of the government and that the government should not abdicate this responsibility by turning over prison operation to private industry" (Shichor 1995: 52). Proponents of privatization argue that state oversight and monitoring will ensure that there is no abuse of rights in the privatization project. However, the administration and staff of private prisons owe a duty to the company that employs them and may give loyalty and allegiance to the company rather than to a set of rules imposed by the state.

Privatization opponents claim it is morally wrong to allow private corporations to profit from the state punishment of citizens. The American Civil Liberties Union has argued that "the profit motive is incompatible with doing justice" (Logan 1990: 72). The issue is whether a private entity is likely to value its own interests over the interests of justice because its dominant purpose is to earn profits for its shareholders. Historically, however, prison systems have linked the profit motive and incarceration through schemes such as convict leasing. This means it is problematic to argue that the management of prisoners privately is more morally objectionable than profiteering from their labor.

Opponents claim that prison corporations may try to influence policy makers and administrators to ensure that private prisons continue to be built and that they continue to profit from a high rate of incarceration. Therefore, expanding the prison system through privatization will be self-perpetuating; if prisons are built, they will be filled (Shichor 1995: 61).

Super-Maximum or "Supermax" Prisons

There is no commonly agreed-upon definition of what constitutes a super-maximum prison—a "supermax"—but the National Institute of Corrections has proposed three qualifying elements:

- Accommodation is physically separated from other prison units.
- There exists a controlled environment that denotes security by separating inmates from staff and other prisoners and restricting their movements.

- It houses inmates who have been committed to a supermax administratively rather than through disciplinary action because they are perceived to require special control on the basis of violent or disruptive behavior in another facility also of high security (Blomberg and Lucken 2000: 217).

Correctional systems give different names to supermax units within regular prisons and to detached supermax prisons. The range of descriptive terms includes control units, administrative maximum prisons or penitentiaries, intensive housing units, intensive management units, maxi–maxi units, maximum control facilities, restrictive housing units, secured housing units, and special housing units (Finn 2005a: 166). Sometimes, supermax conditions can be imposed on an ad hoc basis in regular maximum security. For example, Conover (2001: 29) reports that at Sing Sing Prison inmates for whom there was insufficient space in "the Box" or Special Housing Unit (SHU) were "keeplocked" in their cells for 23 hours a day as if they were in the Box. According to Conover (2001: 127), the SHU at Sing Sing Prison "had the highest testosterone level in the prison" and among the guards, while working in a maximum-security prison was considered "more macho" than working in a medium- or lower-level security prison, working in the SHU was the ultimate macho job.

Need for Supermax Conditions

The justifications for supermax prisons include the following:

- The need to create special and more rigorous conditions of confinement for those inmates who are persistently violent, resistant to discipline, and cannot be housed in normal confinement conditions.
- The means of ensuring good behavior for those housed in conventional maximum security prisons because the more unattractive conditions of a supermax prison or unit will act as a disincentive to bad conduct.

- A less acknowledged reason proposed by Zimring and Hawkins (2004: 168) is that having a supermax prison is a "status symbol" so that when some states began to build and open them, the supermax became "a normative part of any major state prison system" and not having a supermax consigned a state to the minor correctional leagues.

These authors contend that the appeal of the supermax as a corrections status symbol explains the enthusiasm for creating these units in the 1990s. While during the 1980s only one facility could be considered a supermax, by 2000, 34 states maintained them as facilities or units within facilities with a capacity of nearly 20,000 beds.

The common characteristics of these supermax units and prisons include the following:

- Inmates are confined in small cells for 22–23 hours a day and typically spend the short time allowed for outdoor exercise in a small caged-in or cement-walled area referred to as "dog runs."
- Technology is merged with custody in the form of remote-controlled doors and intercom systems that reduce contact and interaction between officers and inmates.
- There are no congregate activities.
- Where treatment programs are offered, these are often delivered through closed-circuit television or cable services to avoid personal contact.
- There are few, if any, work opportunities.
- Visits from family are often conducted through videoconferencing and not in person; only staff enter inmate living pods for cell extractions or to escort inmates to showers and visits, or to use the telephone (King 2005: 120).
- Inmates are placed in restraints when they exit their cells and are usually restrained when in the presence of others through ankle chains, handcuffs, and waist chains (Finn 2005b: 168; Haney 2005: 940).

- Remote 'podular supervision' enables staff in a central security location to exercise 180 or 270 degree visual surveillance over inmate living unit pods (King 2005: 120).

In all respects this modern form of supermax confinement is a reinvention of the practice of solitary confinement employed in the early days of the penitentiary. As Haney describes them, supermax prisons "merge the 19th-century practice of long term solitary confinement with 21st-century technology" (Haney 2005: 938).

Federal Supermax Prisons

Within the federal prison system, the ADX (Administrative Maximum) penitentiary at Florence, Colorado, is the highest-level security prison and satisfies the criteria for a supermax prison. It began operations in November 1994. ADX Florence houses a maximum of 490 inmates in single cells in nine separate units. A Control Unit provides for long-term disciplinary segregation, and an SHU accommodates those in short-term disciplinary segregation (Ward 2005: 16).

Inmates serve a specific term in the Control Unit, for example, 48 months for the offense of assaulting an officer (Ward 2005: 17). About 95 percent of the inmates at ADX have been sent there for misconduct in other federal prisons, including assaulting, murdering, attempting to murder other inmates, escape, assaulting staff, and rioting. Gang membership, hostage taking, and distributing illicit drugs can also be justification for transfer to ADX.

Security at Florence is maintained through 1,400 electronically operated doors and 168 closed-circuit television cameras. Cells are larger than those found in regular prisons, measuring 7 feet by 12 feet with a shower, sink, and toilet. A concrete slab provides the base for a mattress. Each cell is provided with a 12-inch black and white television, and each has a window 2 feet long and 5 inches wide that in the Control Unit and SHU looks out on a solitary exercise yard surrounded by walls. Entry into a cell is through a solid steel door and through a grill door containing slots for food trays (Ward 2005: 16).

Perspectives on Supermax Prisons

Supermax prison conditions are justified on the basis that inmates are "the worst of the worst" and are too dangerous to confine in less secure conditions. However, there is little evidence to support these claims, and inmates are often placed in supermax units, not because of what they have done but because of judgments about their character; for example, they are judged "dangerous" or a "threat" or to be a member of a "disruptive" group (Haney 2005: 941).

The number of mentally ill inmates in supermax is generally higher than that in the general prison population, and it has been estimated that about 30 percent suffer from "severe mental disorders." This may be due to the fact that mentally ill inmates are more likely to be disruptive and "act out," which is punished rather than treated. Many studies have documented the adverse psychological impact of living in supermax conditions. The recorded symptoms include sleep disturbances, loss of appetite, anxiety, panic, rage, paranoia, loss of control, hallucinations, and self-mutilation. One study found that three-quarters or more of a sample of supermax inmates reported suffering a range of adverse psychological effects, including a tendency to withdraw socially, oversensitivity to external stimuli, and irrational anger and irritability (Haney 2005: 941).

The assertion that supermax conditions constitute cruel and unusual punishment in violation of the Constitution was tested in *Madrid v. Gomez* 1995, which investigated confinement conditions at the Pelican Bay Security Housing Unit in California. The Court was unable to find a violation of the Constitution but did bar categories of inmates from being sent there because of the tendency of the facility to render them mentally ill or exacerbate preexisting mental illness.

In *Ruiz v. Johnson* 1999 a federal court ruled that administrative segregation units in the federal prison system were operating at standards less than those mandated constitutionally and that the conditions constituted cruel and unusual punishment.

In *Jones 'El v. Berg* 2001 a federal court granted an injunction to an inmate on the grounds that seriously mentally ill prisoners were at risk of irreparable emotional damage if the state of Wisconsin continued to keep them confined in "extremely isolating conditions." Several inmates were ordered to be removed, and other categories of prisoners were ordered to be evaluated and, if found to be seriously mentally ill, were also to be transferred out of the unit (Haney 2005: 943).

Many of the concerns about supermax prisons and their conditions of incarceration relate to solitary confinement, a defining characteristic of the supermax model. These issues are discussed here.

Solitary Confinement

The U.S. Department of Justice (Beck 2015) explains that inmates may be held in "restrictive housing" (administrative segregation or solitary confinement) for a number of reasons that include the following:

- For their own protection or to protect other inmates
- While awaiting classification or reclassification
- While awaiting transfer to another prison or to a unit within a prison
- While awaiting a hearing for violation of a prison rule or regulation

The use of restrictive housing for disciplinary or administrative reasons varies widely in duration and in the conditions of confinement. Segregation facilities are located in both women's and men's prisons. At the CCWF, the largest women's prison in the world, women were isolated for three reasons: fighting, drug-related activities, and assaults on staff. Women sent to segregation typically served terms of less than a month, but in the case of an assault on staff, they could serve six months or longer (Owen 1998: 114).

There are three main forms of segregation:

- *Punitive segregation* is used for punishing prisoner misconduct and usually imposed for a fixed period following a disciplinary adjudication.
- *Protective segregation* is used to hold vulnerable prisoners apart from the general population for their own protection, for example, sex offenders and convicted former police officers.
- *Administrative segregation* is used to isolate prisoners that fall into certain categories such as escape risks, gang members, predators, high risk, and terrorists. The decision to place an inmate in solitary is almost always made by the prison administration and very rarely by a court (Shalev 2009: 2).

The Federal Bureau of Prisons regulations covering inmates placed in solitary confinement provide that inmates must receive the same standards of cleanliness, hygiene, and nourishment as are granted to the general population and inmates must receive a minimum of five hours of exercise time weekly and have access to showers at least three times a week. However, reports have indicated that these requirements are regularly violated and inmates are often kept in substandard conditions and denied their rights. Inmates held in administrative segregation are entitled to participate in the same programs and religious observances as are enjoyed by the general population, but again these rights are frequently ignored by staff, who cite security of staff shortages as justification (Hannem-Kish 2005: 911). The requirement in the federal system that inmates placed in solitary confinement be assessed every 30 days for psychological deterioration strongly indicates that there are negative aspects to this form of isolation (Hannem-Kish 2005: 911).

The forms of restrictive housing described earlier represent a return to the penal conditions that prevailed in the golden age of the penitentiary. Solitary confinement can be traced back in time to the establishment of the Cherry Hill Prison (Eastern State Penitentiary) in Philadelphia in 1823 where inmates were kept isolated at all times. By the 1830s, reports were being made about a sharp increase in mental disorders among inmates undergoing solitary confinement (Guenther 2013: xi). By the late nineteenth century the penitentiary system of isolation had been dismantled, but by the 1980s with the advent of the supermax prison or unit, it had returned to the U.S. penal system (Shalev 2009: 17).

Solitary confinement was reinvented when prison administrators decided that total control of selected inmates would minimize risks to prison staff from possible inmate violence, reflecting the contemporary view that prisoners for solitary confinement "have become risks to be managed, resistances to be eliminated, and organisms to be fed, maintained and even prevented from taking their own lives" (Guenther 2013: xvi).

On an average day in 2011–2012, up to 4.4 percent of state and federal prison inmates were held in restrictive housing, and in the preceding 12 months or since coming to their present facility, nearly 20 percent of prison inmates had been held in restrictive housing. A survey conducted by the U.S. Department of Justice of the use of restrictive housing over the period 2011–2012 found the following:

- Twenty-nine percent of inmates with current symptoms of serious psychological distress had been placed in restrictive housing units in the preceding 12 months; therefore, use of these units was associated with mental health issues.

- Younger inmates with no high school diploma and those who were lesbian, gay, or bisexual were more likely to have spent time in restrictive housing than older inmates, those with a high school diploma or higher education, and heterosexual inmates.

- More than three-quarters of inmates who were charged with assaulting other inmates or staff spent time in restrictive housing in the preceding 12 months.

• Prison with higher rates of using restrictive housing experienced higher levels of disorder and lower levels of inmate trust and confidence in staff.

Legal Restrictions of Solitary Confinement

The Eighth Amendment prohibits cruel and unusual punishment, and solitary confinement has been challenged as a violation of this prohibition in the courts. The courts have generally been ready to intervene in cases where physical conditions were deficient but have otherwise given deference to prison administrations. Judicial decisions concerning physical conditions included that isolation and deprivation of hot water, soap, and clothing were constitutionally intolerable, but permitting inmates in isolation to shower once every five days was acceptable; and that without additional deprivations solitary confinement did not in itself amount to a violation of the constitution (Shalev 2011: 159).

In 1995 in *Madrid v. Gomez*, a U.S. district court provided an analysis of the conditions prevailing at Pelican Bay Prison, California. The court noted that the meaning of the Eighth Amendment varies according to a test of "evolving standards of decency" and that prisoners are not wholly divested of constitutional rights when incarcerated although rights may be diminished by the nature of the prison environment. To demonstrate a violation of the Eighth Amendment, it would have to be shown that the punishment either "inflicts unnecessary or wanton pain" or is "grossly disproportionate to the severity of the crime warranting punishment" and to meet this test prison officials must have acted with "deliberate indifference" (Shalev 2011: 161). The court found that conditions at Pelican Bay did not violate the Eighth Amendment except in relation to certain categories of inmates, including those "already mentally ill, . . . persons with borderline personality disorders, brain damage or mental retardation, impulse-ridden personalities, or a history of prior psychiatric problems of chronic depression" (quoted in Shalev 2011: 164).

The courts have, however, been reluctant to hold that access to human social contact is protected or that supermax confinement may cause mental illness in persons with no prior history of that illness (Shalev 2011: 167). Philosopher Kimberley Brownlee (2013: 199) argues that such a right exists, which she terms "the right against social deprivation," and explains it as "a persisting lack of minimally adequate opportunities for decent or supportive human contact." She identifies the holding of inmates in long-term solitary confinement as a violation of this right and bases her argument on the duty to respect persons and the inherent worth of social inclusion (2013: 212).

Reform Measures

Most recently, solitary confinement as a penal practice has come under scrutiny at the federal level and in some states with the result that reforms are to take place. California has agreed to review the use of solitary confinement in its prisons with the aim of imposing limits on the duration of such confinement. Reportedly, nearly 3,000 inmates are kept in restricted housing daily. The terms of settlement were agreed to by California following a federal court action mandations that only inmates found to have committed serious violations of prison regulations will be placed in restrictive housing. Gang members will no longer be placed there simply because they have a gang affiliation and indeterminate confinement will cease (Williams 2015). California Corrections has reported that keeping an inmate in restricted housing costs about $70,000 a year compared to an average cost of about $58,000 for inmates kept in the general population (Rodriguez 2016).

New York State reached a similar settlement as the result of a lawsuit brought by the New York Civil Liberties Union on behalf of about 4,000 inmates placed in restrictive housing. Isolation will no longer be imposed for first-time violations of drug use or possession which have previously accounted for up to one-fifth of the confined population. Congregate recreation will be permitted for two hours three times a week, and inmates will be given greater access to reading materials (Williams 2015).

In the federal system, President Obama announced on January 25, 2016, that after a review of solitary confinement in U.S. prisons, while the practice is a necessary tool, it should be limited, made subject to constraints, and used only as a last resort. Solitary confinement for juveniles would be banned, it would not be used to punish "low-level infractions," and the time allowed out of solitary confinement would be increased. The president said about 10,000 federal prisoners held in solitary confinement would be affected and hoped that his plan would serve as a model for the states (Eilperin, *The Washington Post*, 2016).

Prison Rape

Prisoner rape has been defined by the organization Stop Prisoner Rape (2007: 4) as "all forms of sexual violence inflicted on anyone in custody, including someone awaiting trial in a county jail." Rape is an issue in both men's and women's prisons, but in the former, rape of one prisoner by another prisoner, while an act of violence, may also be aimed at establishing male dominance within prison hierarchies. Rape enhances the masculinity of the perpetrator and signals that he is not to be labeled gay (Castle et al. 2002: 16). The male inmate subculture defines male penetrative acts as nongay but regards receptive-penetrated activity as an expression of gay identity (Leighton and Roy 2005: 819). In women's prisons, rape is more likely to involve male staff abusing female prisoners. In both cases, much rape goes unreported.

In male prisons, inmates who perform aggressive penetrative gay acts are known as "wolves" or "daddies" (Castle et al. 2002: 16). The rape victim, referred to as a "punk" or "fag," is transformed by the act of rape into a woman in the eyes of other inmates. A punk or fag who has been raped and has consequently become feminized is liable to repeated brutalization and rape, and may also become the "slave" of another inmate, tasked to satisfy his sexual needs in exchange for protection.

A punk may also be required by his owner to provide sexual services to other inmates (Kupers 1999: 141, 142), and punks may also voluntarily perform gay acts in prison for protection or to obtain goods and services. Punks are located on the lowest level of the prison sexual hierarchy.

Michael Santos, an inmate who received a 45-year sentence for nonviolent drug offenses, describes the "press game," where inmates will attempt to convert a gay inmate into a prison prostitute who can generate income for a gang or crew. This conversion strategy may involve targeting a newly arrived inmate and lending him money, and, when the debt is high, asking him for a favor that they know he cannot deliver, such as stealing a radio from a guard. When the inmate responds that he cannot perform the required favor, the lender demands payment, and when this is not made, he forces the inmate to perform sexual acts and uses him as a prostitute to discharge the debt (Santos 2004: 93, 94).

Different studies report wide variations concerning the incidence of rape in male prisons. For example, research conducted in 1966 in Philadelphia found that 4.7 percent of inmates reported sexual assaults, and a 1980 study of New York State male prisons revealed that while 28 percent of inmates reported being targets of sexual aggression, only one inmate reported being raped. A 1977 study of 400 male inmates in six North Carolina state prisons showed an average report rate of sexual assaults of 2.4 percent; a 1982 study in California found a rate of 14 percent, and a study of 17 federal prisons in 1984 revealed a 2 percent rate of "sexual targets" and a 0.3 percent rape rate (Hensley et al. 2003: 18, 19). In a 2003 study of three Oklahoma prisons, about 14 percent reported being sexual targets and 1.1 percent reported being victims of completed sexual assaults.

As for female prisons, one study of sexual coercion in a female prison in the South found about 4.5 percent had been victims of attempted or completed rapes. Studies from the mid-1990s to 2000 found that 7 percent of women interviewed in three prisons reported instances of coerced sex and that when rapes did take place among women inmates, there were multiple perpetrators rather than a single offender (Kunselman et al. 2002: 35). At one male federal prison in California, women were housed in the segregation unit, and in *Lucas v. White* 1998 the court found that three of these women were essentially sold to male inmates by correctional staff who allowed male inmates access to the women's cells for the purpose of rape (Pollock 2004: 211).

Research indicates that there is a correlation between the size of the inmate population and the incidence of rape because prisons with more inmates are more likely to have official reports of sexual attacks or threats of attacks filed, while this is less likely at minimum-security prisons.

Prison Rape Elimination Act 2003

This law was enacted to address the issue of male prison rape. The law

- sets a zero tolerance standard for prison rape;
- prioritizes the prevention of rape in prison systems;
- devises and implements national standards to detect, prevent, reduce, and punish rape;
- provides for data collection and information on the incidence of rape; and
- increases staff accountability for failing to detect, prevent, reduce, or punish rape (Mair et al. 2003: 602; National Institute of Justice 2006).

The act creates a Review Panel on Prison Rape within the Department of Justice, which is required to hold annual public hearings on operations in three prisons with the highest and two prisons with the lowest incidents of rape. A National Prison Rape Reduction Commission is established comprising nine members with expertise on the subject to conduct research (Mair et al. 2003: 604).

In 2014, the Bureau of Justice Statistics of the Justice Department reported that PREA Data Collection Activities had found the following:

- In 2011 corrections administrators reported 8,763 allegations of sexual victimization, an increase over the 8,404 incidents reported in 2010 and 7,855 in 2009.
- In 2011, 902 allegations of sexual victimization (10%) were determined to have occurred following an investigation into the allegations, and about 48 percent of substantiated allegations involved prison staff with inmates. Females committed more than half of all substantiated incidents of staff misconduct and one-quarter of all incidents of sexual harassment.

A 2001 study by Human Rights Watch on male rape claims that prison rape has a far higher incidence than prison authorities admit to, and inmate victimization surveys reveal wide disparities between rapes reported to, and recorded by, prison administrators and those indicated by such surveys, with the latter revealing far higher rates than the prison data. Underreporting of rape was found in a 1996 Nebraska study, where only 29 percent of victimized inmates officially reported abuses (Human Rights Watch 2001: 132).

Human Rights Watch suggests that non-reporting of rape may reflect prison administrators' indifference toward such reports and that prisoners would be more likely to report rapes if they were certain of receiving protection. It is said that correctional officers typically do not offer protection to those who have been raped but instead advise them to fight their attacker. In this way, it is claimed that prison systems condone rape.

Correctional Responses to Rape Allegations

Human Rights Watch (2001: 153) found that the response of correctional authorities to rape is often to impose minor disciplinary sanctions, such as 30 days in segregation, or to move rapists to another facility and that allegations of rape were often treated callously. Where the rape involved a gay inmate, unless the inmate was able to show clear physical injury, the claim of rape would be rejected, because prison officials generally assume the act was consensual.

Studies have shown that prison rape is often ignored by officers. One sample of officers in Texas found that 46 percent believed that some inmates were deserving of being raped. There is also evidence of the threat of rape being used by officers to punish inmates or create informers. One notorious case occurred in the Corcoran State Prison in California where some officers used an inmate who was a psychopath and serial rapist as their enforcer. When called upon, he would either beat or rape inmates to enforce directions of the officers (Leighton and Roy 2005: 822).

In women's prisons, sexual abuse of inmates by officers takes various forms, including direct assaults and coercing inmates into sexual acts by promising good or services, or under threat of losing privileges, such as denying visits by children, or threatening transfer to a higher-security facility. Sexual assaults occur during searches when male guards fondle inmates. Guards observe women in the showers and while they are using the toilet facilities. In 1999 Amnesty International observed that "sexual relations between staff and inmates are inherently abusive of the inmates . . . and can never be truly consensual" (Leighton and Roy 2005: 821).

In 1994 the Supreme Court ruled in *Farmer v. Brennan* that prison officials were under a duty to prevent prisoners from harming each other and that "deliberate indifference" to a risk of serious harm violated the prohibition against cruel and unusual punishment. The case was brought by a female transgender inmate who was placed with the male general population in an Indiana prison. She was repeatedly raped and beaten by male inmates and contracted HIV as a result (Parenti 1999: 186).

Transgender Prisoners

The terms "transgender" and "transsexual" describe people "who are born with typical male or female anatomies but feel as though they've been born into the 'wrong body.' For example, a person who identifies as transgender or transsexual may have typical female anatomy but feel like a male and seek to become male by taking hormones or electing to have sex reassignment surgeries" (Intersex Society of North America).

While there are few transgender prisoners in America, they present problems for administrators because they are at a high risk of assault or self-harm. Previously, prisons were structured around either male or female gender, and inmates were classified as male or female. However, this is problematic for trans persons, and in practice, the classification applied depends on the policy of the prison. Generally, prisons will categorize a trans person according to sex at birth or to self-identity. Therefore, a prisoner born as male but who self-identifies as female and who exhibits any female characteristics may be placed in a female facility where the prisoner is less likely to suffer harm. A study of assaults in the California prison system found, for example, that 59 percent of transgender inmates reported having been sexually abused, compared with 4 percent of the general inmate population (Nader 2010: 83). Some trans inmates report that they engage in prison prostitution or partner with another inmate for protection in exchange for sex (Jenness and Fenstermaker 2015: 5).

In the United States transgender inmates are often segregated from the general population for "their own protection" (Shah 2010), and according to one recent report of correctional staff and inmates in Pennsylvania, trans prisoners are required to share space with marginalized groups, including sex offenders, mentally ill inmates, and snitches. Trans women are commonly presumed to be gay and are treated with contempt by other inmates and correctional staff (Jenness and Fenstermaker 2015: 6, 7).

In June 2015, the Justice Department reported for the first time accurate estimates of rates of sexual victimization among transgender inmates. It found that

- an estimated 35 percent of transgender inmates in prisons reported experiencing one or more incidents of sexual victimization by another inmate or by a staff person in the past 12 months, or since admission where less than 12 months;

- about one-quarter of transgender inmates in prisons reported an incident involving another inmate and almost three-quarters said the incidents involved nonconsensual sex acts (PREA Data Collection Activities 2015: 2).

Other countries have legislated on gender issues to prevent confusion in their prison systems. For example, in the United Kingdom, the Ministry of Justice (2011) issued a legal mandate that "an establishment must permit prisoners who consider themselves transsexual and wish to begin gender reassignment to live permanently in their acquired gender." This means that self-identified transgender inmates must be permitted to wear their own clothes and be given access to technologies and medications that help confirm their gender. In the United States trans inmates have claimed entitlement to hormone therapy while in prison, arguing that refusal amounts to a violation of the Eight Amendment's prohibition of cruel and unusual punishment and arguing that denial of therapy constitutes "deliberate indifference" to an inmate's serious medical needs (National Center for Lesbian Rights 2006). The U.S. Justice Department supported a claim by a prison inmate in Georgia that the state illegally ceased hormone treatment that she had been taking for 17 years. The department stated its belief that policies prohibiting new hormone treatment for trans inmates violated the Constitution because prison officials must make treatment decisions based on health assessments that are made independently of the prison. In this case, prison records revealed that mental health professionals had diagnosed this inmate with gender dysphoria and the Department therefore contended that gender dysphoria, like any other medical condition, required treatment.

In 2005 Wisconsin enacted a ban on hormone treatment for transgender inmates regardless of whether the treatment was under way when an inmate was arrested. This law was challenged on constitutional grounds and overturned by a federal court in 2011.

In many states so-called freeze frame policies allow inmates to continue any treatment they were receiving before their arrest but ban expanding or commencing new treatments. This policy applied at the federal level until 2011, but new rules require that treatment plans be regularly reviewed, and hormone treatment may be permitted regardless of whether it was ongoing at the time of arrest (Apuzzo 2015).

Life Sentences and Life without Parole (LWOP)

Originally, indeterminate sentences were closely linked to systems of parole. While sentencing is now generally determinate—imposing a fixed term of imprisonment—state laws continue to provide for parole to be granted before the sentence is completed. Therefore, it is possible to serve a life sentence with the possibility of parole, meaning that the offender may be paroled at some future date depending on the decision of the state parole board. However, in many states laws provide for the sentence of life without parole (LWOP). This sentence means exactly what it says: the prisoner given a sentence of LWOP will spend the rest of his or her life in prison and may not apply for parole to obtain an early release, regardless of whether he or she is rehabilitated. Therefore, LWOP is a lifetime sentence. The only possibilities for release are a pardon or a commutation of sentence. Generally, it is the governor of the state (or, in the case of the federal system, the U.S. president), who has the power to award pardons and commutations of sentences. These forms of release are rarely granted.

The sentence of LWOP is currently being served by more than 41,000 inmates, an increase of 28,500 since 1992 (Dolovich 2012: 110). In addition, more than 140,000 persons are serving life sentences with the possibility of securing parole after having served a minimum period of years (Henry 2012: 66). This compares to only about 34,000 inmates serving life sentences in 1984 (Leigey 2011: 153). However, where states have abolished parole altogether, namely Florida, Illinois, Iowa, Louisiana, Maine, Pennsylvania, South Dakota, and the federal system, a life sentence is the functional equivalent of LWOP (Henry 2012: 68). Therefore, even though the sentence imposed is not LWOP but life imprisonment, the abolition of parole in these states and federally means that the prisoner will spend his or her life in prison unless a pardon or commutation is granted. The increase in the number of LWOP sentences and life sentences with the possibility of parole has been attributed to their being used as an alternative to the sentence of death (Leigey 2011: 153).

Perspectives on LWOP

Some now argue that such sentences constitute "uniquely severe and degrading punishments because of the nature of the punishment itself, because they deny human dignity, and because they are de facto irrevocable" (Henry 2012: 72). Research has shown that those serving life sentences become isolated from their families, cease to receive visitations, and, where married, often get divorced (Leigey 2011: 154). It is said that lifetime sentences should be seen as worse than the sentence of death because a lifetime sentence allows for extended periods of suffering, fails to respect the worth and dignity of the individual, and denies all redemptive possibilities.

Generally, this oppositional perspective is supported in developed countries outside the United States. The Council of Europe has stated that imprisoning a person for life without hope of release is inhuman and incompatible with the idea of reintegrating prisoners into society. Consistent with this declaration, while other countries have retained life imprisonment as a sentence, the sentence must be reviewed after a minimum period of years has been served, for example, after 10 years in Belgium and after 15 years in Germany, Austria, and Switzerland, and after 30 years in France (Henry 2012: 78).

In the United States the Supreme Court has generally ruled that life sentences with or without parole do not constitute cruel and unusual punishment. However, in 2010, in *Graham v. Florida*, the Court held for the first time that a noncapital sentence was a violation of the prohibition against cruel and unusual punishment. In that case, a 16-year-old boy who had committed an armed robbery received probation, which he violated. For that violation he received a life sentence, and because Florida had abolished parole he would never be released from prison. The Court determined that such a sentence could not be validly imposed on a juvenile convicted of an offense other than homicide. The Court said that LWOP was the second most severe penalty under the law and said that it deprived the convicted person of "the most basic liberties, without giving hope of restoration" (quoted in Henry 2012: 80).

Opponents of LWOP also argue that despite its severity, the sentence of LWOP receives no special judicial scrutiny and that it ought to be subject to the same kinds of restrictions and protections as apply to death sentences. Also, the greater the number of LWOP sentences and sentences of life imprisonment where there exists no possibility of parole, the more prison systems will be burdened with the costs and challenges of housing an aging and increasingly unhealthy prison population. The costs of confining life-sentenced inmates for an average life sentence of 29 years have been estimated at $1 million per inmate (Leigey 2011: 161).

Those favoring LWOP and life sentences include death penalty abolitionists who contend that life sentences ought to be substituted for death sentences and become the harshest punishment possible. They argue that life sentences are less costly than death sentences and can be reversed if evidence comes to light proving a person's innocence, whereas this is impossible where the death sentence is imposed. There appears to be strong public support for the sentence of LWOP, and surveys show that fewer persons support the death penalty where LWOP is suggested as an alternative. Other supporters of LWOP include victim groups who tend to support life sentences generally because they are aware that the possibility of parole is remote (Leigey 2011: 157).

Abolishing Imprisonment and Prison Reform

Prisons and imprisonment are taken-for-granted aspects of our society, but some scholars and commentators have argued for the complete abolition of imprisonment or for something less: that imprisonment should truly be reserved for the worst of crimes and criminals and that alternative punishments to incarceration ought to be applied in all other cases. The case for abolition has been powerfully argued by Angela Davis in her well-known text *Are Prisons Obsolete?* However, she, like most scholars, does not claim that prisons should be completely abolished. Arguments about abolition usually encompass proposals such as drastically reducing the use of imprisonment so that it is retained only for the most serious crimes, reducing the length of prison sentences, focusing more on rehabilitation, using alternative methods of punishment such as restorative justice, and making more use of community sanctions and restitution (Lippke 2007: 250).

The Persistence of the Punishment of Imprisonment

Davis (2003) argues that "the prison is considered an inevitable and permanent feature of our social lives" and that "in most circles prison abolition is simply unthinkable and implausible" (2003: 9). In light of the mass incarceration that has taken place in the country since the 1980s it is reasonable to ask, why did this occur without first giving consideration to the effectiveness of imprisonment, and why has the policy not significantly reduced the crime rate?

Research shows that mass incarceration policies have had little impact on crime (Pratt 2009: 66–68). The historical record shows that the rise of the penitentiary was linked to the notion that offenders would abandon their criminality when required to reflect upon it in solitude. Over time, the purpose of incarceration was transformed from providing a time of reflection and possible rehabilitation to treating the prison as a site for warehousing offenders, especially drug offenders, for long periods without any pretense that they would refashion themselves through modern forms of rehabilitation. Imprisonment, constructed as a positive act of moral salvation, therefore became detached from its original nature and purpose and is now perceived as the dominant means of exacting retribution for criminal conduct. The foundation of imprisonment as the dominant form of punishment should be seen therefore as a product of a particular set of circumstances in history.

Davis points to the strongly racist dimension of the prison, especially the association between slavery and the Southern convict lease system, the punishment of whipping, and the control over black labor exercised after the Civil War. She notes that the persistence of historical patterns of discrimination in the modern justice system has resulted in the hugely disproportionate incarceration of black men and women and the consequent damage to black families and communities (2003: 37).

The emergence of the prison industrial complex has raised concern that prisons are now an element of the economy and a source of profit. Growing the global prison industry has become part of growing the American economy, and imprisonment has become inextricably linked to externalities other than punishment and rehabilitation. Its racism, sexism, and its reshaping as a warehouse for serious and nonserious offenders are ignored in favor of economic imperatives (2003: 100).

Contemporary dependence on incarceration makes it difficult to imagine alternatives for the 2 million inmates in U.S. prison systems. Davis argues against simply replacing imprisonment, instead proposing that the prison industrial complex should be dismantled and replaced by a set of alternatives to incarceration that would improve adverse social and economic conditions, offer educational opportunities to all persons, and safeguard health. In addition, the justice system would refocus away from retribution and incapacitation toward reconciliation and reparation in line with restorative justice values and beliefs. It would also oppose racism and sexism within the system and pursue techniques to encourage decarceration (2003: 109).

Criminologist Thomas Mathiesen says modern penality is characterized by a major long-term increase in the prison population; the expansion of prison systems worldwide, but especially in the U.S; and a perceived need for greater disciplining of certain populations through laws that impose longer sentences for certain groups of offenders such as drug users. After assessing the value of imprisonment in terms of rehabilitation, deterrence, incapacitation, and justice, Mathiesen concludes that these theories are unable to justify the prison, but nevertheless prisons persist because of an ideology of prison that endorses it as "meaningful and legitimate" (Mathiesen 2006: 141).

Mathiesen believes that the present state of incarceration indicates the need to diminish and eventually abolish prisons, and cites as an example, Norway, which has succeeded in reducing the size of its prison system. One approach to reduction or abolition would be to widen the range of offenses for which imprisonment is not the penalty and also to narrow the scope of the criminal law (2006: 163). Supplementing this action would be a program of early releases, a reduction in maximum sentences, and a plan for closing prisons that would be strictly adhered to.

Abolition and Reform: Some Proposals

Lippke (2007: 251) suggests that where the costs and burdens of incarceration exceed its benefits, it should be abolished. He questions the value of imprisonment in reducing crime and the burdens it imposes when it takes its current form in the United States of "hard treatment, idleness and isolation" (2007: 251). In addition, the costs of building and maintaining prisons and of housing inmates are high, and those costs could perhaps be more beneficially spent on relieving social problems that cause crime and on crime prevention generally.

Arguing the case for prison reform from a psychological perspective, Haney (2006: 303) proposes three categories of reform:

- Imprisonment should be used more sparingly; for example, specialized courts such as those for drugs that are more community based would use treatment-oriented approaches and not impose imprisonment. In this way, prisons would return to being the last resort of criminal justice and their place taken by a host of alternative sanctions that do not involve confinement (2006: 304, 307).
- The nature of incarceration should be reformed so as to remove potentially damaging confinement conditions by, for example, making greater use of community sanctions and restorative justice.
- Because the majority of persons incarcerated are poor and disproportionately of color, crime control ought not to focus on committing persons to prison for deviance but on improving the social and economic conditions that contribute toward that deviance.

Haney argues that penal systems ought to increase social services for inmates, open up prisons to far greater contact with the outside, humanize staff, liberalize inmate self-expression, upgrade educational and vocational programming, and all should align prison with the concept of "civilized standards" (2006: 305). Alignment implies ceasing to warehouse prisoners and re-creating the prison environment to as much as possible resemble the free world. This would include increased contact with the outside by facilitating visitation. Evidence from European prison systems suggests that encouraging a prison regime to offer help to prisoners also benefits staff (2006: 311).

Criminologist Michael Tonry (2004: 21) agrees that prison life ought to closely approximate that existing in the outside community so that prisoners who have not functioned successfully in a community learn the necessary skills during their confinement.

Tonry (2004: 19) proposes that no prison house more than 300 inmates because large numbers of inmates result in dehumanizing conditions, facilitate the victimization of vulnerable prisoners, make security maintenance more challenging, and allow gangs to recruit from a larger inmate population.

Rehabilitation would be reinstated as the primary goal of incarceration, with new rehabilitation programming focusing on the social and economic challenges that inmates will have to meet on release (Haney 2006: 315). Prison ought not to operate as if they were mental hospitals, and adequate treatment ought to be provided in the community outside of prisons so as to avoid imprisoning those who are mentally ill (Haney 2006: 323).

Policies that promote racial tolerance and racial integration should be encouraged in prisons, and institutionally sanctioned racial barriers should be dismantled. Responses to gangs ought to focus on the conditions that give rise to them. The attraction of gang participation is more likely to diminish where facilities are program-oriented and where basic amenities are provided so that gangs are deprived of the opportunity to supply inmates' needs by smuggling in contraband (Haney 2006: 327).

References

Apuzzo, Matt. 2015. "Transgender Inmate's Hormone Treatment Lawsuit Gets Justice Dept. Backing." *The New York Times*, April 3, 2015.

Austin, J., Johnson, K.D., and Gregoriou, M. 2000. *Juveniles in Adult Prisons and Jails: A National Assessment.* Washington, DC: U.S. Department of Justice.

Beck, Allen J. 2015. *Use of Restrictive Housing in U.S. Prisons and Jails 2011–12.* Washington, DC: U.S. Department of Justice, Office of Justice Programs, Bureau of Justice Statistics.

Bishop, D.M. and Frazier, C.E. 2000. Consequences of Transfer, in Fagan, J. and Zimring, F., eds. *The Changing Borders of Criminal Justice: Transfer of Adolescents to the*

Criminal Court. Chicago: University of Chicago Press, pp. 227–276.

Blomberg, Thomas G. and Lucken, Karol. 2000. *American Penology: A History of Control*. New York: Aldine de Gruyter.

Brownlee, Kimberley. 2013. A Human Right against Social Deprivation. *The Philosophical Quarterly* 63(251): pp. 199–222.

Caplow, Theodore and Simon, Jonathan. 1999. Understanding Prison Policy and Population Trends, in Tonry, Michael and Petersilia, Joan, eds. *Prisons: A Review of Research*. Chicago: University of Chicago Press, pp. 63–120.

Carceral, K.C. 2006. *Prison, Inc: A Convict Exposes Life Inside a Private Prison*. New York: New York University Press.

Carrabine, Eamonn. 2005. Riots, in Bosworth, Mary, ed. *Encyclopedia of Prisons and Correctional Facilities*, Volume 2. Thousand Oaks, CA: Sage Publications, pp. 853–856.

Carson, E. Ann. 2015. *Prisoners in 2014*. Washington, DC: U.S. Department of Justice, Office of Justice Programs, Bureau of Justice Statistics.

Castle, Tammy, Hensley, Christopher, and Tewksbury, Richard. 2002. Argot Roles and Prison Sexual Hierarchy, in Hensley, Christopher, ed. *Prison Sex: Practice and Policy*. Boulder, CO: Lynne Rienner, pp. 13–26.

Clear, Todd, R. 2015. The Criminology of Downsizing. *Victims and Offenders* 10: 358–364.

Cole, Mihael Ami. 2005. Recidivism, in Bosworth, Mary ed. *Encyclopedia of Prisons and Correctional Facilities*, Volume 2. Thousand Oaks, CA: Sage Publications, pp. 822–825.

Conover, Ted. 2001. *Newjack: Guarding Sing Sing*. New York: Vintage.

Culp, Richard. 2005. Contract Facilities Prison, in Bosworth, Mary, ed. *Encyclopedia of Prisons and Correctional Facilities*, Volume 1. Thousand Oaks, CA: Sage Publications, pp. 162–164.

Davis, Angela Y. 2003. *Are Prisons Obsolete?* New York: Seven Stories Press.

Dolovich, Sharon. 2012. Creating the Permanent Prisoner, in Ogletree, Charles J. and Sarat, Austin, eds. *Life without Parole: America's New Death Penalty?* New York: New York University Press, pp. 96–137.

Eilperin, Juliet. January 26, 2016. "Obama Bans Solitary Confinement for Juveniles in Federal Prisons." *The Washington Post.* Available at https://www.washingtonpost .com/politics/obama-bans-solitary-confinement-for-juveniles-in-federal-prisons/2016/01/25, accessed March 18, 2016.

Eisikovits, Zvi and Baizerman, Michael. 1982. "Doin' Time": Violent Youth in a Juvenile Facility and in an Adult Prison. *Journal of Offender Rehabilitation* 6: 5–20.

Finn, Mary A. 2005a. Control Unit, in Bosworth, Mary, ed. *Encyclopedia of Prisons and Correctional Facilities*, Volume 1. Thousand Oaks, CA: Sage Publications, pp. 166–169.

Finn, Mary A. 2005b. Violence, in Bosworth, Mary, ed. *Encyclopedia of Prisons and Correctional Facilities*, Volume 2. Thousand Oaks, CA: Sage Publications, pp. 995–999.

Finn, Mary A. 2005c. Disabled Prisoners, in Bosworth Mary ed. *Encyclopedia of Prisons and Correctional Facilities,* Volume 1. Thousand Oaks, CA: Sage Publications, pp. 239–240.

Finn, Peter. 1996. No-Frills Prisons and Jails: A Movement in Flux. *Federal Probation* 60(3): 35–44.

Fleisher, Mark and Decker, Scott H. 2009. Gangs Behind Bars: Prevalence, Conduct, and Response, in Tewksbury, Richard and Dabney, Dean, eds. *Prisons and Jails: A Reader.* New York: McGraw Hill, pp. 159–174.

Gillespie, Wayne. 2004. Crime and Justice in the United States, in Stanko, Stephen, Gillespie, Wayne, and Crews, Gordon A., eds. *Living in Prison: A History of the*

Correctional System with an Insider's View. Westport, CT: Greenwood Press, pp. 3–24.

Gottschalk, Marie. 2015. *Caught: The Prison State and the Lockdown of American Politics*. Princeton, NJ: Princeton University Press.

Guenther, Lisa. 2013. *Solitary Confinement: Social Death and Its Afterlives*. Minneapolis: University of Minnesota Press.

Haney, Craig. 2005. Supermax Prisons, in Bosworth, Mary, ed. *Encyclopedia of Prisons and Correctional Facilities*, Volume 2. Thousand Oaks, CA: Sage Publications, pp. 938–943.

Haney, Craig. 2006. *Reforming Punishment: Psychological Limits to the Pains of Imprisonment*. Washington, DC: American Psychological Association.

Hannem-Kish, Stacy. 2005. Solitary Confinement, in Bosworth, Mary, ed. *Encyclopedia of Prisons and Correctional Facilities*, Volume 2. Thousand Oaks, CA: Sage Publications, pp. 909–912.

Henry, Jessica S. 2012. Death-in-Prison Sentences: Overutilized and Underscrutinized, in Ogletree, Charles J. and Sarat, Austin, eds. *Life without Parole: America's New Death Penalty?* New York: New York University Press, pp. 68–95.

Hensley, Christopher, Koscheski, Mary, and Tewksbury, Richard. 2003. The Impact of Institutional Factors on Officially Reported Sexual Assaults in Prisons. *Sexuality & Culture* 7(4): 16–26.

Hensley, Christopher, Rutland, Sandra, and Gray-Ray, Phyllis. 2002. Conjugal Visitation Programs: The Logical Conclusion, in Hensley, Christopher, ed. *Prison Sex: Practice and Policy*. Boulder, CO: Lynne Rienner, pp. 133–142.

Hindus, Michael Stephen. 1980. *Prison and Plantation: Crime, Justice and Authority in Massachusetts and South*

Carolina, 1767–1878. Chapel Hill: University of North Carolina Press.

Human Rights Watch. 2001. *No Escape: Male Rape in U.S. Prisons*. New York: Human Rights Watch.

Intersex Society of North America. "What's the Difference between Being Transgender or Transsexual and Having an Intersex Condition?" Available at http://www.isna.org/faq/transgender, accessed December 15, 2015.

Irwin, John and Owen, Barbara. 2005. Harm and the Contemporary Prison, in Liebling, Alison and Maruna, Shadd, eds. *The Effects of Imprisonment*. Cullumpton, Devon: Willan Publishing, pp. 94–117.

Jacobs, James B. 1977. *Stateville: The Penitentiary in Mass Society*. Chicago: The University of Chicago Press.

Jenness, Valerie and Fenstermaker, Sarah. 2015. Forty Years after Brownmiller: Prisons for Men, Transgender Inmates, and the Rape of the Feminine. *Gender and Society* 20(10): 1–16.

Johnson, Robert. 2005. Brave New Prisons: The Growing Social Isolation of Modern Penal Institutions, in Liebling, Alison and Maruna, Shadd, eds. *The Effects of Imprisonment*. Cullumpton, Devon: Willan Publishing, pp. 255–284.

Kendall, Kathleen. 2005. Psychiatric Care, in Bosworth, Mary, ed. *Encyclopedia of Prisons and Correctional Facilities*, Volume 2. Thousand Oaks, CA: Sage Publications, pp. 786–789.

King, Roy D. 2005. The Effects of Supermax Custody, in Liebling, Alison and Maruna, Shadd, eds. *The Effects of Imprisonment*. Cullumpton, Devon: Willan Publishing, pp. 118–145.

Kunkel, Karl R. and Capps, Jason S. 2005. Privatization 1996, in Bosworth, Mary, ed. *Encyclopedia of Prisons and Correctional Facilities*, Volume 1. Thousand Oaks, CA: Sage Publications, pp. 768–773.

Kunselman, Julie, Tewksbury, Richard, Dumond, Robert W., and Dumond, Doris A. 2002. Nonconsensual Sexual Behavior, in Hensley, Christopher, ed. *Prison Sex: Practice and Policy*. Boulder, CO: Lynne Rienner, pp. 27–48.

Kupchik, Aaron. 2006. *Judging Juveniles: Prosecuting Adolescents in Adult and Juvenile Courts*. New York: New York University Press.

Kupers, Terry. 1999. *Prison Madness: The Mental Health Crisis behind Bars and What We Must Do about It*. San Francisco, CA: Jossey-Bass Publishers.

Leigey, Margaret, E. 2011. Life Sentence, in Chambliss, William J., ed. *Corrections*. Thousand Oaks, CA: Sage Publications, pp. 151–164.

Leigey, Margaret E., Hodge, Jessica P., and Saum, Christine A. 2009. Kids in the Big House: Juveniles Incarcerated in Adult Facilities, in Ruddell, Rick and Thomas, Matthew O., eds. *Juvenile Corrections*. Richmond, KY: Newgate Press, pp. 113–135.

Leighton, Paul and Roy, Jennifer. 2005. Rape, in Bosworth, Mary, ed. *Encyclopedia of Prisons and Correctional Facilities*, Volume 2. Thousand Oaks, CA: Sage Publications, pp. 819–822.

Lenz, Nygel. 2002. "Luxuries" in Prison: The Relationship between Amenity Funding and Public Support. *Crime and Delinquency* 48(4): 499–525.

Levinson Robert B. and Greene, John J. 1999. New "Boys" on the Block: A Study of Prison Inmates under the Age of 18. *Corrections Today*: 61(1): 60–64.

Liebling, Alison and Maruna, Shadd. 2005. Introduction: The Effects of Imprisonment Revisited, in Liebling, Alison and Maruna, Shadd, eds. *The Effects of Imprisonment*. Cullumpton, Devon: Willan Publishing: pp. 1–32.

Lippke, Richard L. 2007. *Rethinking Imprisonment*. New York: Oxford University Press.

Logan, Charles. 1990. *Private Prisons: Cons and Pros.* New York: Oxford University Press.

Lyman, M.D. 1989. *Gangland.* Springfield, IL: Charles C. Thomas.

Mair, Julie Samia, Frattaroli, Shannon, and Teret, Stephen. 2003. New Hope for Victims of Sexual Assault. *Journal of Law: Medicine & Ethics* 31: 602–606.

Mathiesen, Thomas. 2006. *Prison on Trial.* Winchester, UK: Waterside Press.

Mays, G. Larry and Winfree, L. Thomas. 2005. *Essentials of Corrections.* Belmont, CA: Wadsworth.

Mentor, Kenneth. 2005. College Courses in Prison, in Bosworth, Mary, ed. *Encyclopedia of Prisons and Correctional Facilities*, Volume 1. Thousand Oaks, CA: Sage Publications, pp. 141–144.

Ministry of Justice, United Kingdom. March 2, 2011. *The Care and Management of Transsexual Prisoners* (PSI2011-007). London: National Offender Management Service.

Morash, Merry and Schram, Pamela J. 2002. *The Prison Experience: Special Issues of Women in Prison.* Prospect Heights, IL: Waveland Press.

Nader, Christine. 2010. Correctional Facilities. *The Georgetown Journal of Gender and the Law* 11(1): 77–95.

National Center for Lesbian Rights. June 2006. "Rights of Transgender Prisoners." Available at www.nclrights.org, accessed August 11, 2011.

National Institute of Justice. 2006. NIJ's Response to the Prison Rape Elimination Act. *Corrections Today* 68(1): 60–61.

Owen, Barbara. 1998. *"In the Mix": Struggle and Survival in a Women's Prison.* New York: State University of New York Press.

Parenti, Christian. 1999. *Lockdown America: Police and Prisons in the Age of Crisis.* New York: Verso.

Pollock, Jocelyn M. 2004. *Prisons and Prison Life: Costs and Consequences*. New York: Oxford University Press.

Pollock, Jocelyn. 2010. Afterword, in George, Erin. *A Woman Doing Life: Notes from a Prison for Women*. New York: Oxford University Press, pp. 176–185.

Pratt, Travis C. 2009. *Addicted to Incarceration: Corrections Policy and the Politics of Misinformation in the United States*. Thousand Oaks, CA: Sage Publications.

PREA Data Collection Activities, 2015. U.S Department of Justice, Office of Justice Programs, Bureau of Statistics, Washington, DC.

Rodriguez, Sal. January 8, 2016. "California Expects to Save $28 Million by Reducing Solitary Confinement." Solitary Watch. http://solitarywatch.com/2016/01/08/california-expects-to-save-28-million-by-reducing-solitary-confinement/, accessed January 9, 2016.

Ross, Jeffrey Ian and Richards, Stephen C. 2002. *Behind Bars: Surviving Prison*. Indianapolis, IN: Alpha Books.

Santos, Michael G. 2004. *About Prison*. Belmont, CA: Wadsworth.

Shah, Benish. 2010. Lost in the Gender Maze: Placement of Transgender Inmates in the Prison System. *Journal of Race, Gender and Ethnicity* 5(1): 39–56.

Shalev, Sharon. 2009. *Supermax: Controlling Risk through Solitary Confinement*. Devon, UK: Willan Publishing.

Shalev, Sharon. 2011. Solitary Confinement and Supermax Prisons: A Human Rights and Ethical Analysis. *Journal of Forensic Psychology Practice* 11(2, 3): 151–183.

Shelden, Randall G. 2005. Prison Industrial Complex, in Bosworth, Mary, ed. *Encyclopedia of Prisons and Correctional Facilities*, Volumes 1 and II. Thousand Oaks, CA: Sage Publications.

Shichor, David. 1995. *Punishment for Profit: Private Prisons/ Public Concerns*. Thousand Oaks, CA: Sage Publications.

Sickmund, Melissa. 2004. *Juveniles in Corrections*. OJJDP. National Report Series Bulletin.

Skarbek, David. 2014. *The Social Order of the Underworld: How Prison Gangs Govern the American Penal System*. New York: Oxford University Press.

Stop Prisoner Rape. 2007. *Stories from Inside: Prisoner Rape and the War on Drugs*. Los Angeles, CA: Author. Available at http://www.spr.org, accessed March 23, 2007.

Sykes, Gresham. 1999. *The Society of Captives: A Study of a Maximum Security Prison*. Princeton, NJ: Princeton University Press (original work published in 1958).

Tonry, Michael. 2004. Has the Prison a Future? in Tonry, Michael, ed. *The Future of Imprisonment*. New York: Oxford University Press, pp. 3–26.

Walters, Joanna. December 2, 2015. "Illinois Inmates Increasingly Sued by State to Recoup Incarceration Costs." *The Guardian*. Available at http://www.theguardian.com/us-news/2015/dec/02/illinois-inmates-sued-incarceration-costs, accessed December 3, 2015.

Ward, David A. 2005. ADX (Administrative Maximum): Florence, in Bosworth, Mary, ed. *Encyclopedia of Prisons and Correctional Facilities*, Volume 1. Thousand Oaks, CA: Sage Publications, pp. 15–18.

Welch, Michael. 2005. *Ironies of Imprisonment*. Thousand Oaks, CA: Sage Publications.

Welch, Michael. 2011. *Corrections: A Critical Approach*. New York: Routledge.

West, Heather C. and Sabol, William J. 2009. *Prisons Inmates at Midyear 2008—Statistical Tables*. Washington, DC: Department of Justice, Bureau of Justice Statistics.

Williams, Timothy. 2015. "The High Cost of Calling the Imprisoned." *The New York Times*, March 30, 2015.

Wolff, Nancy, Blitz, Cynthia L., Shi, Jing, Shi, Siegel, Jane, and Bachman, Ronet. 2009. Physical Violence Inside Prisons: Rates of Victimization, in Tewksbury, Richard and Dabney, Dean, eds. *Prisons and Jails: A Reader*. New York: McGraw Hill, pp. 111–120.

Wozniak, Kevin H. 2014. American Public Opinion about Prisons. *Criminal Justice Review* 39(3): 305–324.

Zimring, Franklin E. and Hawkins, Gordon. 2004. Democracy and the Limits of Punishment: A Preface to Prisoners' Rights, in Tonry, Michael, ed. *The Future of Imprisonment*. New York: Oxford University Press, pp. 157–178.

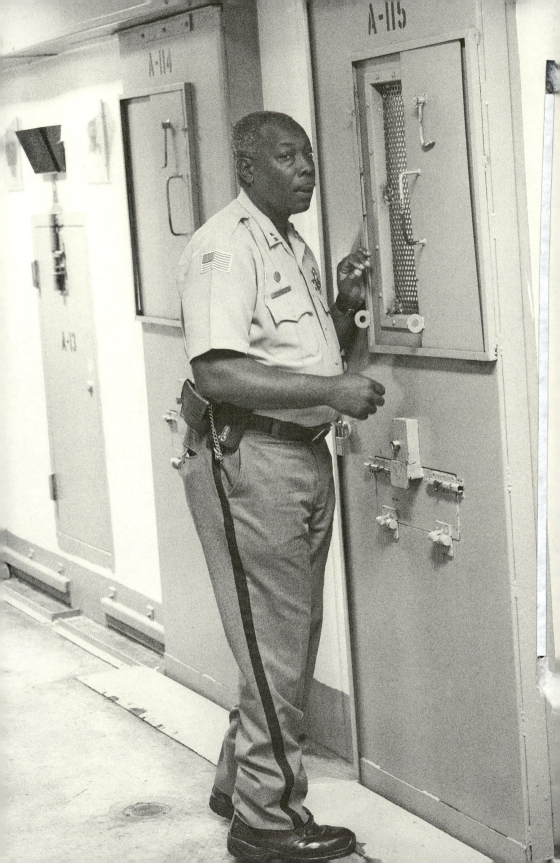

3   Perspectives

This chapter comprises a set of essays giving perspectives on prisons. The essay authors are voices from academia, prison administration, education, former prisoners, and private non-profit institutions concerned with sentencing policy. Their perspectives add an additional dimension to this book by highlighting important aspects of the prison experience and articulating the policy debate about sentencing. All contributions link to the issues and controversies discussed in Chapter 2 or to the historical account in Chapter 1.

The perspectives begin with an argument from Ashley Nellis that the current U.S. mass incarceration is an outcome of state and federal crime control policies and that those policies are in need of reform to reduce racial disparities and the current imprisonment rate. That argument is echoed by Christine Arazan, who not only highlights racial disparities but also points to the high proportion of offenders who are serving sentences for drug offenses, especially in the federal prison system. She points to the war on drugs as a major causal factor in mass imprisonment but sees hope for the future in the new "smart on crime" approaches being developed in the states and federally. Michael Costelloe critiques supermax incarceration, canvassing arguments for and against and contending that, overall,

Captain Dwain Williams checks on a prisoner in the Special Management Unit, known as "high-max" at a Georgia prison in 2015. Face-to-face interaction with inmates is rare. The cells are only 7 by 13½ feet, and inmates can't see out unless guards slide back a metal cover over the grated opening on the door. (AP Photo/David Goldman) this model of incarceration has failed to satisfy its claims to reduce violence and unrest and that in any event, it is morally highly problematic.

Shifting from issues of policy to problems of administration and professionalism, Deborah Mitchell Robinson asks whether a college degree should be a requirement for all correctional officers. Currently, it is required only in the federal system of corrections for entry level. In state systems, the entry-level qualification is a high school diploma. It is not clear why the federal system has higher requirements than the state system, since the work is essentially the same. Robinson stresses that a college education provides a new correctional officer with a stock of knowledge than his or her high school counterpart will not possess. Subjects such as mental health, psychology, and most of all interactions with diverse cultures are commonly part of the college experience and would add greatly to a correctional officer's ability to work within prison environments.

Former prison warden Susan Jones continues the administration theme by addressing the challenges of managing female inmates. Her comprehensive and insightful essay shares her perspective that female officers who supervise female inmates (often because they are required by law to supervise such activities such as searches of the person) are regarded as having less status than other officers and have fewer management options than those that can be applied to male inmates. She calls for greater recognition of the challenges faced by these officers and for solutions to be found to their perceived lower status. Angel Medina, another prison administrator, presents an overview of the benchmarks he regards as important in effectively administering prisons. He identifies the need for a senior management team, for trust among staff, for staff to perform to the highest standard, for every incident report to be reviewed for lessons to be learned, and, most of all, for administrators to have a complete understanding of their staff and their motivations.

Vince Guerrero addresses a key issue in corrections, that of mentally ill inmates. His perspective is informed by his experience as a lieutenant in the security staff at a facility expressly designated for men with mental illness. He stresses the need for the security and clinical staff to form an alliance in their own interests and that of the inmates so that, for example, instances of violent conduct are not read solely as violence but are also viewed as symptoms of mental illness. He describes techniques of verbal de-escalation that can be employed to preempt violence by both inmates and officers. His perspective offers valuable insights into managing this specific population of inmates.

The final perspective is a vivid and engaging essay from James J. Hamm, a former prisoner, who calls upon his inside knowledge of a prison to describe the dramatic experience of entering an institution for the first time. Hamm gives readers an understanding of inmate interactions at a point in time within the prison environment, of the prison culture, and offers advice on coping with both. The discussion of prison gangs in Chapter 2 provides specific additional context for this remarkable essay.

Imprisonment in America
Ashley Nellis

The United States holds 2.2 million people in prisons and jails around the country, a development that has been called "historically unprecedented and internationally unique." The main causes of the U.S. position in the world are the punitive crime policies that have produced an overreliance on incarceration and an underinvestment on prevention, early intervention, and diversion from imprisonment. The U.S. prison population has been driven upward up by more than 500 percent over the past four decades, creating both overcrowded prisons and substantial fiscal problems for states. Today, states spend $55 billion annually in corrections expenditures. Since 2010, the overall imprisonment rate has receded slightly for the first time in decades, declining from 2.3 million to 2.2 million. At the present rate of decline, however, it will take nearly 90 years to return the prison population to its pre-mass incarceration level.

The United States is also the world leader in lengthy imprisonment, such as life sentences. One in nine inmates is serving a life sentence in the United States, and 31 percent of lifers will never have the opportunity for parole. California, which leads the nation in terms of life-sentenced inmates, has more than 40,000 inmates serving life terms. In addition, more than 10 percent of the prison populations in Louisiana, Massachusetts, and Pennsylvania are serving parole-ineligible life sentences. Compare this to other western countries, where a life sentence is exceedingly rare and typically equates to 25 years before release for even the most serious offenses (Appleton 2015).

A range of crime control policies at the federal and state levels have created the system of mass incarceration now firmly in place. At the federal level, the elimination of judicial discretion as part of the 1984 Sentencing Reform Act established the federal sentencing commission and subsequent guidelines that removed the ability of judges to use individual judgment to decide appropriate prison sentences for federal defendants. Several states followed suit, establishing the first markings of the new generation of mandatory minimum laws that would greatly accelerate mass incarceration. In 1986, the Anti-Drug Abuse Act established a 100 to 1 sentencing disparity between crack and powder cocaine, mandating a minimum the same sentence of five years for possession of 5 grams of crack cocaine versus 500 grams of powder cocaine, despite the fact that the two drugs are pharmacologically identical. In 1994, the Violent Crime Control and Law Enforcement Act further accelerated the incarceration boom through incentivizing state prison construction and allocating several billion dollars for law enforcement initiatives and resources, along with enhancements to the federal death penalty and support to states for lengthening prison terms through "truth-in-sentencing" laws (Mauer 2006). At the state level, policies were also supported to both prioritize incarceration over prevention and diversion for persons convicted of crimes and extend prison sentences they received. These were accomplished chiefly through passing new habitual offender laws, expanding mandatory minimum sentences, deprioritizing prevention and intervention strategies, and abolishing or greatly restricting access to parole.

Today, just over half of state inmates have been convicted of a violent offense, 16 percent have been convicted of a drug offense, 19 percent have been convicted of a property offense, and 11 percent have been convicted of a public order offense (Carson 2015). At the federal level, more than half of the inmates in the federal system have been convicted of a drug offense, while 7 percent have been convicted of a violent crime, 36 percent have been convicted of a public order offense, and 6 percent have been convicted of a property crime (Carson 2015). At the federal level, the average sentence for federal prisoners convicted of a drug offense has tripled from 22 months to 62 months. The majority of prisoners are male, but the rate of imprisonment of women has been increasing at a rate that is 50 percent higher than that of men since 1980. In 1980 there were 13,258 women in federal prisons and jails; as of 2014, this figure stood at 106,232 (The Sentencing Project 2015). The racial dynamics of female incarceration have shifted in recent years, with white females outpacing black females.

Racial disparity is widespread in the U.S. prison system. Nationally, African Americans are overrepresented in comparison to whites at a rate of 5 to 1, and Hispanics are incarcerated at 1.5 times the rate of whites. State-level disparities show a range in black/white disparity, that is 3 to 1 on the low end and over 12 to 1 on the high end (Nellis 2016). For black men in their thirties, 1 in every 10 is incarcerated on any given day. Despite modest improvements in prison decarceration in some states recently, racial disparity endures as a glaring example of injustice.

Scholarly research has shown for decades that unequal treatment based on race and ethnicity begins at the point of arrest, through tactics such as racial profiling, and continues to the point of imprisonment and well beyond. In the U.S. punishment system, the period of incarceration is only the beginning of years of penalties that are applied to those with a criminal conviction. Commonly known as collateral consequences, there are in place a series of additional constraints that follow individuals well past their prison experience, including barriers to employment and housing, loss of voting rights, and termination of public benefits to assist needy individuals in their efforts to get back on track.

The American carceral state is in great need of serious attention and reform, for both moral and fiscal reasons. To begin to accomplish this, it has been proposed that reforms must occur not only at the various stages of the criminal justice system—and ideas about how to tackle needed reforms are plentiful—but also more fundamentally at what lies beneath, which is largely racially stratified income and social inequality.

References

Appleton, C. 2015. *Life without Parole*. Oxford: Oxford University Press.

Carson, E. 2015. *Prisoners in 2014*. Washington, DC: Bureau of Justice Statistics.

Mauer, M. 2006. *Race to Incarcerate:* New York: The New Press.

Mauer, M. and Ghandnoosh, N. 2013. "Can We Wait 88 Years to End Mass Incarceration?" Available at http://www.huffingtonpost.com/marc-mauer/88-years-mass-incarceration_b_4474132.html.

National Association of State Budget Officers. 2015. *State Expenditure Report: 2013–2015*. Washington, DC: National Association of State Budget Officers.

National Research Council. 2014. *The Growth of Incarceration in the United States: Exploring Causes and Consequences*. Washington, DC: The National Academies Press.

Nellis, A. 2013. *Life Goes On: The Historic Rise in Life Sentences in America*. Washington, DC: The Sentencing Project.

Nellis, A. 2016. *State Rates of Disparity*. Washington, DC: The Sentencing Project.

The Sentencing Project. 2015. *Fact Sheet: Trends in U.S. Corrections*. Washington, DC: The Sentencing Project.

Ashley Nellis, PhD, is senior research analyst at The Sentencing Project. Her work focuses largely on the study of racial disparities in the justice system, the overuse of lengthy prison sentences, and juvenile justice. She is the author of A Return to Justice: Rethinking Our Approach to Juveniles in the System.

Mass Injustice: The War on Drugs, Institutional Discrimination, and the Impact on U.S. Prisons
Christine Arazan

Prison rates in the United States have increased steadily for nearly four decades beginning in the early 1970s. In 2014, over 1.5 million people were in the nation's state and federal prisons—an increase of over 600 percent since the mid-1970s (Carson 2015). Incarceration rates are so high in the United States that we have earned the dubious honor of imprisoning more people proportionally than any other nation in the world. And yet these summary statistics obscure a disturbing disparity in terms of *who* is incarcerated and for *what* offenses.

The Who: Racial and Ethnic Minorities
In 2014, whites comprised 33.6 percent of the people in state and federal prisons, blacks 35.8 percent, Hispanic 21.6 percent, and "other" 9 percent. Black men are nearly six times as likely to be incarcerated as white men and Hispanic men 2.3 times (The Sentencing Project 2015). Bonczar (2003) provides an interesting analysis of the likelihood of imprisonment for individuals born in the United States. He concludes that if our incarceration rates continue, an estimated one in every nine males born today can expect to go to prison in his lifetime. Specifically, 1 of every 3

African American males would go to prison as would 1 of every 6 Latino males, compared to 1 in 17 white males. The same general pattern of racial/ethnic disparity is found for women: 1 of every 18 African American females, 1 of every 45 Hispanic females, and 1 of every 111 white females could expect incarceration in their lifetime given our current incarceration rates.

For What: Drug Offenses

The number of Americans incarcerated for drug offenses in state and federal prisons exploded from an approximate 23,700 in 1980 to over 304,500 in 2014—an increase of 1,183 percent (The Sentencing Project 2015). The federal prison system in particular has been overwhelmed with the sheer quantity of convicted drug offenders, with just over half of the federal prison population comprised of individuals incarcerated on a drug conviction.

*How We Got Here: Institutional Discrimination
and "The War on Drugs"*

In 1971, then president Richard Nixon identified drug abuse as "public enemy number one" and declared a War on Drugs, a war that by the 1980s had firmly bonded the linkages between minorities, drugs and crime in public and political rhetoric and in the media. In 1984 Congress created the United States Sentencing Commission with the passing of the Sentencing Reform Act. The Sentencing Reform Act tasked the Sentencing Commission with distributing guidelines to dictate the sentence to be imposed in criminal cases, including drug offenses. The application of these sentencing guidelines and mandatory minimum sentencing structures resulted in the institutionalization of discriminatory sentencing policies.

The most commonly cited example of this institutional discrimination is the Anti-Drug Abuse Act of 1986 that differentiated crack cocaine, most prevalent in inner-city drug markets where it was sold and most often within minority communities, from other forms of cocaine (like powder) and established a 100 to 1 weight ratio as the threshold for requiring a five-year mandatory minimum penalty if convicted of possession (United States Sentencing Commission 2016). Ultimately, the penalty for possessing 100 grams of powder cocaine, typically used by more affluent drug users, was comparable to possessing only 1 gram of crack cocaine, typically used by ethnic and racial minorities.

The passage of the Fair Sentencing Act in 2010 reduced this sentencing disparity to 18 to 1, clearly decreasing yet not eliminating the punishment disparity. The enactment of these federal sentencing policies created by the U.S. Sentencing Commission resulted in disparate incarceration rates for crack versus powder cocaine users that disproportionately affected African American users and their urban communities.

Undeniably there are a variety of factors responsible for these unprecedented and unparalleled incarceration rates. There is a large body of research that documents and examines the interplay between an increasingly punitive public, the relative contribution of crime rates, disparate law enforcement practices, and mandatory sentencing practices and policies. However, the research overwhelmingly points to the impact of the War on Drugs and the set of policies adopted within the possessive framework. These policies include law enforcement practices (e.g., racial profiling, civil asset forfeiture laws, and Terry frisks, in which police can stop and search individuals as long as there exists a reasonable cause for suspicion, without a warrant or even probable cause) and prosecutorial decision making and the imposition of mandatory minimum sentencing structures, school zone drug enhancements, and three strikes laws. (Because urban centers are so densely populated, it is more likely that a drug offense occurs within an area defined as a school zone and disproportionately impacts offenders in urban centers—individuals who are racial/ethnic minorities [Mauer 2011].) These policies, once considered "race neutral," have been shown to be anything but neutral and are a striking example of institutional discrimination.

In large part it was the policy "reforms" triggered by the war on drugs that have resulted in a justice system overwhelmed by the sheer quantity of arrests, a backlogged court system, and unprecedented rates of incarceration, coupled with high rates of recidivism. And not surprisingly, it is disproportionately individuals who lack access to legitimate opportunities and power, those already marginalized by structural inequalities, who are the most likely victims of this mass injustice. These disparities are not the result of greater criminal involvement in drug offenses for these populations but rather of institutionalized law enforcement and sentencing policies enacted by state and federal lawmakers during the 1980s (Mauer 2011).

The Pendulum Begins to Swing, Perhaps

Clearly the sheer quantity of individuals incarcerated in the United States is just unsustainable from a fiscal standpoint. While still too early to know definitively, there are some indications that the era of mass incarceration may slowly be coming to an end. Incarceration rates have been, albeit inconsistently, declining since approximately 2004 in both state and federal prisons. The federal prison population decreased by over 5,000 inmates from 2013 to 2014, marking the second consecutive year of decline and the second-largest decline in more than 35 years (Carson 2015).

Declining crime rates coupled with the implementation of several key legislative attempts to reform sentencing policies may result in declining incarceration rates. Arguably, the most significant example of legislative change to date is the 2013 "Smart on Crime" plan. The United States attorney general Eric Holder announced that the Department of Justice will no longer charge certain low-level and nonviolent drug offenders with crimes that carry a mandatory minimum sentence. In lieu of mandatory minimum sentences that mandate incarceration, the Department of Justice recommended pursuing alternatives to incarceration to eliminate unfair disparities and reduce overburdened prisons. Holder (2013) commended states like

Texas, Georgia, Arkansas, Ohio, and Pennsylvania for taking action to reduce incarceration of low-level offenders by seeking alternatives to prison.

While fiscal constraints may have been the initial impetus for reexamining the current state of mass incarceration, decreasing crime rates, key changes in sentencing laws and policies coupled with shifts in public opinion, have opened the door for lawmakers in key states and federal positions to rely on research-based alternatives like specialty courts, diversion programs, and treatment options as legitimate alternatives to incarceration.

References

Bonczar, T. 2003. *Prevalence of Imprisonment in the U.S. Population, 1974–2001* (NCJ 197976). Washington, DC: Bureau of Justice Statistics. www.bjs.gov/content/pub/pdf/piusp01.pdf.

Carson, A.E. 2015. *Prisoners in 2014* (NCJ 248955). Washington, DC: Bureau of Justice Statistics. www.bjs.gov/content/pub/pdf/p14.pdf.

Holder, E. 2013. "The Attorney General's 'Smart on Crime' Initiative." Available at www.justice.gov/sites/default/files/ag/legacy/2014/04/11/ag-smart-on-crime-fact-sheet.pdf. Accessed June 15, 2016

Mauer, M. 2011. Addressing Racial Disparities in Incarceration. *The Prison Journal*, doi:10.1177/0032885511415227.

The Sentencing Project. 2015. "Trends in U.S. Corrections." Available at www.sentencingproject.org/wp-content/uploads/2016/01/Trends-in-US-Corrections.pdf. Accessed June 15, 2016

United States Sentencing Commission. 2016. "Chapter 6: Report on Cocaine and Federal Sentencing Policy. The National Legislative and Law Enforcement Response to Cocaine." Washington, DC. Available at www.ussc.gov/report-cocaine-and-federal-sentencing-policy-2, accessed March 23, 2016.

Christine Arazan earned a PhD in criminology and criminal justice from the Florida State University in 2007 and is currently assistant professor in the Department of Criminology and Criminal Justice at Northern Arizona University. Her research interests include drugs and drug policy, and intervention, program, and policy evaluations.

Supermax: A Troubling Trend in Incarceration
Michael Costelloe

The use of supermax prisons is a relatively new and controversial correctional strategy. While supermax housing has its historical roots in the federal penitentiaries of Alcatraz and Marion, Illinois, it has become increasingly popular in state correctional facilities. There is considerable diversity regarding how "supermax" is defined, how it operates, who is housed there, and what is its primary purpose. However, supermax is generally defined as a stand-alone prison or a unit within a prison that provides secure control over inmates who are considered violent, disruptive, or a threat to the safety and well-being of other inmates and prison personnel. Supermax inmates are generally confined for an indefinite period of time to individual cells for an average of 23 hours a day and have little or no interaction with other inmates and limited contact with prison staff. Inmates thus eat, exercise, and program individually. Supermax security is touted to achieve a number of goals, but its primary objectives are order, control, safety, and the incapacitation of dangerous or disruptive inmates. The process for determining admissions and release from supermax also varies across jurisdiction, with the final authority generally resting with either the warden or the head of the state correctional system (Butler et al. 2012).

The use of supermax housing is objectionable on both pragmatic and principled grounds. Pragmatically, it has not been empirically demonstrated that the use of supermax housing is cost effective and efficient, or even that it provides for a more secure prison environment. In terms of cost, what is clear is that the use of supermax housing is more expensive to build, operate, and maintain than are other forms of prison housing due to the advanced and extensive security measures that are required. What is not as apparent, however, is whether any derived benefit from its use outweighs this increase in cost given the paucity of research in this area (Mears 2008; Mears and Watson 2006). Furthermore, supermax incarceration operates under the assumption that some inmates pose such a threat to the well-being of other inmates and prison personnel that they must be kept in isolation.

However, recent research shows that this may not necessarily be the case. It has been noted that not only do classification procedures vary considerably across states and prisons, but they are also often not clearly outlined. Therefore, it has been difficult for researchers to assess the claims that supermax units house the "worst of the worst" inmates and thus whether they actually achieve the goals of creating more secure and controlled prisons. Finally, the use of supermax housing may be counterproductive to rehabilitation efforts. Access to educational and vocational programs for supermax residents, those who may more acutely need it, is severely limited due to increased security measures. Often, these kinds of rehabilitation programs are available only by accessing videos or by one-on-one interaction with correctional personnel through a locked steel door or while shackled.

However, even if the effectiveness of supermax units could be demonstrated, there are legal, idealistic, and humanistic reasons for discontinuing or reducing their use. In fact, there are many who argue that their use is a violation of both constitutional rights and human rights. In terms of constitutional rights, it has been charged that unclear classification processes result in arbitrary decision making and do not afford an inmate an adequate process for refuting the decision to place them in an extended control environment. The Supreme Court has ruled that prisoners are entitled to notification of the decision to place them in supermax, an opportunity to respond to that decision, and meaningful periodic reviews in order to keep them there. Nevertheless, the criteria for supermax placement were left in the hands of prison administrators, and the rights of inmates remained largely limited, informal, and symbolic.

Because judges do not sentence individuals to supermax facilities, sending someone there seemingly increases the severity of punishment (and a greater deprivation of liberty) beyond what was initially imposed and thus could be considered a violation of the Fifth Amendment of the U.S. Constitution, which prohibits the deprivation of liberty without due process of the law. Moreover, there are many who argue that the use of supermax facilities, and particularly its reliance on solitary confinement, is a violation of the Eighth Amendment's protection against cruel and unusual punishment. Among some of the more common conditions that have been presented as cruel are the conditions and length of isolation; lack of recreation; noncontact visitation; and the undue emotional, psychological, and physical harm long periods of solitary confinement have been shown to inflict.

Supermax prisons are not merely correctional or legal issues; they are just as importantly a human rights issue. Inmates already lose a great deal of freedom when they enter prison; in supermax institutions, they lose even more, and, for many, there may be long-term consequences such as psychological and physical health problems. In fact, supermax prisons have been shown to diminish inmate mental health and increase suicide attempts (Haney 2008). Maybe even more disconcerting, however, is that mentally ill inmates are at times placed in supermax facilities/units, as they are often deemed disruptive. Furthermore, the nature of supermax housing often impedes inmates from receiving the adequate mental health treatment that they need, thus exponentially exacerbating the problem (Mears and Castro 2006: 413).

According to Human Rights Watch, supermax prisons are "perhaps the most troubling" human rights trend in U.S. corrections. Of particular concern is the use of solitary confinement. International law contends that long-term isolation in solitary confinement is torture, inhuman, and degrading (Lobel 2008: 4). The Committee Against Torture recommends that the practice of using solitary confinement as punishment should be abolished because of the mental and physical health problems it can produce (Lobel 2008). Both the Human Rights Committee and the Committee Against Torture have voiced their concerns on the harsh conditions inmates have to endure in supermax prisons and that solitary confinement should be used only in exceptional cases, not as a primary form of punishment (Human Rights Watch 2009).

References

Butler, D.H., Griffin III, O.H., and Johnson, W. 2012. What Makes You the "Worst of the Worst?" An Examination of State Policies Defining Supermaximum Confinement. *Criminal Justice Policy Review* 24(6): 676–694.

Haney, C. 2008. A Culture of Harm: Taming the Dynamics of Cruelty in Supermax Prisons. *Criminal Justice and Behavior* 35(8): 956–984.

Human Rights Watch. September 22, 2009. "Mental Illness, Human Rights, and US Prisons." Available at https://www.hrw.org/news/2009/09/22/mental-illness-human-rights-and-us-prisons, accessed April 19, 2016.

Lobel, J. 2008. Prolonged Solitary Confinement and the Constitution. *Journal of Constitutional Law* 11: 118–119.

Mears, D.P. 2008. An Assessment of Supermax Prisons Using an Evaluation Research Framework. *The Prison Journal* 88(1): 43–68.

Mears, D.P. and Castro, J.L. 2006. Wardens' Views on the Wisdom of Supermax Prisons. *Crime & Delinquency* 52(3): 398–431.

Mears, D.P. and Watson, J. 2006. Towards a Fair and Balanced Assessment of Supermax Prisons. *Justice Quarterly* 23(2): 232–270.

Michael Costelloe is associate professor of criminology and criminal justice at Northern Arizona University. His research interests are in the area of drug policy, immigration, policing, and public attitudes toward crime and punishment.

Should a College Degree Be Required for Correctional Officers?
Deborah Mitchell Robinson

Should correctional officers at local and state correctional institutions be required to have a college degree for an entry-level position? I am specifically not questioning federal corrections because the requirements are already set at a four-year college degree or at least three years of full-time general experience or one year of specialized experience. At present, educational requirements for local and state correctional officers begin with a high school diploma or a General Educational Development (GED) equivalent, and rise to the level of some college, a two-year college degree, or a four-year college degree, depending on the state and specific institution. In other words, the educational requirement for entry-level federal correctional officers is a college degree or substantial experience, while the educational requirement for most entry-level local or state correctional officers is a high school diploma.

My question, then, is, what is so special or unique about the federal correctional system, run by the Bureau of Prisons, which would require a college degree? Aren't correctional officers in all types of correctional institutions essentially engaging in the same duties and responsibilities, namely the care, custody, and control of inmates? Granted, correctional institutions at the various levels house different types of inmates, and in addition, jails house those who are awaiting trial or who are not able or eligible to post bail/bond. However, the overall responsibilities are the same. All correctional officers need to understand institutional policies and procedures, the Eighth Amendment, and any jurisdictional statutes that pertain to custody, including the humane treatment of those confined.

If federal correctional officers are engaging in the same types of duties and responsibilities as local and state correctional officers, then why the varying levels of educational requirements? The importance of the correctional officer cannot be understated. Correctional officers are on the front lines within the confines of the correctional institution. From the local jail to the supermax prison, correctional officers are required to maintain order, while also understanding the unique environment posed by institutional confinement.

Being in higher education for 20 years, I understand that I might be biased in terms of education. However, also having a husband who has worked in both corrections and law enforcement at local and state levels, and in numerous discussions and interactions with those in corrections, from entry level to warden, I truly see the value of what a college education brings to the job. There is just something about the college experience that those who graduate only from high school do not obtain. It is more than simply the degree awarded; it has to do with the overall learning and growing as an individual that takes place within the college environment.

For example, mental illness is an ever-present and growing issue at all levels of corrections. The issues raised in handling those inmates with a mental illness can be confusing and sometimes difficult to manage, even for those with specific training. Not only are these individuals in need of treatment and/or medication, but also many have symptoms that will worsen in a confined environment. A misdiagnosis or identification of a mental health issue can be devastating to the inmate, the correctional officer, and the institution. College students in various fields and majors are exposed to courses that deal directly or indirectly with the psychology of human behavior. In fact, many colleges require, or at least offer as an elective, a general psychology course as part of the lower-division core curriculum. This puts the correctional officer with a college degree in a better position to be able to identify, recognize, and understand the unique issues related to the mentally ill. On the other hand, these are courses high school students are not routinely exposed to, putting those correctional officers at a disadvantage when issues with mental illness and associated behaviors arise in the correctional setting.

The K-12 system is at the local level. This means that students will typically see the same students and teachers year after year, while remaining in the same cultural environment of the school system and community. This is not to say that there is anything wrong with growing up and eventually working in the same community, but rather what college provides is an invaluable experience into diverse cultures and diverse individuals. Students in college have the chance to interact with, learn from, work with, and engage in conversation and dialog with individuals from different states and regions of the country, as well as students from all over the world. This experience provides a potential correctional officer with a vast knowledge and understanding of, or at least some familiarity with, many of the same diverse cultural values as inmates he or she will encounter in jail or prison.

We are truly a multicultural society, and inmates in jails and prisons reflect that multicultural diversity. Correctional officers who have been successful in obtaining a college degree will invariably be in a better position to understand those they supervise. Being confined in jail or prison is, in and of itself, one of the most stressful situations for any human being. Correctional officers can make this situation better for inmates and themselves with understanding, knowledge, and respect for their fellow man, traits that can be better developed through the college experience. Therefore, incorporating a minimum requirement of a college degree for entry-level correctional officers, at any institution, will make for a better correctional officer and a more positive institutional environment.

Deborah Mitchell Robinson, PhD, is professor of criminal justice at Valdosta State University. She obtained her MS and PhD degrees from Florida State University and her BSPR degree from the University of Florida. She has taught and developed a wide range of criminal justice courses, including several based on her research interests of crime prevention, sexual deviance, and historical aspects of crime and offenders. She has written, along with numerous articles, three textbooks, the latest on Georgia's Criminal Justice System.

Challenges Faced by Female Prison Officers Working with Female Prisoners
Susan Jones

The number of female inmates confined in correctional facilities makes up 22.5 percent of the inmate population in the United States and constitutes a rate of 770 women prisoners per 100,000 population as compared to 3,530 per 100,000 for men (Kaeble et. al. 2015: 19; Human Rights Watch 1996). The population of female inmates was first housed historically with male inmates, and later they were moved into separate wings. Eventually, separate women's prisons were built that were managed and supervised, for the most part, by female staff. This practice started to change in the 1980s as a result of court decisions regarding equal employment issues, the Law Enforcement Education Program, and changes in the available workforce. When the number of female officers increased in male facilities, the number of male officers also increased in female facilities.

In 2003, the Prison Rape Elimination Act (PREA) was enacted. This legislation was pursued, in part, due to litigation. More than one class action suit was brought against state systems (i.e., Georgia), regarding the systemic abuse of female inmates by male staff members. The standards required by PREA for adult jails and prisons were published in 2013; these standards mandated changes in the way female inmates were to be supervised. Specifically, PREA requires that female inmates must be pat-searched only by female officers (facilities with less than 50 inmates do not have to comply with this standard until August 2017); all inmates must be allowed to shower, perform bodily functions, and change clothing without nonmedical staff of the opposite gender viewing their breasts, buttocks, or genitalia; and opposite gender staff must announce their presence when entering an inmate housing unit (Prison Rape Elimination Act 2003, § 115.15). The last two of these three requirements affect the management of male facilities also, but the numbers and size of these male institutions make the required scheduling adjustments more manageable.

It is difficult to argue the necessity of PREA based on the evidence that has been collected detailing sexual abuse and violence in prisons; however, PREA has had a disproportionately negative effect on the staffing of female prisons. Now, due to the need for maintaining a larger female workforce in female prisons, it can be more difficult for female officers to transfer to other facilities. It has also made it more difficult for female officers to move to positions outside of the housing units within the same female prison. Normally, posts in housing units and where inmate searches are conducted are often among the least desirable posts in an institution. This can lead officers, especially female officers, to avoid applying for work at a female unit because they know they will be "stuck" in posts that do not provide a great deal of variety and experiences.

The real impact of PREA standards is that they have magnified the stigma and lack of status associated with working with female inmates. The lower status of working with female inmates can be traced back to the 1800s when female officers were referred to as matrons and paid substantially less than male guards/officers. Even though differences in title and pay have been eliminated in most jurisdictions, the correctional culture still sees working with female inmates as "less than" (Rasche 2007). This cultural value is directly tied to the ability of correctional employees to promote outside of a female facility and can directly impact individual employees' career paths.

The smaller population of female inmates is also directly linked to resources and management options. Correctional administrators must allocate resources efficiently, and this usually translates into far fewer program options at female facilities compared to male facilities. Male inmates can be moved between facilities to accommodate their program needs, but the number of institutions housing female inmates is usually very limited, so program choices are also limited.

Along with the reduced availability of programs, officers within the female facilities have fewer options when managing inmates. A primary management approach in male facilities is to disperse problem or vulnerable inmates throughout the system. This separation can be an effective tool to reduce violence, gang activity, and victimization. When a female facility is one of only a few options in a system, it is not possible to separate inmates as effectively. As a result, managers of female facilities rely on creative scheduling or increased supervision and communication by the assigned officers. Sometimes rival female inmates are placed in separate wings of the same unit, and it becomes the officers' job to maintain the safety of all the inmates. This type of management requires a great deal more skill when communicating and interacting with the inmate population than what is often seen in male facilities.

Female inmates are not the only special population that demands attention in corrections. The needs of the mentally ill, sex offenders, sexually vulnerable, elderly, or youthful offenders present tough challenges for correctional leaders. Each of these types of special needs inmates is also found within the female population. Consequently, officers assigned to a female unit must be able to draw upon training and experience to provide the necessary supervision and safety for this small population.

The challenges faced by officers in female prisons can make it difficult for a system to recruit and retain officers who want this assignment and who can be positive change-agents. The need for professional and effective female officers goes beyond the mandates of PREA. Female officers are also needed to provide role models for the inmate population and to serve the needs of this special population of inmates. The correctional system must work to find a way to recognize the value of the work of female correctional officers in order to change the cultural belief that working with female inmates is a second-class assignment. Increasing the value of working with female inmates can help to recruit and retain professional female officers who can fulfill the mandates of PREA while working to improve the correctional outcomes with this population.

References

Human Rights Watch. 1996. "All Too Familiar: Sexual Abuse of Women in U.S. State Prisons." Available at https://www .hrw.org/reports/1996/Us1.htm, accessed May 15, 2016.

Kaeble, D., Glaze, L., Tsoutis, A., and Minton, T. 2015. "Correctional Populations in the United States, 2014." Bureau of Justice Statistics, U.S. Department of Justice. NCJ 249513.

Prison Rape Elimination Act. 2003. PREA; Public Law 108-79. Available at https://www.ojjdp.gov/about/ PubLNo108-79.txt, accessed on May 15, 2016.

Rasche, C.E. 2007. The Dislike of Female Offenders among Correctional Officers: A Need for Specialized Training, in Roslyn, Muraskin, ed. *It's a Crime: Women and Justice* (fourth ed.). 237–252. Pearson Prentice Hall.

Susan Jones is former warden, Colorado Department of Corrections, and currently adjunct professor, University of Colorado, Colorado Springs. She retired in July 2012 after working for 31 years in Colorado Corrections. Dr. Jones began her career in corrections in 1981 as a community corrections counselor. Her assignments included training, programs, custody/control, administration, and case management.

Threads of Correctional Leadership: A Warden's Perspective
Angel Medina

Every successful correctional agency understands that its greatest and most important resource is its staff. However, this idea seems to drift and lose its importance as "the run of the day and the 11th hour incident" creeps in as the priority of the agency.

The ways we introduce staff and send them off in our profession and correctional facilities speak volumes about the character of our organization and the leadership in place. The warden sets the tone, expectation, and the pace of his or her correctional facility. In my everyday practice, as an organizational norm, every newly hired, promoted, or transferred staff is scheduled to meet with my senior management team (SMT). The intent is to (1) allow new staff to introduce themselves, their previous work history, what they do for fun, and as much as they want to share about their family; (2) to allow the SMT to share the same information about themselves; and (3) to share the mission and philosophy, culture mapping, decision making process, and expectations. This effort helps bring out the individuality and personality of the new staff and helps to remove the notion that new staff are just another employee number, a filled vacancy, or a spot on a schedule. Instead, we hope new staff will see our genuine interest in their talents and the value they bring to the workplace. It also helps the new staff to realize that the SMT is an important group in the leadership of the institution and not just a "title" on an organizational chart. We begin in this way to forge a relationship between the new employee and the senior leadership and to send the message that staff are indeed our greatest resource and our leadership is committed to their growth and development.

As my team meets with new staff, my first message to them is that our SMT serves them and is accountable to them. Staff do not serve the SMT but serve our mission of safety, security, and service to others. This often provokes some disbelief and indications that they are thinking, "but you're the warden." Yes I am the warden, but I know in order for me to lead effectively I need to ensure my staff are provided every resource—policy, training, guidelines, information, equipment, and leadership—to ensure and support their success. Line staff do the heavy lifting required to carry out our mission through their daily deliberate efforts to provide safety, security, and service, and this is what defines our success.

Trust is central to our organizational success. New staff have been selected not only because of their qualifications but also because *we trust them*. As a warden I do not put a time line on when I will begin to trust staff. I tell them from the first day that they have my trust—just don't lose it. I tell them if they lie to the agency on any level by omission or admission they have compromised the profession and have become a liability to the organization. Mistakes of the "head" we can assist you with, but mistakes of the "heart" are with you alone.

Much has been said about leadership and organizational excellence in the field of corrections. Leadership is everyone's business. If we review the formula of success for many of the Fortune 500 companies, we will find the common threads of leadership, trust, collaboration, discipline, mission, and vision woven into the very foundation and framework of these corporations. These sets of values represent the fabric of every high-functioning organization.

In our "company" or profession we are charged with confining, managing, and "fixing or repairing" the offender's criminal behavior. This correctional challenge has become the society's riddle wrapped in the human flesh of complexity. The lives we are entrusted with have been banished or ignored by society, and some have been convicted of some of the most horrific transgressions against society. We don't get to choose our clientele and we don't have a five-star menu of resources, but we aim to have staff with the highest levels of character and integrity. Our staff take on this mission knowing that all else has seemingly failed: the individual, the family, the community, and the criminal justice system. And still, our workforce day after day and shift after shift take on this enormous challenge of reducing and interrupting an offender's criminality. Staff truly are the builders and protectors of our profession.

Just as local, state, and federal governments roll out policy and legislation to stop the violence, correctional systems follow stride with similar attempts to reduce the rates of recidivism with innovative or "refreshed" programs and approaches. I suggest that it's not as much about the lack of resources in corrections as it is about a lack of our "all-inclusive will" within our prison systems to work at the highest levels of our allotted resource capacity.

The true measure of our success is not the individual offender's accomplishment or failure, but our ability to leverage to capacity the organizational capital passed on to us by our various governmental agencies. If we are able to successfully "set the correctional table" for an offender to develop successfully, this should be our measure of organizational success. It is when we fail to effectively case plan and/or fail to correctly exercise our correctional assets that we become inept or commit correctional malpractice. Organizational success should be measured by our ability to shape and sustain a fully engaged and holistic correctional system. If an offender takes advantage of our menu of service and fails to thrive first in our institutions and then in the community, it is at this juncture of our correctional relationship the recidivating offender owns the failure. In short, when we set the correctional table correctly, we have satisfied our governmental mandate.

Our mission has grown beyond the highest levels of public service, safety, and security. It now strives for a deeper understanding and an even more committed effort to ensure that programmatic services for offenders are evidence based, organizationally aligned, delivered in collaboration with all stakeholders, and proven to reduce offender recidivism. The heavy lifting of this vision must be completed with a strong commitment to staff development centered on trust, respect, knowledge, and attitudes congruent with best practices in contemporary corrections.

Our willingness and ability to work on a razor's edge will determine our success in delivery of correctional programming. It means providing safety and security without being punitive or compromising constitutional integrity. It means delivering services and programs in a manner where safety and security is never compromised—short cuts kill and offender idleness leads to incident. How do we begin to capture the essence of our work force?

One vehicle of organizational assessment is to religiously review *every incident report*. This level of commitment and understanding allows for the leadership to quickly identify which incidents are being confronted; the report tells us what the writer knows about policy and practice, their capacity to de-escalate and problem solve, and their overall ability to communicate their actions taken during their tour of duty. The review of incident reports also provides a way to measure how *responsive the chain of command* is, their understanding of regulation, their ability to get ahead of or anticipate further behavior or incident, and their overall application of leadership and management. As problems are identified in the incident report by the SMT, further organizational assessment and insight lead to greater understanding of leadership gaps or where breakdown is occurring in the organization. The agency is now in a better position to understand if there is "drift" in the application of mission, policy, and *actual practice*. Clearer communication and fewer barriers should result as the chain of command becomes even more responsive and accountable to the agency. And along the way the organization becomes more engaged and inter-reliant rather than simply passive or indecisive. By demonstrating a commitment to the value of the incident report, we can interrupt the ratcheting of tolerance for poor performance, offender misconduct, and overall mission creep. At the end of the day, we should be creating as many mission-driven feedback loops as possible to validate good work by staff and the value they bring to our agency.

The incident report allows senior leadership to step back and determine if the organization is promoting a mission-driven response to the institutional challenge. The report and our response to it enhance what we do well as well as the work ahead. Every time we give meaningful direction and recognition to all levels of the organization, we create an opportunity for staff to *come closer to meeting the organizational mission.* Our response should be delivered in a manner that creates dialog rather than barriers. The overall credibility and effectiveness of an SMT is determined by its willingness to support and be accountable to line staff, thus *setting the correctional table.* In short, the organization's collective leadership starts to realize the outcomes and conditions of the agency's vision.

The real question is, are we promoting mission, vision, and organizational values through our words and actions within the everyday business of corrections? Mission statements, strategic plans, and organizational charts are important and useful, but are meaningless if we fail to truly understand our staff and their motivations. The more staff experience situations when they influence the organization in concrete ways, the more successful we will become. It is at this level of leadership that mission and vision become meaningful and alive within the correctional work environment.

Angel Medina has worked with the Colorado Department of Corrections (CDOC) for nearly 30 years. During that time he has worked his way up through the ranks from entry-level correctional officer to his current position of warden over the Canon Minimum Centers located in Canon City, Colorado. During his tenure with the CDOC he has worked at over 10 different facilities and offices. Some of those functions have included Special Operations Response Team, Colorado Correctional Training Academy, Offender Services, major, associate warden, and warden at five different facilities.

Working with Chronically Mentally Ill Inmates:
A Shift Commander's Perspective
Vince Guerrero

The San Carlos Correctional Facility (SCCF) is one of 20 Department of Correction's (DOC) facilities within the state of Colorado. This very unique facility was opened in 1995 and was designed to provide therapeutic interventions to DOC inmates with a diagnosed mental illness. The designed capacity is 250 with a security-level rating of maximum although there are mixed-custody inmates housed at SCCF. Prior to the activation of SCCF, many forward-thinking professionals within our correctional system and legislative branch realized the importance of properly addressing the dramatic increase in inmates entering the system with significant mental health diagnosis. When left unchecked, inmates with significant mental health issues are often victimized or are used to victimize others within mainline facilities. By providing inmates with the intensive treatment that is needed, mental health issues are addressed and overall system safety is enhanced.

As a lieutenant attached to the security team, my specific duty was that of shift commander. The most essential duty of this role was to serve as senior operations authority for an assigned shift.

Working within a correctional facility that provides treatment to the inmate population can be extremely challenging on several fronts. A primary challenge for all staff is to establish and *maintain* a strong working alliance between security staff and clinical staff. In all institutions, cooperation between teams is vital to the overall success of your institution. The ability of everyone on the team to invest in, and a willingness to understand, and respect each other's role is essential. Without strong safety and security protocols and practices, inmates do not feel safe, staff do not feel safe, and programming is ineffective. Conversely, without a well thought-out and meaningful mental health treatment intervention system, an inmate's ability to work through his or her illness is considerably hampered.

The challenges for today's correctional officers within this environment are many. One of the biggest challenges that I saw on a daily basis was the ability of staff to interact with many different inmates with differing mental health diagnosis that were often displayed in a variety of different ways. Many of these behavioral expressions were in the form of anger directed at staff, at other inmates, or at themselves. A continual challenge of all of us was to not solely focus on the immediate behavior being displayed but to also keep in mind, in particular, the diagnosis driving the behaviors. In concert with the treatment staff, we needed to find the best ways of providing effective interventions while maintaining safety and security. One of the most challenging aspects of working in this type of prison is the way in which verbal de-escalation and non-escalation approaches must be delivered. With this very unique population, words over force can still be, and should be, used to guide inmates to voluntary compliance even though they may be in a psychotic state of mind. Many times it was only because of the verbal skills of solid correctional officers that emergencies were avoided, physical managements were limited, and inmates were treated humanely and respectfully.

The method of this non-escalation and de-escalation technique that we trained to was at the time called "Verbal Judo." This intervention is now called "Verbal Defense and Influence" (VDI). The main premise of this tool is to deflect words, similarly to how a martial arts expert might deflect physical blows. The fundamentals of VDI are not new, but they are designed and taught in a manner that allows correctional officers to interact with inmates and use this tactical form of communication to generate voluntary compliance and to sequentially illustrate the exhaustion of all available efforts prior to going "hands on." For example, as shift commander, I would be called to an area of the facility where there was an incident either brewing or in progress. When I arrived at the scene, the vast majority of the time I was able to stand by while our correctional officers utilized VDI. It would typically go something like this: inmate is in his cell refusing basic orders to come out of the room. First responder would make contact through introduction and state the reason for them being there; when exchanging dialogue, make requests as opposed to giving orders, offer options not threats, give a second chance to make the right choice, and confirm any noncompliance. In this common scenario, it was energizing to see staff use this sequence to walk the inmate through this decision making process where they felt like they were in control to make good choices. This process allowed for a meaningful dialogue that slowed the intensity of the situation down and allowed the inmate "an out" that was acceptable for him, because it was his choice.

As effective as verbal skills were the vast majority of the time, we still needed to prepare for the eventuality of words failing. On rare occasions that our VDI was not effective, we still had solid, articulate, legally defensible, and nonphysical efforts that were exhausted prior to initiating force.

When this occurred, our preestablished protocols were initiated, and the situation was dealt with as expediently and professionally as possible. Due to the very unique mission of SCCF and our function as a mental health treatment facility, we were licensed to initiate interventions that were not approved for use at more typical facilities. The interventions included the initiation of emergency medications, use of emergency restraint, and emergency seclusion. Continuing therapeutic interventions also included a process for petitioning the court for involuntary administration of psychotropic medications beyond the immediacy of emergency medications.

Due to the intensive regimen of cognitive behavioral interventions, the appropriate use of psychotropic medications, and the daily interventions of correctional officers, successful discharges were realized. The vast majority of inmates discharging from SCCF were able to return to a more traditional facility that was appropriate for their individual security level. Some inmates were able to successfully attain parole. Some inmates were successfully discharged back to society.

As we continue to see time and time again, untreated mental health issues continue to drive many significant events in all aspects of our communities. With that in mind, it was essential that staff approach the mission of SCCF with a sense of urgency and belief that addressing the mental health of offenders *is* public safety. As we all know, the vast majority of offenders will be released one day.

Vince Guerrero is associate professor of criminal justice studies at Colorado Technical University. He obtained his undergraduate degree from Colorado State University-Pueblo and later obtained a master's degree in organizational management. He has taught a variety of criminal justice classes with a special emphasis on juvenile and adult corrections. He has been working in the state government for over 24 years with the Colorado Department of Corrections and the Division of Youth Corrections under the Department of Human Services. He is currently working with the mentally ill population in the high-security forensics unit at the Colorado Mental Health Institute in Pueblo.

Roll Call
James J. Hamm

In the Arizona prison system, the vast majority of prisoners are male, and newly arriving prisoners (new to the system, new to any particular yard) are informally subjected to an interview, referred to as "roll call." This article provides a view of what a new prisoner must consider as he negotiates his place in the prison population.

As a newly arriving prisoner gets onto a general population "yard," a person of the same race who is a shot-caller or a representative of the shot-caller on that yard will meet him either immediately or shortly after arrival. In prison lingo, that person is "political," meaning gang connected. The purpose of roll call is to identify sex offenders, snitches, and other people who are down at the bottom of the prison population's informal social hierarchy, in preparation for running those people off the yard, extorting them, or even attacking them.

The shot-caller will demand to see your "paperwork," which means paperwork showing the offense(s) for which you were convicted, the sentence(s) imposed, the names of codefendants, and perhaps the PSR (presentence report), a document which provides a narrative of the offense and a summary of the offender's participation. PSRs are prepared by the County Adult Probation Department for the sentencing judge's consideration in determining the sentence to be imposed.

On the one hand, it might well be true that you don't have connections within the population who will welcome or assist you or provide some sort of vouching for you. But the people whom you are meeting—in a potentially not-so-friendly fashion—don't really know what to expect from you, either. The person(s) speaking to you do not know who you are and are hoping for a routine interaction, in which you either came prepared and promptly hand over your paperwork or you promptly agree to get the paperwork and let someone review it. Therefore, when you are asked for your paperwork, slow the interaction down, deliberately, obviously, openly, intentionally—stop moving, stop talking, stop whatever you were doing or about to do, and just stop, period. Look at the guy or the group meeting you, not in fear, not aggressively, not in an excessively defensive way; just look like you would if someone just pointed out the dining room ("chow hall") and you wanted to remember the building so you can get back there on your own, later.

Realize that the persons looking back at you *do not know what you are intending at that moment*, and the possibilities range from one extreme (you memorizing the people you might want to beat within an inch of their lives with a weapon you have not yet acquired) to the other extreme (identifying the first group of people to whom you are willing to pay "protection" for the privilege of staying on the yard). They don't *know* what you are doing, what you are thinking, who you are, why you are here, what you intend to do while you are here, whether you have friends on whom you can count, who those friends are, and so on. All they *know* is that you stopped and you are now looking at them. If they introduce themselves, they will do so with nicknames (Baldy, Tiny, Black Joe, Two Times, Big Dog, etc.). They will ask you where you are coming from (court, county jail, private prison, other state prison facility, etc.)—if you are truly a first timer, you will be coming from court or jail or court via jail. Jail information can be checked out through their contacts, one of their compatriots at that jail—and that will take a bit of time.

Stretch that stop-moment out. In the privacy of your mind, work at being neutral, functioning in an information-gathering mode, especially about how these people are reacting to you and what you have just done (stopping, looking, stretching the moment). Whether you realize it or not, it will be obvious to them that you are "doing *something*" in your mind, but it will not be obvious *what* you are doing, and that is truly valuable to you.

Ambiguity is your friend. Your "reputation" within the social structure has just started to form, and you deliberately want to incorporate as many ambiguities and unknowns as possible into that sense of who others think you are or who you might be. Deliberately try not to fit into any preexisting category (gang member, wimp, Jesus freak, moron, wealthy, broke, lost, sexual victim, terrified, wanna-be tough guy, etc.). What you want to strive for is to leave the impression (without ever saying so) that you are evaluating the prison environment (and the people who populate it) to see what you want to do and how you might handle anyone who has a different idea about your status. You want the "unknown" to be a part of your persona, and that starts with not giving out a single piece of information about yourself more than what is absolutely required. You do not have to take the ultimate hard line (i.e., "My right to privacy supersedes your right to live"), but it's not hard to communicate *nonverbally* that your privacy is important to you.

Semi-compliance with roll call is possible. If, in fact, you are (1) not a sex offender (unlikely, because the prison classification system would have routed you to a sex offender yard and roll call is a different thing on those yards when it exists at all), (2) not a snitch (did not roll over on anyone else, did not testify against a codefendant, etc.), and (3) not convicted of what might be viewed as a "low-life crime" (shooting a woman or a child, burning down a house with people inside, beating an elderly woman, etc.), then you might want to seriously consider semi-noncompliance with the roll call. After stretching the moment out, you might say something like, "I'll tell you what. I'll give you my name and case number from (fill-in-the-blank) county and you can look it up. I'll even show you a document with my name and that case number. After you look it up, if you have a problem with what you found out, come and see me and we'll 'talk' about it. But I'm not interested in just giving out information to someone I don't know and to who I owe nothing." While you might decide to provide some paperwork for review, you might not want to give up your PSR. For the PSR, you can simply say, "no," and walk away—after all, what are they *really* going to do, shank you right then? Not a chance, especially if you have gone even one inch in terms of complying with the roll call that will allow them to check you out.

Remind yourself that it is not only others who do not know what you are capable of—you do not know what you are capable of. You only find out the outer limits of your abilities when you are faced with the absolute necessity of going through something. You do not have to behave as though you are ready to tear someone's head off; all you have to do is leave that question unanswered; let other people's imagination work its magic in their minds. And if someone actually threatens you, just look at them and wait to see if they are going to actually "jump," or if they are just going to shoot off their mouths. If someone actually attacks you (the first one will be a physical altercation intended to "tune you up"), go into full defensive mode, backing up, blocking punches and kicks, dodging tackles, until you believe that it has been made clear to any observers (guards, other prisoners) that you are just defending yourself, and then "take steps to interfere with the assailant's ability to continue the confrontation." This does not mean taking things to an extreme, or "teaching him a lesson," or "finishing the fight"; it might mean putting him on the ground (trip him, overbalance him, push him down, hit him in the solar plexus, kick him in the kneecap, grasp his hair, and drag him to the ground) and then walking away (after all, you didn't start the fight). If asked by other prisoners or by prison officials, you "don't know why he attacked [you], but [you] don't think he's stupid enough to try it again."

You will find that you will "grow" into your new, temporary persona and that you can both manage that persona and use it to create a larger personal space around you than you would otherwise be allowed.

James Hamm spent 17½ years in Arizona's state prison system, obtaining a bachelor of science degree in applied sociology with an extended major from Northern Arizona University, graduating summa cum laude. After his release, he obtained a juris doctor degree from Arizona State University's College of Law. He is self-employed as a private criminal justice consultant for attorneys on criminal appeals and civil rights and is an expert witness on prison gangs, the inmate code, and the realities of prison life.

This chapter describes the major federal agencies, some state agencies, and a range of private organizations concerned with the operation, policies, and practices of U.S. corrections systems. The federal correctional system is a key component in the corrections network and is located within the U.S. Department of Justice. It operates as the Federal Bureau of Prisons responsible for the federal prison system and the National Institute of Corrections, which promotes information sharing and good practices in corrections and offers training, funding, and resources across the entire spectrum of corrections. States have their own correctional systems; there are sometimes linkages between private organizations and state corrections; for example, the Correctional Association of New York is empowered to inspect and report on the New York State prison system. One important federal agency, the U.S. Sentencing Commission, has its counterparts among the states, many of which have created their own State Sentencing Commissions.

There are numerous private nonprofit independent organizations involved in prison work. These range from scholarly research-type organizations such as The Sentencing Project to activist groups that are focused on specific aspects of the prison experience, such as the conditions in supermax prisons and the

James Bain, center, walks down the Polk County Courthouse steps with Melissa Mantle, left, and Seth Miller of the Innocence Project in Bartow, Florida, in 2009. With help from the Innocence Project and new DNA evidence, Bain was exonerated and released after spending 35 years in prison for a rape conviction. (AP Photo/Steve Nesius) protection of inmate rights. In addition, there are a number of organizations that collectively make up the prison/commercial/industrial complex, which have a vested interest in the continuance of substantial correctional systems as purchasers of goods and services. Professional associations for correctional officers and groups such as health professionals working in corrections have been established to provide information and services to corrections systems and individuals working in those systems.

American Civil Liberties Union National Prison Project

Founded in 1920 the American Civil Liberties Union (ACLU) is the primary private organization in the nation undertaking the protection of constitutional rights. ACLU activities include the National Prison Project (NPP), which has been in operation since 1972 and has the following goals:

- Domestic torture: the NPP litigates against conditions found in supermax prisons that it characterizes as torture. These conditions include sensory deprivation and extreme isolation. The NPP also focuses on abuse, assault, retaliation, and other forms of torture that occur during incarceration. As well as litigating such conditions, the NPP is involved in the StopMax Campaign, devoted to ending extreme conditions of solitary confinement.
- Protecting and enforcing inmate rights to health and safety in prisons through litigation that challenges deficient medical care, both physical and mental.
- Protecting the right to human dignity through means such as litigation, public education, and advocacy. The NPP is concerned to ensure that human dignity and constitutional rights are respected inside prisons. This work encompasses ending rape and assaults, promoting equal treatment regardless of race and gender, and protecting the rights of inmates who suffer from mental illness or other disabilities.

- Securing prisoner access to the courts, especially by amending the Prison Litigation Reform Act enacted in 1996 which erected numerous barriers to prisoner access to the courts on the rationale that many prisoner lawsuits amounted to frivolous litigation. The NPP heads a coalition of more than 50 groups that argue for amendments to this law.
- In line with its mandate to protect constitutional rights, the NPP aims to protect freedom of thought, association, belief, and religion in prisons. The NPP believes that the strict rules applied in prisons can amount to violations of First Amendment rights.

The NPP primarily uses the mechanism of class action law suits to further its aims and goals. In addition, the NPP publishes data on prison conditions, organizes training and awareness conferences, and provides expert advice to a wide range of stakeholders, including lawyers and community organizations. The NPP has won lawsuits in more than 25 states, including cases in the U.S. Supreme Court concerned with the lawfulness of prison beatings that have judged them to be cruel and unusual punishment. NPP has represented more than 100,000 men, women, and children in confinement.

American Correctional Association

The American Correctional Association (ACA), up until 1954 known as the National Prison Association, was formed in 1870 and is the oldest correctional organization in the United States serving correctional professionals. In 1870, the then NPA formulated the first set of corrections principles in the country. Those principles were later revised in 1982 and in 2002.

The ACA states that its vision is to "shape the future of corrections through strong, progressive leadership that brings together various voices and forges coalitions and partnerships to promote the concepts embodied in its Declaration of Principles." It provides a professional organization for persons and groups, public and private, that share the common aim of improving the justice system.

Over time the ACA has developed significant roles in professional development and education, standards and accreditation, and research and education. The association has formulated and disseminated a code of ethics for corrections professionals, adopted in 1994, that describes the standards of conduct expected of correctional professionals, including protection of the civil and legal rights of all persons, members to refrain from accepting gifts or favors, and members to report corrupt or unethical behavior to the appropriate authority.

The ACA fulfills an important function in granting accreditation to elements of correction systems. In 1954 the ACA published the first operational standards for corrections in its Manual of Correctional Standards, which has now grown to 22 different manuals covering many aspects of correctional services such as standards for facilities, programs, prison industries, food, and administration. ACA standards have been incorporated into U.S. institutions and are applied worldwide. Today, standards are formulated by the Standards Committee comprising 20 experienced justice professionals. Most recently, the committee has been addressing standards for restrictive housing (located in maximum and supermax facilities) explained as "a placement that requires an inmate to be confined to a cell at least 22 hours per day for the safe and secure operation of the facility." Gaining ACA accreditation involves an ACA audit of the facility by correctional professionals approved by the Director of Standards and Accreditation. On average, an auditor will have at least 18 years of experience in corrections, and every auditor is required to pass the ACA auditor orientation course.

In relation to professional development, the ACA offers online and onsite training and a self-study program that enables a person to become a certified corrections professional. There are more than 200 online courses. Onsite training involves ACA staff visiting a facility and custom designing training according to the expressed needs. The most requested training subjects include basic and advanced hostage negotiation, managing security threat groups (prison gangs), preventing sexual misconduct, managing female offenders, and correctional management. The most recent training courses are on use of force and health care.

The ACA publishes *Corrections Today*, a magazine for correctional professionals, *Corrections Compendium*, a peer-reviewed journal of correctional research, and *Correctional Heath Today* for health professionals working in the corrections sector. In addition, the ACA conducts annual conferences and numerous workshops. The ACA Web site offers a marketplace for the sale of various correctional products such as mattresses, gate systems, and dental and health contractors.

American Correctional Health Services Association

The American Correctional Health Services Association (ACHSA) is the organization for correctional health care professionals. It was formed in 1976 with the aim of providing education, skill development, and support for persons, organizations, and decision makers involved in correctional health services. It therefore provides a sense of community for health care workers and strives to provide positive changes in health for persons detained and incarcerated. Membership extends to numerous categories of health care professionals, including nurses, physicians, psychiatrists, nurse practitioners, mental health professionals, and administrative and ancillary personnel who work in a correctional setting, as well as individuals and companies that support its aims. The organization is administered by an elected board of directors.

In its statement of ethics ACHSA declares that correctional health professionals should never be involved in any aspect of the carrying out of the death penalty, participate in escorting inmates, forced transfers, security supervision, and strip searches, or in witnessing use of force. They should also evaluate an inmate as a patient or client and provide health care to all inmates regardless of their custody status.

In line with its ethical declarations ACHSA has adopted a set of Position Statements concerning inmates. An example is that concerned with shackling pregnant inmates, a common practice among correctional systems. In a 2009 Position Statement, the organization states that "only three states and the Federal Bureau of Prisons have policies that expressly prohibit the use of restraints or shackles during labor and delivery; many states' policies do not specifically address the issue." Noting that the American College of Obstetricians and Gynecologists has publicly supported a ban on the use of shackles during labor and delivery, ACHSA declares that it "supports banning the use of leg irons/shackles and restraints for pregnant women during labor and delivery and immediately after they have given birth."

In a further declaration on the use of forced and involuntary psychotropic medication adopted in August 2006, the organization states that inmate patients have no absolute right to refuse treatment because court decisions have held that this right can be qualified for inmates in the interests of the safety and security of the correctional institution, in preventing unnecessary inmate death, and in preventing self-harm to the inmate or to others. In an emergency, where there exists an imminent danger of harm to self or others, a physician may order a one-time involuntary administration of a psychotropic drug. As in all cases of forced medication, an effort must first be made to obtain informed consent. After further detailing the circumstances in which psychotropic drugs may be administered without consent, the statement goes on to declare that correctional health care programs must contain policies, procedures, and multidisciplinary education/training covering forced and involuntary medication.

ACHSA issues a newsletter that includes discussions of topics of interest to correctional health care professionals. The June 2016 newsletter contains a paper discussing whether health care for inmates is a right or a privilege, which concludes that in the view of the author, it is a right. Some commentators claim that under the principle of less eligibility, an inmate has no rights, including health care.

American Friends Service Committee

American Friends Service Committee (AFSC) is a Quaker organization founded in 1917 that promotes justice as a practical expression of faith in action. The committee shared the Nobel Prize for peace in 1947. The committee comprises a board of directors, a board executive committee, and officers of the board of directors. Along with a range of national and international issues focused on nonviolence and peace, and ensuring that government action is fair and is kept accountable, the FSC advocates an end to mass incarceration, the improvement of prison conditions, and a halt to prison privatization, and generally promotes a reconciliation and healing approach to criminal justice issues.

The committee has documented its finding about private prisons. In 2012 it published *Private Prisons: The Public's Problem: A Quality Assessment of Arizona's Private Prisons*. In addition, in relation to Arizona private prisons, the committee investigated the contracting out of prison health care to the country's largest private prison health care provider, asserting that illegal and deadly health care was provided to inmates. In 2015, the FSC published an independent assessment of riots that took place in July 2015 in the Kingman, Arizona, prison complex. The report uncovered persistent problems in this private prison that were in place before the riots in the form of inadequate staffing, inmates suffering mistreatment by guards, and poor management. As a result of these reports, Arizona terminated its contract with the private prison provider. In 2013 in New Hampshire, FSC and others were instrumental in halting a proposal by the state to have private corporations run the state prison system.

FSC has documented the effects of mass incarceration in the United States and published numerous accounts and fact statements designed to increase public awareness of this issue. The FSC has especially focused on the nexus between racial disparities and incarceration and argued that there is an association between the practice of slavery and the modern form of mass incarceration. In 2006 two members of AFC published *Beyond Prisons*, tracing the history and features of the penal system, offering moral and ethical assessments of its policy and practices, and suggesting radical alternatives.

FSC has also documented the conditions and nature of solitary confinement in the United States. In 2014 FSC submitted a "shadow report" to the UN Committee Against Torture that described inhumane conditions in prisons. Part of its report comprised Survivors Speak, the testimonies of inmates who suffered cruel treatment or who witnessed abuses committed against other inmates. The FSC Prison Watch Program located in Newark, New Jersey, has collected testimony from prisoners in the form of letters for more than 20 years, documenting abuses in the prisons of that state. In August 2012 FSC published *Lifetime Lockdown: How Isolation Conditions Impact Prisoner Reentry*, documenting the linkages between spending time in isolation and the challenges of reentry into the community.

Conditions of confinement is a key concern of the FSC, and it operates programs in numerous states that document and publish aspects of prison conditions and advocate and encourage dialogue between ex-prisoners and members of the community. Generally, the data collection, programs, awareness-raising activities, and advocacy of the FSC represent an important element in enhancing public knowledge of prisons and prison systems. The concerns of FSC reflect its desire to reduce violence, ensure peace, and maintain accountability by and to government.

Association of State Correctional Administrators

After beginning as an informal gathering of state correctional administrators in 1960, this association (Association of State Correctional Administrators [ASCA]) was formed in 1972 as a formalization of those informal arrangements. As the name suggests, the organization provides a point of contact and a meeting place for professional correctional administrators. According to its constitution, ASCA aims to improve correctional services and practices through promoting and facilitating the exchange of ideas and philosophies at the top administrative level of correctional planning and policy making; and to enhance correctional techniques, especially in the fields of programming, design of facilities, staff training, and correctional management. In addition, ASCA promotes public support for corrections and reentry, conducts some research in correctional practices, develops correctional standards and accreditation, and fosters exchanges of information with international agencies and organizations interested in correctional programs. The actual operations of the organization are contracted out to the Criminal Justice Institute, and the organization is headquartered in Maryland. In addition to correctional administrators in the United States, the Canadian Correctional Service is a member.

ASCA runs a number of projects through specific project committees, for example, the Program and Training Committee, Racial Disparity Committee, and the Reentry and Community Corrections Committee. The function of the Racial Disparity Committee is to analyze correctional policies that generate racial disparities and promote the elimination of racial discrimination in corrections. The Training Committee has produced a Prison Staffing Analysis Manual that contains a model staffing analysis process and offers detailed guidelines for developing and evaluating posts and special guidelines for staffing housing units. ASCA has published a number of papers and reports that are of practical use to correctional administrators, including a *Guide on Contracting for Correctional Services Provided by Private Firms.*

In common with other organizations, ASCA has recently turned its attention to the topic of segregation in corrections. A report on *Prisoners in Administrative Segregation* was prepared by ASCA jointly with Yale Law School in September 2015. The report essentially captures baseline data on prisoners placed in segregation (isolation) and is the first to provide updated information, as of September 2014, on both the numbers and the conditions in restrictive housing nationwide. Thirty-four jurisdictions provided data on persons in restricted housing, revealing that 80,000–100,000 people were, in 2014, in restrictive housing settings in prisons. The report found that in many jurisdictions, prisoners were required to spend 23 hours in their cells on weekdays and, in many, 24 hours on weekends. In addition, most jurisdictions did not limit the time that an inmate could spend in segregation, and only one state imposed a one-year limit. Several jurisdictions did not track the number of continuous days a person was held, but in those that did, in a substantial number, prisoners remained in segregation for more than three years.

In 2016, following a survey of correctional administrators, ASCA found that the top five critical issues in corrections were staffing, restrictive housing, mental health, budgets, and overcrowding.

Bureau of Justice Statistics

The Bureau of Justice Statistics is the primary source of data on justice systems, state and federal, including correctional systems, within the United States. The bureau is part of the U.S. Department of Justice and was established in 1979. The bureau, which is housed within the department under the function Office of Justice Programs, researches and reports annually on the imprisonment rate and the prisoner population in the state and federal systems. It also provides special reports on specific topics such as mental health in prisons and prison rape under the Prison Rape Elimination Act. The special reports are often mandated by specific laws that aim not only to counter a problem, such as prison rape, but also to set up data systems for the collection and analysis of information for future policy making. The bureau therefore fulfills a vital role in providing the baseline data crucial for criminal justice policy making.

Administratively, the bureau is headed by a director who is assisted by a statistical adviser. There are three deputy directors who report to the director. One is responsible for statistical planning, operations, and policy; another for law enforcement, prosecution, courts, and special projects; and the third for victimization and corrections. Statistical units report to the deputy directors and conduct the major work of the agency.

The bureau publishes annual reports on criminal victimization, correctional populations, federal criminal offenders, and case processing. Periodically, it publishes on the following topics: administration of law enforcement agencies and correctional facilities, prosecutorial practices and policies, state court case processing, felony convictions, characteristics of correctional populations, criminal justice expenditure and employment, civil case processing in state courts, and special studies on other criminal justice topics.

In relation, specifically, to corrections, the bureau publishes administrative data on state and federal prisoners collected twice a year; annual survey of jails; annual survey of probation and parole; administrative data on offenders under community supervision; administrative data on admissions to and releases from state prisons, collected annually; and census of state and federal adult correctional facilities, collected periodically.

In addition, the bureau conducts a number of recurrent national surveys of prison and jail inmates. These surveys are typically conducted every five to seven years and are broad in scope. They collect a wide range of data on the personal and criminal histories of criminal offenders. Topics cover childhood experiences, family structure, educational background, prior criminal activity, substance abuse experiences, mental and physical health problems, and conditions of current confinement.

Correctional Association of New York

This association, known as "the CA," was founded in 1844 by the then president of the Board of Inspectors of Sing Sing Prison, New York. It is a nonpartisan, nonprofit organization that advocates for a more humane and effective criminal justice system and a more just and equitable society. Its original mission was to improve the conditions of defendants and inmates, improve the discipline and administration of local jails and state prisons, and provide assistance and encouragement to people on their reentry after incarceration. Today, the CA's objectives are to reduce the use of incarceration as a response to socioeconomic problems, ensure that humane conditions are found in prisons and that inmates' rights and those of their families are protected, and ensure accountability for all aspects of the corrections system.

The CA is the sole private organization in New York State with the power to conduct examinations of state correctional facilities and report findings and recommendations to governmental authorities and the public.

Over time, the CA has been instrumental in reforming the criminal justice system in the state. In terms of the corrections function, the CA created the first probation and parole systems in the state (in about 1875) and argued for the provision of separate facilities for youth convicted of crimes. In the 1900s the CA worked to ensure that inmates had opportunities to acquire formal education and advocated for the creation of prison libraries. It also argued that inmates should learn a trade while incarcerated. Other policies promoted by the CA were a prison classification system, opposition to corporal punishment, special care facilities for people in prison afflicted with tuberculosis, establishment of a psychiatric clinic at Sing Sing Prison, creation of the New York City Parole Commission, development of policies that enabled incarcerated people to contribute to the war effort by working in war-related industries, and creation of an adequate public defender system.

During the 1980s and 1990s, the CA addressed the issue of HIV/AIDS in prison; campaigned against severe prison overcrowding; and worked to repeal mandatory minimum sentencing laws for people convicted of drug crimes, to create public awareness of the costs incurred by city, county, and state correctional agencies, and to promote alternatives to incarceration.

By exercising its significant power to inspect state correctional facilities, the CA has been able to uncover specific issues in corrections in the state. These include the fact that prisons inadequately respond to inmates' medical and mental health problems and fail to treat their substance abuse needs and that relations with families are impacted by inmates' distance from home, and the absence of significant job training and educational programs and the dramatic reduction in funding for college education.

The CA Prison Visiting Project has been operational since 1846. Each year this project visits 7–10 New York State's male prisons and other facilities and publishes a facility-specific report on prison conditions. For example, in June 2016 the project issued a highly critical report concerning the Clinton Correctional Facility following an escape in 2015 that identifies and describes violence and abuse by officers against inmates that occurred prior to the escapes.

As well as this general inspection function, this project undertakes research on issues in corrections and publishes comprehensive reports of findings and recommendations. The project also receives, logs, and responds to thousands of letters each year from individuals confined in New York prisons. Based on this data, the project campaigns for reforms by working at different levels of government, such as at the state level, asking that the state adopt agency-wide policies, replicate model programs, and institutionalize best practices. The project also works with ex-prisoners, service providers, and community organizations to develop more humane prison policies. Project staff also give presentations and expert testimony at conferences and public forums across the country, and conduct public awareness and education about prison issues.

The CA has also been active on issues affecting women in prison. In December 2015 the CA Women in Prison Project released a video advocating the end of the practice of shackling incarcerated pregnant women in New York prisons. The project is promoting the Anti-Shackling Bill, which will prohibit shackling women during all stages of as pregnancy—currently laws prohibit shackling only during labor and childbirth.

Among the other multiple public interest issues associated with corrections that the CA is involved with are families and incarceration, HIV and health care, mental health care for inmates, substance abuse in prisons, prison downsizing, and survivors of abuse and incarceration. The access enjoyed by the CA to state prisons, a legacy of history, gives the CA the opportunity to collect prison data and apply it to its advocacy efforts. This compares to the situation in other states where inspections are not generally conducted by independent bodies (one exception is Illinois where inspections are conducted by the John Howard Association) and researchers are usually not given any access at all.

Corrections Technology Association

The Corrections Technology Association (CTA) was formed as a nonprofit association in 1999 with a mission to promote the use of technology in correctional systems. Its members are professionals who are involved with some aspect of technology in corrections. For example, technologies are very much in evidence in supermax prisons. As such, CTA is another element in the corrections/commercial/industrial complex interested in the stability and growth of corrections as a field of entrepreneurship. The other stated aims of CTA are to identify further technologies that have an application to corrections, use technology to improve corrections operations and to promote public safety, promote information sharing among relevant agencies, develop standards for technology solutions in corrections, and provide educational opportunities to technology professionals associated with the field of corrections.

In terms of standard setting, in 2014 CTA published a set of standards of 508 pages covering numerous aspects of the corrections function and operation from intake to release, including topics on discipline and medical and parole release, with annotations for each function that identify the data generated by each function or operation. There is an accompanying glossary of terms and a list of actors and description of function. In several places, these standards refer to standards set by the Association of State Correctional Administrators.

Numerous technology companies sponsor CTA activities, including an annual technology summit organized by CTA since 2010. Typically, these summits are focused on corrections and technology and provide an opportunity for sponsors and others to market their products and services to the state correctional services that attend.

Families Against Mandatory Minimums

State and federal mandatory minimum sentences have impacted correctional systems greatly, especially in terms of overcrowding, the growth of an elderly inmate population, and the need for additional resources. Advocacy and awareness organizations that campaign against mandatory minimum sentences are therefore of interest to correctional systems because they lobby against the very sentences that have presented so many challenges to those systems. The organization titled Families Against Mandatory Minimums (FAMM), headquartered in Washington, D.C., works nationally to advocate the repeal of these sentences for nonviolent offenses. It was founded in 1991 as a nonprofit organization and now claims 70,000 supporters.

Headed by a president and vice president and responsible to a board of directors, FAMM maintains a substantial staffing, including a general counsel, director of legislative affairs, director of state policy, communications director, and a storyteller and research manager, whose function is to determine how best to narrate the stories of prisoners and their families who have been impacted by mandatory minimum sentencing laws.

FAMM claims that its efforts have benefited more than 310,000 people since 1991. This is based on federal prisoners having received lesser sentences than the mandatory minimum following the enactment of an exception to federal drugs laws imposing mandatory minimums, an amendment that was enacted due to the lobbying efforts of FAMM, and to other similar actions advocated by FAMM and associated with drug laws generally.

FAMM activities include a federal project and a state project. The former advocates a federal sentencing system that provides fair punishment according to the circumstances of each individual offender. FAMM argues for the reform of mandatory minimum sentencing laws, amendments to the federal sentencing guidelines, and presidential clemency. The latter project advocates similar policy changes at the state level and argues for more flexible, cost-effective sentencing options and alternatives. In another project, FAMM worked with the conservative American Legislative Exchange Council to formulate a model language that can be incorporated into state sentencing reforms.

The FAMM Web site publishes important information about sentencing as an aid to public awareness and prisoner profiles that describe the circumstances of individuals serving mandatory minimum sentences. Here FAMM attempts to add a human context to the debate about sentencing, recording instances where judges imposed a mandatory sentence against their own judgment, and describing the individual circumstances of convicted drug offenders.

Federal Bureau of Prisons

The bureau was created by law in 1930 within the U.S. Department of Justice and is tasked with the "management and regulation of all Federal penal and correctional institutions." At the time of its creation, this gave the agency responsibility for the operations of 11 federal prisons. By the end of 1930 the bureau was operating 14 prisons with just over 13,000 prisoners and by 1940, 24 facilities and more than 24,000 inmates. Starting from the 1980s changes in legislation described in this book vastly increased the size of the federal prison system so that by year-end 2014, the federal prison population was 210,567. The federal inmate population decreased by 5,300 inmates (down 2.5%) from 2013 to 2014, the second consecutive year of decline. Half of male federal prisoners (50%) and more than half of female federal prisoners (59%) were serving sentences for drug offenses on September 30, 2014.

The bureau employs almost 40,000 staff to operate its facilities, which are classified as minimum security, low security, medium security, high security, and administrative security. Facilities are found throughout the country. There are currently 22 facilities classed as penitentiaries, of which 17 are categorized as high security. Federal Prison Camps (or camps) house minimum-security inmates who are generally nonviolent offenders with minimal criminal histories and have less than 10 years remaining to serve. Roughly 18 percent of federal prisoners reside in camps, and, of that population, approximately 70 percent are drug offenders. Almost 90 percent of federal prisoners housed in high-security population have a history of violence, more than 60 percent have been sanctioned for violating prison rules, and 14 percent have been convicted of murder, aggravated assault, or kidnapping.

Numerous facilities fall under the "administrative" umbrella, including ADX Florence, Colorado, which is a supermax prison. The bureau contracts with state correctional systems and private providers for community-based facilities (i.e., Residential Reentry Centers [or halfway houses]) and for prisons to house non-U.S. citizens who are the subject of deportation proceedings. Facilities provided under contract house approximately 17 percent of the total prisoner population.

The bureau classifies every prisoner on intake at its Designation and Sentence Computation Center, located in Texas, and the bureau, and not the court that sentenced him or her, is solely responsible for determining an offender's appropriate level of security. Classification decisions are regulated by the Inmate Security Designation and Custody Classification

Manual. While classification is a complex process, basically a prisoner is assessed according to the level of security and staff supervision required; the level of security and staff supervision the institution provides; medical needs; treatment needs, such as substance abuse treatment; and various other factors, including bed capacity, any court recommendations, and any special security needs.

The problem of overcapacity caused by an increasing prison population resulted in the bureau housing 40,000 prisoners in private secure and nonsecure facilities at year-end 2014, a number that represents 19 percent of the total federal prison population. This privatization rate is far in excess of that found in the states and makes the bureau the highest user of private prison companies. On August 19, 2016, the Department of Justice announced, following a review of their use, that it would reduce and ultimately eliminate the housing of federal prisoners in private prisons, judging them to be less safe and less effective than public prisons.

In a report to Congress in May 2016, the Congressional Research Service noted that a report from the Government Accountability Office (GAO), stating that the increased number of federal prisoners had caused an increased use of double and triple bunking, and waiting lists for education and drug treatment programs, limited meaningful work opportunities and increased inmate-to-staff ratios. Overcapacity had also increased bureau costs, and appropriations increased more than $7.1 billion from FY1980 ($330 million) to FY2016 ($7.479 billion). The bureau's appropriation has, over time, taken a larger share of the entire budget of the Department of Justice.

Administratively, the bureau operates from Washington, D.C., and through regional offices in regions designated as follows:

- Western—Dublin, California
- North Central—Kansas City

- South Central—Dallas
- Southeast—Atlanta
- Mid-Atlantic—Annapolis Junction
- Northeast—Philadelphia

Senior management comprises the director, assistant directors, and regional directors. The bureau also maintains community corrections offices in the regions, which operate halfway houses and supervise home confinement for prerelease prisoners. The bureau posts current statistical data on its Web site and publishes data on the characteristics of the federal prison population.

While serving a sentence in a federal facility, an inmate will interact primarily with the Unit Team located in his or her housing unit, comprising the unit officer, counselor, case manager, and unit manager. Concerns, requests, and grievances are submitted to the team, often in writing, and decisions can be appealed to the warden. Wardens are given wide discretion in a facility's daily activities, and their decisions are generally final. Visits to a federal facility must be preapproved. The approval process requires the prisoner to mail a standardized form to the prospective visitor, who then must return the completed form to the Unit Team, which conducts a background check.

The bureau permits prisoners to maintain accounts at a prison commissary from which they can purchase approved items at allotted times (e.g., food, cigarettes, clothing, personal hygiene products, hand-held radios, watches, fans) and pay for telephone calls. There are no limits on the balance that can be maintained in such an account.

Most federal prisoners are required to work but wages are minimal, in the range of 12–40 cents per hour. About 12 percent of the prison population is responsible for food preparation. Employment within Federal Prison Industries (UNICOR) provides a higher rate of pay between 23 cents to $1.15 per hour. Many institutions also offer vocational training through work assignments. Programs include heating, ventilation, and air conditioning; plumbing; motor vehicle maintenance; welding; dental assistant; carpentry; culinary arts; and electrician.

The Inmate Financial Responsibility Program (IFRP) requires inmates to use their earnings to satisfy court-ordered fines, victim restitution, child support, and other monetary judgments. Also, some inmates are assessed a cost of incarceration fee, which is collected under the IFRP. Inmates working in Federal Prison Industries with financial obligations must pay 50 percent of their earnings to the IFRP.

Human Rights Watch

Human Rights Watch (HRW) was formed in 1988 in a consolidation of various projects and programs operating in different parts of the world concerned with the protection of human rights. In 1997 HRW shared the Nobel Peace Prize. It now operates in 90 countries, including the United States. With 80 staff researchers HRW conducts regular, systematic investigations of human rights abuses around the world. In 1998 HRW created The Human Rights Watch Council, a global network of volunteers—currently 850 members in three cities—to support HRW through fund raising, advocacy, and outreach. There are 20 major committees within the structure of the council, and in the United States they are located in Chicago, Los Angeles, New York, Santa Barbara, and Silicon Valley.

Since the 1990s in its role as a leading international nongovernment organization, HRW has campaigned and highlighted prison conditions and specific aspects of incarceration in the United States. HRW's Prison Project is congruent with its concern for national and international standards of human rights and withholding all governments accountable for violations of those rights. Therefore, HRW works with partners monitoring conditions of imprisonment and pressuring governments generally to bring their prison conditions into compliance with international rights standards.

In April 2001, HRW published a groundbreaking study of male rape in U.S. prisons, and in April 1999 and October 1997, it published reports on supermax security confinement in Virginia and Indiana, respectively. Gender has also figured in HRW research; for example, it published a report on retaliation against women in Michigan women's prisons in 1998 and in 1996 reported on sexual abuse in state women's prisons.

The concern about prison conditions was recently expressed in HRW's 2015 report on the use of violence against inmates with mental disabilities in U.S. prisons and jails. Mental illness among inmates is prevalent and presents significant challenges to correctional staff. In its investigation HRW found that prison staff sometimes responded with violence when inmates exhibited behavior that was symptomatic of a mental health condition. This is true even when responding to incidents that are nonthreatening, such as urinating on the floor, using profane language, and repeatedly banging on a cell door.

The international repute of HRW is undoubted, and it remains a highly influential organization in the field of human rights protection in both the United States and worldwide.

The Innocence Project

This nonprofit organization was founded in 1992 by lawyers Barry Scheck and Peter Neufeld. Its focus is on exonerating innocent people wrongfully convicted by using DNA testing and generally reforming the justice system to prevent further injustice. According to the Innocence Project, 343 people convicted of crimes have been exonerated by using DNA testing, including 20 who served time on death rows. Of this number, the average time spent in prison before release was 14 years. The project was the first organization to use DNA testing to provide conclusive evidence of innocence. The record of exonerations established by the project has shown that wrongful convictions result from systemic faults in the justice system, especially in the trial process, and that these cases are not mere aberrations in an otherwise smoothly functioning system of justice.

The process followed by the project is for its intake and evaluation staff to carry out extensive research into each case referred to or coming to the notice of the project to determine whether conducting DNA testing is likely to prove innocence and therefore exoneration. The project Web site features some of the cases where it has proved the innocence of a convicted person. One such case is that of Andre Hatchett, an African American, who served 25 years for the crime of second-degree murder, a crime he did not commit and whose conviction for which was reversed in March 2016. At the time of the crime, Hatchett, who has special needs and was then 24, was recovering from severe gunshot wounds to his throat and leg. His right leg was in a cast, requiring crutches on the night of the crime. Despite these physical limitations and an alibi, Hatchett's lawyers in two separate trials failed to submit his medical records that would have shown the virtual impossibility of him having committed the crime. His conviction rested solely on the evidence of one witness, and he was convicted despite his physical constraints and his alibi.

The project notes that attempts to enact legislation to reform so-called eye witness identification procedures by imposing strict requirements as to documentation and the videotaping of confessions continue to meet with great resistance.

The project has identified through its research and cases several causes for wrongful conviction. These are as follows:

- Statements from persons with an incentive to testify such as money or a reduction in sentence (in 15% of exonerations through DNA testing, statements from incentive persons resulted in the wrongful conviction). This practice is known as "snitching."
- Inadequate defense—here, the wrongful conviction was brought about because of a lawyer's incompetence. Examples

include a lawyer sleeping during the trial, failing to investigate alibis, failing to attend hearings, and failing to call forensic evidence at trial.

- The use of untested and unproven forensic techniques that have not been adequately evaluated. For example, in about half of exonerations through DNA testing, improper or non-validated forensic science played a role in the wrongful conviction.

- Law enforcement and prosecutorial misconduct such as failing to produce exculpatory evidence that would assist the accused, police coercing false confessions, and prosecutors putting pressure on defense witnesses not to testify.

- False confessions or admissions by an accused resulting in a wrongful conviction—more than one in four persons exonerated through DNA testing made a confession that was false due to circumstances such as duress, the threat of a severe sentence, or ignorance of the law.

- Misidentification by persons claiming to be eyewitnesses to a crime—contrary to popular belief, this kind of identification is often wrong and inaccurate. In an astonishing 70 percent of convictions overturned by DNA testing, the conviction was the outcome of a misidentification.

The project supports and advocates for law reforms that will reduce or eradicate these causes of wrongful conviction. In the meantime, it will continue to take up cases that fall into the aforementioned categories by acting through a network of independent organizations set up in U.S. states as well as overseas, which are often university based.

National Association of Sentencing Commissions

The National Association of Sentencing Commissions (NASC) is a nonprofit organization incorporated in Delaware. The objective of the organization is to facilitate the exchange and sharing of information, ideas, data, expertise, and experiences and to educate individuals on issues related to sentencing policies, sentencing guidelines, and sentencing commissions.

NASC is governed by an Executive Committee elected by the membership at the annual meeting. The Executive Committee comprises seven members and includes a president, vice president, treasurer, secretary, and members at large. Executive Committee members may serve two consecutive three-year terms.

NASC came into being following informal meetings and discussions between states that established sentencing commissions in the 1970s and early 1980s. Those states exchanged views and information about sentencing and sentences practices, and as states became interested in creating sentencing commissions, the need for information sharing became greater. Following a sentencing symposium in 1992, State Sentencing Commissions began to hold annual meetings as a means of providing a site for learning and sharing sentencing information, including sentencing policies. In 1993 the first informal sentencing commission conference was held in Washington State in 1993. By the late 1990s participants had agreed to formalize the informal arrangements for meeting and information by incorporating under the title of the National Association of Sentencing Commissions. All State Sentencing Commissions as well as the U.S. Sentencing Commission were invited to participate in the newly formed organization.

Currently, the NASC membership includes representation from about 24 states, which have by law established sentencing commissions or policy councils, and states considering the creation of a sentencing commission. There is no requirement that a state actually have a sentencing commission to join the organization. NASC members include states with or without sentencing guidelines, states with presumptive or voluntary guidelines, and states with determinate or indeterminate sentencing practices. Therefore, while sentencing commissions such as those in Alabama, Connecticut, and Delaware are members of NASC, Alaska is represented by its Judicial

Council, Missouri by its Sentencing Advisory Commission, and Oregon by its Criminal Justice Commission.

NASC has been holding annual conferences since 1995. In 2013 the conference topic was Merging Sentencing Research and Policy, in 2014 Guiding Shifts in Sentencing Policy, and in 2015 Transforming Research to Results. Since 1995 NASC has been issuing a biannual newsletter that provides valuable information on changes in sentencing policy taking place in the states. NASC therefore constitutes a forum complementary to the federal sentencing commission and has established itself as a point of contact nationwide on this important topic.

National Correctional Industries Association

The National Correctional Industries Association (NCIA) is a nonprofit industry organization concerned with professional development and business solutions in the field of corrections generally. Its headquarters is in Maryland, and it is affiliated with the American Correctional Association. It operates according to bylaws, a strategic plan, and a set of policies that relate to correctional industries.

The bylaws state that the specific purposes of the organization are to establish an organization of persons and public and private agencies who are engaged in rehabilitation programming for inmates; to establish, develop, and improve correctional industries; to use correctional industries to promote rehabilitation, training, and education of inmates; to promote relations between labor, private enterprise, and chambers of commerce for the benefit of correctional industries; and generally to promote and facilitate programs, public awareness, and the exchange of ideas that will benefit correctional industries.

NCIA operates through a board of directors, an executive director, specialist committees, and regional associations. NCIA states that it is a "powerful legislative and lobbying voice" and is in the business of providing marketing and advertising opportunities for vendors to correctional services systems. It holds an annual conference and issues a quarterly newsletter. Corporate members pay an annual fee of $500 or $1,200 for a higher class of corporate membership, and correctional institutions that may or may not maintain correctional industries pay the same fee annually of $500. Its strategic plan states that it "strives to serve as the bridge between correctional industry professionals and interested parties by providing information and facilitating members' access to the resources they need to shape the future of their organizations."

According to its 2015–2016 Public Policy on Correctional Industries, NCIA "promotes the use of best and promising practices to support successful offender reentry, reduce recidivism and enhance public safety." In addition, "correctional industries produce a well-trained offender that is equipped to enter the workforce upon release and become a productive employee and tax-paying citizen." NCIA points to the fact that in 2014, sales from prison industries funded the salaries and benefits for more than 6,900 civilian staff and purchased raw materials, supplies, and services from local businesses in the amount of $1.3 billion.

The NCIA legislative Position Statement approved in 2015 urges legislative bodies to support legislation that promotes correctional industries, arguing that such industries enhance public safety, support local businesses, lower prison operating costs, and prepare offenders to successfully reenter the community post-release from prison. The NCIA Web site includes a "buyer's guide" that lists specific items used in correctional systems generally.

NCIA is a part of the correctional industrial complex and has a vested interest in the growth of prison industries and, therefore, of prisons, not only in the United States but worldwide.

National Institute of Corrections

Following the 1971 riots at Attica Prison, the then attorney general of the United States convened a National Congress on Corrections in Virginia in December that year. Support was expressed for a national training academy for corrections that would bring about greater professionalism in corrections, provide a means of exchanging information, encourage policy formulation, and provide high-quality training for corrections professionals. These ideas were a response to the events at Attica, which were a watershed in the field of corrections in the United States as they exposed numerous deficiencies in corrections.

In 1974 the National Institute of Corrections (NIC) was created as an agency within the U.S. Department of Justice, Federal Bureau of Prisons. The NIC is headed by a director who is appointed by the U.S. attorney general. The NIC receives policy direction from a 16-member advisory board, the members of which are also appointed by the attorney general. The function of the NIC is to provide training; technical assistance; information services; and policy/program development assistance to federal, state, and local corrections agencies. The NIC is also a leader in influencing correctional policies, practices, and operations throughout the country where issues of concern to correctional administrators and public policy makers are raised.

The NIC coordinates and provides consulting, research, funding, and training in addressing key issues in the corrections field. Current projects include providing information on the Prison Rape Elimination Act; promoting a cognitive behavioral change program for groups that include prisoners; funding for the study *Adults with Behavioral Health Needs under Correctional Supervision: A Shared Framework for Reducing Recidivism and Promoting Recovery* designed for state and local correctional administrators and community-based mental health and substance abuse agency leaders to plan and develop service responses that make efficient use of resources; and providing resources on victim offender services post-conviction including forms of victim and offender dialogue.

In terms of services, the NIC maintains a Technical Assistance Program designed to assist state and local correctional agencies. The NIC's technical assistance includes onsite guidance, support, consultation, or training provided by an experienced technical resource provider or NIC staff member who serves in an advisory capacity and works with agency staff. Assistance can include assessing programs and operations; implementing effective practices; improving management, operations, and programming; reviewing the design, delivery, management, and evaluation of staff training programs; and assisting in the development of offender job training and placement efforts. The NIC also offers a Corrections Community on its Web site as a site for corrections professionals to interact, share knowledge, and network generally.

In the field of training, the NIC offers numerous online courses ranging from computer skills to working with difficult people. In addition, it hosts popular courses, which include courses on suicide prevention and responding to sexual abuse.

The Sentencing Project

The Sentencing Project was formed as a national nonprofit in 1986 to work for a fair and effective justice system by advocating for sentencing reforms and alternatives to incarceration. The organization produces and publishes research relevant to its field of action and engages in media campaigns and advocacy arguing for specific reforms. Headquartered in Washington, D.C., The Sentencing Project has gained a national reputation for the quality of its research and advocacy. The project is headed by an executive director, currently Mark Mauer, who has a national reputation for his publications on sentencing, especially through the book *Race to Incarcerate* which maps the development of policies and practices that have resulted in mass imprisonment in the United States. The board of directors includes Angela Davis, herself an author on this topic. Other experienced staffs fill the advocacy, communication, research, operations, and programming functions of the organization.

The project has published numerous reports. Examples are "Felony Disenfranchisement," "Juvenile Life Imprisonment without Parole," "Black Lives Matter and Public Safety," and the "State of Sentencing 2015." These publications draw attention to significant issues in sentencing and criminal justice and constitute a valuable resource for researchers, academics, and policy makers.

The organization focuses on a set of issues, namely sentencing policy, incarceration, racial disparity, felony disenfranchisement, drug policy, juvenile justice, women in prison, and collateral consequences (meaning the intended or unintended outcomes of sentencing and other justice policies), for example, the consequence that 1 in every 50 children in the United States has a parent in prison and that 5.8 million citizens cannot vote due to having a conviction for a felony.

The Sentencing Project promotes a set of sentencing reform objectives that comprise the following:

- Eliminate mandatory minimum sentences and reduce severe sentences by, for example, allowing a maximum prison sentence of 20 years.
- Treat substance abuse in the community rather than punishing it through incarceration.
- Invest more resources in interventions that promote youth development and reduce juvenile delinquency.
- Examine and eliminate policies and practice that produce racial disparities in criminal justice systems.
- Eliminate barriers to the successful reintegration of released persons in the community.

The organization has allied or affiliated with numerous state and local organizations for communication and advocacy purposes such as the American Civil Liberties Union and nonprofits operating in the same fields as The Sentencing Project such as John Howard societies in various states.

Solitary Watch

Solitary Watch (SW) is a web-based organization with the stated aim of publicizing the widespread use of solitary confinement in the nation. This aim is implemented by providing the public, practicing attorneys, legal scholars, law enforcement and corrections officers, policy makers, educators, advocates, people in prison, and their families with a centralized source of unfolding news, original reporting, firsthand accounts, and background research on solitary confinement in the United States. SW is governed by editors and directors and makes use of reporters, researchers, and contributing writers in its data presentation. SW provides links to a wide array of resources associated with solitary confinement, including court cases, and law review and journal articles.

An article published by SW in August 2016 reports on the Red Onion State Prison, a supermax prison in Virginia. Reforms were to have been implemented at the prison complex in 2011, including an Administrative Segregation Step Down Program, which provided a means for inmates to work their way out of solitary confinement and return to the general population. The State Department of Corrections reported in 2016 that the reforms had been successful and had reduced the segregated population by 72 percent. However, according to the author, a closer examination of the department's claims suggests that the improvement claimed was problematic and that in any event conditions in isolation had not improved.

SW has recently published a book *Hell Is a Very Small Place: Voices from Solitary Confinement* comprising 21 essays and academic papers that describe the severe physical and mental effects of solitary confinement, the solidarity expressed between individuals who live side by side for years without ever meeting one another face to face, the likelihood of madness and suicide, and challenge of maintaining hope and humanity.

Transgender Law Center Detention Project

Founded in 2002 by an organization working for lesbian rights, the Transgender Law Center (TLC) is based in Oakland, California, and its mission is to work for the rights of transgender persons. Its stated aim is to bring about changes to law and policy and to public attitudes that will enable all persons to live safely, authentically, and free from discrimination regardless of their gender identity or expression. The organization looks forward to the time when gender self-determination is seen as a basic right and an aspect of human dignity. The center believes that the law has the power to assist it to achieve its goals. The center is governed by a board of directors and is headed by an executive director.

In 2015, the TLC launched a Detention Project that aims to end the abuses experienced by transgender and gender nonconforming (TGNC) people in prisons, jails, immigration detention, state hospitals, and other forms of detention, and at the hands of law enforcement. The strategy pursued by the project is to offer legal information to transgender inmates and in some cases to provide them with legal representation in lawsuits based on civil rights law that challenge abuse and mistreatment of transgender persons. In addition, the project partners with other organizations to advocate for humane and fair policies for incarcerated TGNC people.

The project publishes details of its lawsuits on behalf of transgender inmates. An example is the case of Shiloh Quine, a transgender woman held in a male prison, who on August 7, 2015, settled a claim with the California Department of Corrections and Rehabilitation. In the terms of settlement, the department agreed to relocate her to a women's facility and provide medical care, including gender-affirming surgery, determined necessary by several medical and mental health professionals. The state also agreed to policy changes that enable transgender prisoners to access clothing and commissary items consistent with their gender identity.

U.S. Sentencing Commission

This commission plays a key role in determining for how long an offender against federal law will be imprisoned and what factors will be taken into account and what factors will be disregarded in making sentencing decisions.

The commission was created by law in 1984 to formulate sentencing guidelines for federal crimes so as to reduce sentencing disparities and promote transparency and proportionality in sentencing practice. Prior to the creation of the commission, judges at the federal level had a wide discretion as to the sentence to impose for a federal crime and what factors should be taken into account in making that decision. In practice, sentences varied widely, and Congress therefore legislated to achieve standardized and proportionate sentencing. Legislating sentencing guidelines therefore effectively removed the wide discretion that the judges previously enjoyed in sentencing federal criminals. However, the work of the commission extends beyond simply determining sentencing guidelines for federal crimes since it also gives advice to the executive and legislative branches of government on crime policies, and analyzes criminal justice data. It that way it provides a data resource to a wide range of stakeholders in the criminal justice system.

Organizationally, the commission comprises seven voting members appointed by the president and confirmed by the Senate, who hold office for a six-year term. At least three commissioners must be federal judges, and the attorney general and the chair of the U.S. Parole Commission are ex officio members. The commission employs about 100 staff divided into offices under the general control of a staff director, who is responsible to the commission chair. The offices are general counsel, education and sentencing practice, research and data, legislative and public affairs, and administration. Four advisory groups assist the commission, representing the views of justice practitioners, probation officers, victims, and tribal lands.

The sentencing guidelines promulgated by the commission comprise a complex set of formulae, which federal judges must apply in determining sentences. The two key factors that judges look at are the offense conduct (this fixes the level of the offense so the correct sentence can be worked out) and the defendant's criminal history. There are 43 offense levels and 6 criminal history categories. Sentences are calculated based on the number of points scored by a defendant according to the offense conduct and the criminal history. Four sentencing zones fix the sentence range: Zone A: 0–6 months; Zone B: not exceeding 12 months; Zone C: a minimum penalty of 12 months; and Zone D: in excess of Zone C. Where a defendant has been helpful to the government, his or her sentence can be reduced. Conversely, where, for example, the crime is found to be a hate crime or involves a vulnerable victim, the sentence may be enhanced. Upward and downward departures from the guidelines can be granted where specific criteria are satisfied. Controversial aspects of the guidelines include the very heavy sentences for child pornography offenses, which many judges refuse to apply, and the disparity of treatment between crack cocaine and cocaine, which has now been addressed by changes in the law in 2010.

Up until 2005 when the case of *United States v. Booker* was decided by the U.S. Supreme Court, it was generally believed that sentencing guidelines were mandatory, but the *Booker* case found that the guidelines violated the Sixth Amendment right to trial by jury and the guidelines are now considered to be advisory only. However, when a judge determines to depart from the guidelines, he or she must explain the factors that warranted the increased or decreased sentence.

Many states have legislated to establish their own sentencing commissions following the model of the U.S. Sentencing Commission. For example, by 1999, 18 states had developed some form of sentencing guidelines. Other countries such as Canada, Australia, and United Kingdom have followed suit. In some states, guidelines are advisory only, but in others they must be considered and there is a presumption they will be applied. In some states, guidelines provide for a wide range of sentences, and in others the range is narrow. Some states require offenders to serve the full sentence imposed, and some allow parole boards to determine the length of time served. In some states, guidelines deal only with felonies; others deal with both felonies and misdemeanors. The guidelines have presented multiple challenges to correctional systems. For example, the widespread abolition of parole, and the abolition or reduction of "good time," has eliminated valuable tools for managing inmates and has required that correctional systems develop new ways to sanction inmate indiscipline. The guidelines, both at the federal and at the state levels, have contributed to the aging prison population, higher health care costs, and loss of work productivity, which have given rise to a need to segregate older, vulnerable inmates from younger, aggressive ones.

The commission issues an annual report and frequently issues reports on other topics associated with crime and sentencing. For example, it has issued reports on campaign finance, career offenders, computer crime, aspects of drug laws, mandatory minimum penalties, and sex offenses. It keeps the guidelines under constant review and in April 2016 approved significant changes to the sentencing guidelines, including expanding the categories for compassionate release from prison so that federal inmates may be eligible for compassionate release based on four categories relating to medical conditions, age, family circumstances, and other extraordinary and compelling reasons. These changes have yet to be approved by Congress.

The controversial child pornography guidelines were first promulgated in 1987 and have been revised nine times as Congress repeatedly expressed its abhorrence of such offenses and required them to be dealt with in a punitive manner. After publishing a report on the history of the guidelines for child pornography in 2009, in 2012 the commission submitted a report to Congress recommending changes that would better contextualize particular child pornography offenses by reference to an offender's collecting behavior, the degree of his or her involvement in a child pornography community, and any history of sexually dangerous behavior.

Women's Prison Association

Located in New York, the Women's Prison Association (WPA) was founded in 1845 where it began its existence as the Female Department of the Prison Association of New York. It was the first national organization to work solely with women who come into contact with the criminal justice system. The organization opened the first halfway house for women called the Hopper Home for Criminal Justice-Involved Women, named after Abby Hopper Gibbons (1801–1893), an executive member of the Female Department. At the home, residents were free to leave but had to comply with the house rules, which provided for a strict schedule of activities each day. Gibbons was involved with the operation of the house up until she reached the age of 92 years. In 1992 the Hopper Home was renovated as a residential home and an alternative to incarceration.

Today, the WPA's perspective is that adopting a gender-neutral approach toward women and criminal justice as if they had the same needs as men is incorrect. Instead, the WPA promotes a strategy that uses empirically tested gender-specific tools to respond to the needs of women in contact with the criminal justice system. This approach means that services to women and their families before, during, and after incarceration can be customized to explicit needs. In 1994 the WPA published *The Rights and Responsibilities of Incarcerated Parents*, which became the foundation for A Mothers Law Project to aid inmate mothers with visitation and family court issues. In 2001 the WPA began operating its program WomenCare, providing mentoring services to women exiting the prison system. This program was later expanded, and in 2013 the WPA started another program, JusticeHome, the first of its kind in New York concerned with keeping women out of prison. Its focus is to provide a community-based alternative to imprisonment for women facing felony charges and a minimum sentence of four years. WomenCare operates at the Taconic and Bedford Hills prisons for women.

The WPA is governed by a board of directors assisted by an honorary council. Its operations are under the control of an executive director, who is assisted by a number of directors responsible for specific WPA programs and for the general functions of the organization. The WPA is supported by corporate partners and individual and corporate volunteers and maintains an Emerging Philanthropists Program, a group of professional New Yorkers committed to the work of the WPA. Support is also provided by a number of foundations and agencies within local government in the city of New York.

The information presented in this chapter supplements and illustrates the discussion in Chapter 2 of issues and problems relating to corrections. The data presented here should therefore be read in conjunction with and in the context of that discussion.

Incarceration Trends and Numbers

The United States leads the world in the number of persons it incarcerates as measured by the rate of incarceration per 100,000 persons of a country's population. While the United States has only 5 percent of the world population, it has more than 20 percent of the world's incarcerated population. Figure 5.1 describes this by comparing the U.S. rate to those of selected other countries.

What has been the trend of incarceration in the United States over time? As discussed in Chapters 1 and 2, up to the early 1970s the prison population remained relatively stable at a level of about 200,000 a year or less. Figure 5.2 shows the trend from 1925 and reveals the dramatic upward movement in the number of prisoners that has occurred. In the case of drug offenses alone, there was an increase in the number of

---

A prisoner faces a mural painted by inmates on a cinderblock wall inside the Georgia Diagnostic and Classification Prison in 2015. When visitors approach, inmates in the hallways turn their backs and stand close to the walls. This makes it easy for guards to spot anyone who steps out of line. (AP Photo/David Goldman)

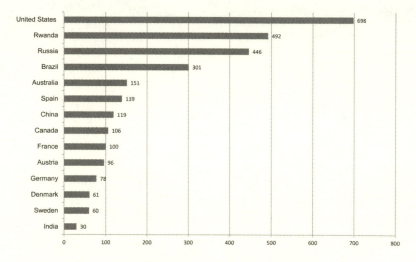

Figure 5.1   International Rates of Incarceration per 100,000

Source: The Sentencing Project, http://www.sentencingproject.org/criminal-justice-facts/. Used by permission.

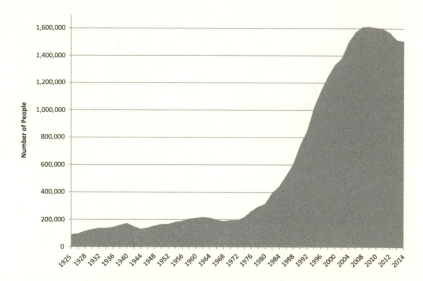

Figure 5.2   U.S. State and Federal Prison Population, 1925–2014

Source: The Sentencing Project, http://www.sentencingproject.org/criminal-justice-facts/. Used by permission.

persons imprisoned for such offenses from 41,000 in 1980 to almost 500,000 by 2014. Only recently has this trend begun to level off.

The U.S. Department of Justice publishes data each year on the number of prisoners in federal and state prisons. The most recent data available is that for the year ending 2014.

Table 5.1 shows the latest count of state and federal prisoners for that year and for previous years commencing in 2004. Again, these figures demonstrate the trend toward greater use of incarceration as a punishment, with the resulting pressure on correctional systems throughout the country.

In 2014, 6 percent of all black males in the age range 30–39 were in prison, compared to 2 percent of Hispanic and 1 percent of white males in the same age group, and half of males (50%) and more than half of females (59%) in federal prison were serving time for drug offenses as of September 30, 2014. Over the past decade, females have made up about 7 percent of the total prison population, and in 2014 female prisoners

Table 5.1 Prisoners under the Jurisdiction of State or Federal Correctional Authorities, December 31, 2004–2014

Year	Total	Federal	State	Male	Female
2004	1,497,100	180,328	1,316,772	1,392,278	104,822
2005	1,525,910	187,618	1,338,292	1,418,392	107,518
2006	1,568,674	193,046	1,375,628	1,456,366	112,308
2007	1,596,835	199,618	1,397,217	1,482,524	114,311
2008	1,608,282	201,280	1,407,002	1,493,670	114,612
2009	1,615,487	208,118	1,407,369	1,502,002	113,485
2010	1,613,803	209,771	1,404,032	1,500,936	112,867
2011	1,598,968	216,362	1,382,606	1,487,561	111,407
2012	1,570,397	217,815	1,352,582	1,461,625	108,772
2013	1,576,950	215,866	1,361,084	1,465,592	111,358
2014	1,561,525	210,567	1,350,958	1,448,564	112,961

Source: Bureau of Justice Statistics, National Prisoner Statistics, 2004–2014.

totaled 113,000, the largest number of female prisoners since 2009. In 2014 rates of imprisonment among the states varied widely. Table 5.2 shows how some states have very high rates of imprisonment while others maintain low rates.

The disparities between states are accounted for by their differing punishment and sentencing policies. Generally, while incarceration rates for males are much higher in the South than in other parts of the country, with a few exceptions, rates for females tend to be broadly equivalent. Oklahoma had the highest rate of female prisoners at 142 per 100,000.

What was the relationship between prison capacity and inmate populations in 2014? As discussed in Chapters 1 and 2, mass imprisonment policies that came into effect in the mid-1970s began to put pressure on prison capacity throughout the country. This was especially evident in states like California and resulted in numerous court actions claiming that overcrowded prisons violated constitutional rights. The year ending 2014 continued this trend as the federal inmate population and those of 18 states exceeded the maximum capacity of their prison systems.

Table 5.2 Imprisonment Rates for Sentenced Prisoners under the Jurisdiction of State and Federal Correctional Authorities per 100,000 U.S. Residents, December 31, 2014

Jurisdiction	Male	Female
Alabama	1,203	97
California	670	33
Florida	976	71
Louisiana	1,577	87
Massachusetts	373	15
Mississippi	1,146	78
New Hampshire	407	36
Rhode Island	354	12
Texas	1,081	93

Source: Bureau of Justice Statistics, National Prisoner Statistics, 2014.

Prison overcrowding was one of the factors that caused the expansion of private prisons. While there has been a gradual increase in the use of private prisons except at the federal level (where the increase has been more accelerated) from 1999 to 2014, at year-end 2014, seven states accommodated at least 20 percent of their inmates in private facilities, including New Mexico (44%), Montana (39%), Oklahoma (26%), and Hawaii (24%). Since 1999, the size of the private prison population has increased 90 percent, from 69,000 inmates at year-end 1999 to 131,300 in 2014. The use of private prisons was at a maximum in 2012, when 137,200 (almost 9%) of the total U.S. prison population were housed in private facilities.

Demographic Characteristics

Tables 5.3 and 5.4 show the imprisonment rate by age and race, of male and female federal and state prisoners, respectively for year-end 2014. Among the significant factors appearing in this data are the following:

- Imprisonment rates for black males were higher than those for other races within every age group.

- Imprisonment rates for black males were 3.8 to 10.5 times greater at each age group than those for white males and 1.4 to 3.1 times greater than those for Hispanic males.

- The largest disparity between white and black male prisoners occurred among inmates aged 18–19. Black males (1,072 prisoners per 100,000 black male residents aged 18–19) were more than 10 times more likely to be in state or federal prison than whites (102 per 100,000).

- Imprisonment rates by race were the highest for males aged 30–34 (6,412 per 100,000 black males, 2,457 per 100,000 Hispanic males, and 1,111 per 100,000 white males). More than 1 percent of white male residents aged 30–39 were in state or federal prison at year-end 2014. Black males

Table 5.3 Imprisonment Rate of Sentenced State and Federal *Male* Prisoners per 100,000 U.S. Residents, by Demographic Characteristics, December 31, 2014

Age Group	All Male	White	Black	Hispanic	Other*
18–19	317	102	1,072	349	542
20–24	1,365	584	3,868	1,521	1,755
25–29	1,912	958	5,434	2,245	2,022
30–34	2,129	1,111	6,412	2,457	2,193
35–39	1,982	1,029	6,122	2,272	1,878
40–44	1,689	942	5,105	1,933	1,619
45–49	1,417	815	4,352	602	1,444
50–54	1,081	633	3,331	1,320	1,112
55–59	698	400	2,178	978	832
60–64	422	252	1,265	680	483
65 or older	158	109	418	299	208

*"Other" includes American Indians and Alaskan Natives; Asians, Native Hawaiians, and other Pacific Islanders; and persons of two or more races.

Sources: Bureau of Justice Statistics, National Prisoner Statistics, 2014; Federal Justice Statistics Program, 2014; National Corrections Reporting Program, 2013; Survey of Inmates in State and Federal Correctional Facilities, 2004; and U.S. Census Bureau, postcensal resident population estimates for January 1, 2015.

Table 5.4 Imprisonment Rate of Sentenced State and Federal *Female* Prisoners per 100,000 U.S. Residents, by Demographic Characteristics, December 31, 2014

Age Group	All Female	White	Black	Hispanic	Other*
18–19	14	8	32	17	12
20–24	96	72	152	94	109
25–29	170	150	244	165	208
30–34	185	163	264	174	225
35–39	155	138	229	137	189
40–44	132	119	213	107	174
45–49	111	90	203	94	161
50–54	72	57	128	67	124
55–59	37	27	72	42	63
60–64	20	15	37	25	37
65 or older	5	4	8	7	12

*"Other" includes American Indians and Alaskan Natives; Asians, Native Hawaiians, and other Pacific Islanders; and persons of two or more races.

Sources: Bureau of Justice Statistics, National Prisoner Statistics, 2014; Federal Justice Statistics Program, 2014; National Corrections Reporting Program, 2013; Survey of Inmates in State and Federal Correctional Facilities, 2004; and U.S. Census Bureau, postcensal resident population estimates for January 1, 2015.

exceeded 6 percent of their total U.S. population in prison for persons aged 30–39.

- Female prisoners aged 30–34 had the highest imprisonment rates among black (264 per 100,000 black females of the same age), white (163 per 100,000), and Hispanic inmates (174 per 100,000). Black females were between 1.6 and 4.1 times more likely to be imprisoned than white females of any age group.

Type of Offense

Data provided by the federal prison system reveals the types of serious offenses for which prisoners have been sentenced and identifies their race and sex by offense nature.

The dramatic effects of the federal war on drugs are made explicit in this data, with 50 percent of sentenced prisoners in the federal system serving time for drug offenses. Significantly, as compared to state correctional systems where 53 percent of inmates were serving sentences for violent crimes, violent offenders made up only 7 percent of the federal prison population. Of the female offenders, 59 percent were serving sentences for drug offenses, 18 percent for property offenses, and only 4 percent for violent crimes. Among Hispanics in the federal system, two offense types were dominant: immigration offenses (16,100) and drug crimes (36,000) or 57 percent. Among black offenders the dominant offenses were drug offenses (53%) and weapons offenses (25%).

Table 5.5 Estimated Percentage of Sentenced Prisoners under Federal Correctional Authority, by Most Serious Offense, Sex, Race, and Hispanic Origin, September 30, 2014

Most Serious Offense	All Inmates	Male	Female	White	Black	Hispanic
Violent	**7.3%**	**7.5%**	**4.4%**	**7.1%**	**9.9%**	**2.0%**
Homicide	1.5	1.5	1.3	0.7	2.4	0.3
Robbery	3.8	3.9	1.7	5.0	5.6	0.9
Other violent actions	2.1	2.2	1.4	1.5	2.0	0.8

(continued)

Table 5.5 *(continued)*

Most Serious Offense	All Inmates	Male	Female	White	Black	Hispanic
Property	**6.0%**	**5.2%**	**18.3%**	**10.0%**	**5.9%**	**2.7%**
Burglary	0.2	0.2	0.2	0.2	0.4	0.0
Fraud	4.7	3.9	15.5	7.8	4.4	2.3
Other property	1.1	1.0	2.7	2.0	1.1	0.4
Drug	**50.1%**	**49.5%**	**58.8%**	**40.3%**	**52.5%**	**56.9%**
Public order	**35.9%**	**37.1%**	**17.9%**	**41.2%**	**31.2%**	**38%**
Immigration	8.9	9.3	3.7	1.2	0.4	25.5
Weapons	15.8	16.6	4.3	14.8	24.8	7.1
Other	11.1	11.2	9.8	25.3	6.1	5.4
Other unspecified	**0.7%**	**0.7%**	**0.6%**	**1.4%**	**0.5%**	**0.4%**
Total number of sentenced inmates	192,663	180,140	12,523	51,600	71.300	63,700

Source: Bureau of Justice Statistics, Federal Justice Statistics Program, 2014.

Recidivism

According to the National Institute for Justice of the U.S. Department of Justice, recidivism "refers to a person's relapse into criminal behavior, often after the person receives sanctions or undergoes intervention for a previous crime. Recidivism is measured by criminal acts that resulted in rearrest, reconviction or return to prison with or without a new sentence during a three-year period following the prisoner's release." Offenders are returned to prison when they commit a new crime or for breach of a supervision order such as failing to report to a probation or parole officer or failing a drug test.

The Bureau of Justice Statistics of the U.S. Department of Justice collects criminal history data from the FBI and the states in order to establish and study the recidivism patterns of various offenders. The latest study by the bureau was in 2005 of about 400,000 offenders released from prison in 30 states. That study found the following:

- There were high rates of recidivism among released prisoners.
- Within three years of release, 67.8 percent of released prisoners were rearrested.
- Within five years of release, 76.6 percent of released prisoners were rearrested.
- Of those prisoners who were rearrested, 56.7 percent were arrested by the end of the first year.
- Property offenders were the most likely to be rearrested, with 82.1 percent of released property offenders arrested for a new crime compared with 76.9 percent of drug offenders, 73.6 percent of public order offenders, and 71.3 percent of violent offenders.

A study of recidivism among federal prisoners conducted by the U.S. Sentencing Commission and published in 2016 found that recidivism rates were the highest for federal firearms offenses and for robbery. The rates for various crimes are described in Table 5.6.

Table 5.6   Rearrest Rates for Recidivism Study Offenders by Federal Offense Type

Offense Type	Rearrest Rate (%)
Drug trafficking	49.9
Firearms	68.3
Fraud	34.2
Robbery	67.3
Larceny	44.4
Immigration	55.7
All others	42.0

Source: U.S. Sentencing Commission, "Recidivism among Federal Offenders: A Comprehensive Overview," March 2016.

In terms of recidivism among the states, rates vary widely. An example from Texas shows the recidivism rates for the fiscal years 2009–2011 in Table 5.7.

Recently, states have increased efforts to reduce recidivism and violations of probation and parole because reducing recidivism offers significant potential cost savings to state criminal justice systems, including their correctional systems. Policy approaches are focused on what is termed "rentry," meaning employing strategies to begin preparing people for release as soon as they enter prison, using a screening instrument that helps staff identify priority areas for intervention and develop case management plans.

For example, in Oregon and Michigan, community supervision officers communicate with inmates before their release to describe the expectations for their behavior in the community and establish continued programming priorities. The aim is to achieve desistance, that is, a situation where the released person has reached a permanent state of non-offending. In Michigan, the Prisoner Reentry Initiative was started in 2003 and begins at intake into prison when risk assessments are conducted. Before being released on parole, a prisoner is transferred to a reentry facility where a transition plan is formulated, which addresses aspects of life outside the prison, including housing, transportation, mentoring, and treatment required for physical or mental illness.

Table 5.7   Texas: Rearrest Rates by Fiscal Year of Release or Start of Supervision, Fiscal Years 2009–2011 Showing Percentage Rearrested within Three Years

	2009	2010	2011
Prison	47.2	47.3	46.5
Jail	51.4	60.7	62.0

Source: Texas Statewide Criminal and Juvenile Justice Recidivism and Revocation Rates, Legislative Budget Board, February 2015.

Mandatory Minimum Sentences

Federal and state laws that impose mandatory minimum sentences require that offenders convicted of specified offenses be incarcerated for a minimum period of time. The offenses that are subject to mandatory minimum sentences commonly include drug trafficking and using weapons to commit crimes. These laws limit judicial powers to impose a sentence and, in effect, transfer the sentencing power of the judge to the prosecutor who is responsible for deciding whether or not to indict a person for a crime that carries such a penalty. Some argue that these sentences are harsh and inconsistent with a rational sentencing system, but others support them because they incapacitate offenders for lengthy periods. Initially, starting from 1986 the federal justice system began enacting mandatory minimum penalty laws, and the states followed suit aided by federal funds appropriated to the states that enabled them to build more prisons to cope with increased sentences.

Within the federal system, the United States Sentencing Commission (USSC) reported in 2011 that the enactment of more federal mandatory minimum sentences since 1986 has, in part, contributed to the growing federal prison population. Mandatory minimum penalties have contributed to federal prison population growth because they have increased in number, have been applied to more offenses, required longer terms of imprisonment, and are used more frequently than they were 20 years ago.

The USSC reported that the number of federal mandatory minimum penalties nearly doubled from 98 in 1991 to 195 in 2011. In addition, offenders convicted of offenses with mandatory minimums are being sent to prison for longer periods. For example, the USSC found that, compared to 1990 (43.6%), a larger proportion of defendants convicted of offenses that carried a mandatory minimum penalty in 2010 (55.5%) were convicted of offenses that carried a mandatory minimum penalty of five years or more.

Increases in the federal prison population attributable in part to the enactment of mandatory minimum sentences resulted in overcrowding in federal facilities, as shown in Table 5.8. As the data indicates, while federal prisons have been operating 30 percent or more in excess of design capacity since 1999, the overcrowding issue is significantly more problematic in medium- and high-security male facilities. Specifically, since 1996, overcrowding in male high-security facilities has generally been at the level of 50 percent or greater.

Table 5.8 Overcrowding in All Federal Facilities and Low-, Medium-, and High-Security Male Facilities, FY1995–FY2012

Fiscal Year	All Federal Facilities (%)	Male Low Security (%)	Male Medium Security (%)	Male High Security (%)
1995	25	33	52	40
1996	24	31	42	65
1997	22	23	37	52
1998	26	27	48	56
1999	31	37	51	51
2000	32	42	50	54
2001	32	38	58	42
2002	33	39	58	41
2003	39	39	59	58
2004	41	45	62	49
2005	34	43	42	35
2006	36	41	37	53
2007	37	35	42	53
2008	36	35	44	50
2009	37	40	47	49
2010	37	37	43	53
2011	39	37	51	55
2012	38	40	47	51

Source: U.S. Department of Justice, Bureau of Prisons.

Life Sentences and Life without Parole

In its 2015 report on life sentences of imprisonment within the federal system, the U.S. Sentencing Commission notes that while the proportion of federal prisoners serving life sentences comprised only 2.5 percent of all federal prisoners in January 2015 (4,436 prisoners), other federal offenders are serving such extremely lengthy sentences that they can be regarded for all practical purposes as "de facto" life sentences. The commission has adopted a measure of a sentence of 470 months or greater as being a de facto life sentence. Table 5.9 describes the federal offenses for which life sentences were imposed in 2013, and Table 5.10 describes de facto life sentences.

In fiscal year 2013, 45 percent of offenders receiving a life imprisonment sentence were black, compared to white 24.8 percent, and Hispanic offenders 24.2 percent. In contrast, for federal offenders generally, the racial composition was 51.5 percent Hispanic, 23.8 percent white, and 20.6 percent black.

Data by offense type for de facto life sentences is provided in Table 5.10. The report notes that the demographic characteristics of offenders sentenced to de facto life imprisonment sentences differed substantially from that of federal offenders generally. In fiscal year 2013, 39.9 percent of offenders receiving a term of imprisonment of 470 months or longer were black, followed by white offenders (36.9%) and Hispanic offenders (17.3%).

Table 5.9   Offenses for Which Life Imprisonment Was Imposed in the Federal System in FY2013

Federal Offense Type	Number of Life Sentences	Percentage of All Life Sentences Imposed
Drug trafficking	64	41.8
Firearms	27	0.3
Murder	19	21.3
Extortion and racketeering	16	1.8

Source: U.S. Sentencing Commission.

Table 5.10   Offenses for Which De Facto Life Sentences Were Imposed in the Federal System in FY2013

Federal Offense Type	Number of Cases	Percentage of All Federal De Facto Life Sentences
Firearms	76	45.2
Child pornography	55	32.7
Drug trafficking	10	6.0

Source: U.S. Sentencing Commission.

Table 5.11   State Enactment of Life without Parole Laws

1970 and Earlier	1971–1990	1991–2012
Massachusetts	Alabama	Arizona
Michigan	Arkansas	Florida
Mississippi	California	Georgia
Montana	Colorado	Indiana
Pennsylvania	Connecticut	Kansas
South Dakota	Delaware	Kentucky
West Virginia	District Columbia	Minnesota
	Hawaii	Nebraska
	Idaho	New Jersey
	Illinois	New York
	Iowa	North Carolina
	Louisiana	North Dakota
	Maine	Ohio
	Maryland	Tennessee
	Missouri	Texas
	Nevada	Utah
	New Hampshire	Wyoming
	New Mexico	
	Oklahoma	
	Oregon	
	Rhode Island	
	South Carolina	
	Vermont	
	Virginia	
	Washington	
	Wisconsin	

Source: The Sentencing Project, Life Goes On: The Historic Rise in Life Sentences in America, 2013. http://sentencingproject.org/wp-content/uploads/2015/12/Life-Goes-On.pdf. Used by permission.

Numerous states as well as the federal system, which eliminated parole in 1987, have enacted life without parole laws, as described in Table 5.11.

The Aging Prison Population

Data from the Bureau of Statistics on the aging of the state prison population reveals that between 1993 and 2013 the number of state prisoners aged 55 or older increased 400 percent from only 3 percent of the total state prison population in 1993 to 10 percent in 2013. Another way of expressing this increase is to state it in terms of the imprisonment rate for persons 55 years and older who were sentenced to one year or more in state prisons. Here, the rate increased from 49 per 100,000 in 1993 to 154 per 100,000 in 2013. Two factors contributed to this increase in the aging of the inmate population: a greater proportion of prisoners were sentenced to, and were serving, longer periods of imprisonment in state prisons; and the admission of older persons increased. Between 1993 and 2003, increases in the number of persons in state prison at year-end and in the number of admissions disproportionately affected persons aged 45–49; however, from 2003 to 2013, growth occurred predominantly among those aged 55 or more.

The age distribution by race of state prisoners for 1993 and 2013 is shown in Tables 5.12 and 5.13. Data shows that

Table 5.12   Sentenced State Prisoners, by Age, Race, and Hispanic Origin, December 31, 1993

Age at Year-End	White	Black	Hispanic
Total	302,600	380,900	150,500
18–19	6,500	15,700	4,700
20–24	51,600	77,500	31,600
25–29	67,100	96,400	40,600
30–34	63,600	82,000	29,100
35–39	41,200	52,400	20,600
40–44	29,800	29,900	10,600
45–49	17,500	9,700	6,200
50–54	10,300	5,000	2,800
55–59	6,800	3,000	2,400

(continued)

Table 5.12 (*continued*)

Age at Year-End	White	Black	Hispanic
60–64	4,300	2,300	800
65 or older	3,000	2,700	200
40–54	57,700	44,600	19,600
55 or older	14,100	8,000	3,400

Source: Bureau of Justice Statistics.

Table 5.13 Sentenced State Prisoners, by Age, Race, and Hispanic Origin, December 31, 2013

Age at Year-End	White	Black	Hispanic
Total	468,600	497,000	274,200
18–19	2,700	7,100	3,500
20–24	41,900	70,700	37,700
25–29	67,900	81,600	49,900
30–34	73,900	79,500	50,900
35–39	61,400	66,400	41,000
40–44	58,800	55,600	31,300
45–49	54,400	51,100	23,600
50–54	47,300	41,800	17,000
55–59	28,700	25,000	9,800
60–64	15,500	11,100	5,000
65 or older	16,000	6,500	4,200
40–54	160,400	148,500	71,800
55 or older	60,200	42,500	18,900

Source: Bureau of Justice Statistics.

over the period 1993 to 2013, arrests of persons aged 40–54 increased 44 percent (up to 739,000) and arrests of persons aged 55 or older increased 77 percent (up to 260,800). The prison population will grow when inmates are serving longer sentences and prisoners aged 55 or more had consistently mean higher sentence lengths, increasing from 76 months in 1993 to 82 months in 2013.

Changes in the age structure in the state prison population have significant implications for the future management and care of inmates and for the allocation of correctional resources.

Mental Health

In its 2005 survey of the mental health of prison and jail inmates, the Bureau of Statistics states that at midyear 2005 more than one half of all inmates suffered a mental health problem. In relation to prison, the data showed that 56 percent of state prisoners and 45 percent of federal prisoners were estimated to have mental health issues. Evidence of a mental health problem was based on a recent history or symptoms of a mental health problem that occurred in the 12 months prior to the interview with an inmate. Almost a quarter of state prisoners who had a mental health problem had served three or more prior incarcerations, and almost in 75 percent of state prisoners the mental health problem was associated with substance dependence or abuse. More than one in three state prisoners with a mental health problem had received treatment since admission.

The range of symptoms of mental disorder and their prevalence in Table 5.14 gives a broad picture of the kind of problems suffered by inmates. The mental health symptoms described

Table 5.14   Prevalence of Symptoms of Mental Health Disorders among State and Federal Prisoners, 2004

Symptoms in Past 12 Months or Since Admission to Prison	Percentage of Inmates in State Prison	Percentage of Inmates in Federal Prison
Major depressive or mania symptoms		
Persistent sad, numb, or empty mood	32.9	23.7
Loss of interest or pleasure in activities	35.4	30.8
Increased or decreased appetite	32.4	25.1
Insomnia or hypersomnia	39.8	32.8

(continued)

Table 5.14   (*continued*)

Symptoms in Past 12 Months or Since Admission to Prison	Percentage of Inmates in State Prison	Percentage of Inmates in Federal Prison
Psychomotor agitation or retardation	39.6	31.4
Feelings of worthlessness or excessive guilt	35.0	25.3
Diminished ability to concentrate or think	28.4	21.3
Ever attempted suicide	13.0	6.0
Persistent anger or irritability	37.8	30.5
Increased/decreased interest in sexual activities	34.4	29.0
Psychotic disorder symptoms		
Delusions	11.8	7.8
Hallucinations	7.9	4.8

Source: Bureau of Justice Statistics.

here should be assessed in the context of the discussion of prisonization in Chapter 2.

In the survey, mental health problems among prisoners are also presented by gender, age, and race. The data indicates that mental health problems were more prevalent among women inmates as compared to male inmates and among white inmates as compared to black and Hispanic inmates. Inmates aged 24 or less had the highest rates of mental health problems and those aged 55 or more had the lowest rates.

The data also revealed a correlation between homelessness and foster care and mental health. State prisoners (13%) with mental health problems were twice as likely as inmates without a mental health problem (6% in state prisons) to have been homeless in the year before their incarceration. About 18 percent of state prisoners who had a mental health problem, compared to 9 percent of state prisoners who did not have a mental problem, said that they had lived in a foster home, agency, or institution while growing up. In addition, past physical or sexual abuse was more prevalent among inmates who had mental health problems. State prisoners with a mental health problem

Table 5.15 Prisoners Who Had a Mental Health Problem, by Characteristic of Gender, Age, and Race

Characteristic	State Prison (%)	Federal Prison (%)
All inmates	56.2	44.8
Gender		
Male	55.0	43.6
Female	73.1	61.2
Race		
White	62.2	49.6
Black	54.7	45.9
Hispanic	46.3	36.8
Other	61.9	50.3
Age		
24 or younger	62.6	57.8
25–34	57.9	48.2
35–44	55.9	40.1
45–54	51.3	41.6
55 or older	39.6	36.1

Source: James, Doris and Laren Glaze. 2006. Special Report. "Mental Health Problems of Prison and Jail Inmates." Bureau of Justice Statistics. September 2006, NCJ 213600.

(27%) were over two times more likely than those without (10%) to report being physically or sexually abused in the past.

Drug abuse was a significant factor in mental health problems, with an estimated 42 percent of inmates in state prisons being found to have both a mental health problem and substance dependence or abuse.

Chapter 2 discusses the correlation between mental health issues and violence and indiscipline by inmates with such problems. The survey data supports this association, showing that violations of prison rules and injuries from fighting were more common among inmates who had a mental health problem. Also, prisoners with a mental health problem were more likely than those without to have been charged with breaking facility rules. Among state prisoners, 58 percent of those who had a mental health problem, compared to 43 percent of those without, had been charged with rule violations.

An estimated 24 percent of state prisoners who had a mental health problem, compared to 14 percent of those without, had been charged with a physical or verbal assault on correctional staff or another inmate. Among federal prisoners who had a mental health problem, 15 percent had been charged with a physical or verbal assault on correctional staff or another inmate compared to 7 percent of those without a mental problem.

Documents

Colonial Punishments

Punishments imposed during the colonial period did not include a sentence of imprisonment and were commonly applied in public. They included shaming punishments, especially spending time in the pillory, as the following reports attest.

Boston Post-Boy, February 1763:

At the Superior Court held at Charlestown last week, Samuel Bacon . . . and Meriam Fitch . . . were convicted of being notorious Cheats, and of having by Fraud, Craft, and Deceit, possess'd themselves of . . . the property of a third Person; were sentence to be each of them set in the Pillory one Hour, with a Paper on each of their Breasts and the words A CHEAT wrote in Capitals thereon, to suffer three months' imprisonment, and to be bound to their good Behaviour for one Year and to pay Costs.

Boston Chronicle, November 20, 1769:

We learn from Worcester that on the eighth instant one Lindsay stood in the Pillory there one hour, after which he received 30 stripes at the public whipping-post, and was then branded in the hand; his crime was Forgery.

Source: Alice Morse Earle, "Curious Punishments of By-Gone Days." *The Chap-Book*, Vol 5, No. 10, 1896, 448–449.

U.S. Constitution

Prisoner litigation has relied heavily on the rights granted by the Constitution. Examples are the right to freedom of religion, which is an issue for prisoners holding the Muslim faith, and freedom from cruel and unusual punishment, a right that continues to be argued, especially in claims arising out of solitary confinement in supermax prisons. These rights are reproduced here.

First Amendment (1791)

Congress shall make no law respecting an establishment of religion, or prohibiting the free exercise thereof; or abridging the freedom of speech, or the press; or the right of the people peaceably to assemble, and to petition the government for a redress of grievances.

Eighth Amendment (1791)

Excessive bail shall not be required, nor excessive fines imposed, nor cruel and unusual punishments inflicted.

Source: National Archives.

Benjamin Rush on Public Punishments (1798)

Benjamin Rush, a signatory of the U.S Constitution, was a renowned physician of the time as well as a social and moral reformer. He argued against slavery and the imposition of the death penalty for murder and opposed public punishments in a collection of essays entitled Essays, Literary, Moral and Philosophical. *Rush believed in the power of religion to combat wrongdoing and, as a physician, believed that crime, like disease, could be cured. He regarded a penitentiary as analogous to a church and stressed the*

value of habitual labor as a virtuous habit that would resist idle-
ness or the urge to criminality and bring about rehabilitation.

. . . all public punishments tend to make bad men worse, and
to increase crimes, by their influence upon society.

1. The reformation of a criminal can never be effected by a
    public punishment.

2. As it is always connected with infamy, it destroys in him
    the sense of shame which is one of the strongest outposts
    of virtue.

3. It is generally of such short duration, as to produce none
    of those changes in body or mind, which are absolutely
    necessary to reform obstinate habits of vice.

4. Experience proves that public punishments have increased
    propensities to crime. A man who has lost his character at a
    whipping post, has nothing valuable left to lose in society.
    Pain has begotten insensibility to the whip; and infamy to
    shame. Added to his old habits of vice, he probably feels
    a spirit of revenge against the whole community, whose
    laws have inflicted his punishment upon him; and hence
    he is stimulated to add to the number and enormity of his
    outrages upon society. The long duration of the punish-
    ment, when public, by increasing its infamy, serves only
    to increase the evils that have been mentioned. . . .

Public punishments make many crimes known in persons who
would otherwise have passed through life in a total ignorance of
them. They moreover produce such a familiarity, in the minds
of spectators, with the crimes for which they are inflicted that,
in some instances they have been known to excite a propensity
for them. . . .

Let a large house be erected in a convenient part of the state.
Let it be divided into a number of apartments, reserving one
large room for public worship. Let cells be provided for the solitary confinement of such persons as are of refractory temper.

Let the hours be supplied with the materials and instruments for carrying on such manufactures as can be conducted with the least instruction or previous knowledge. Let a garden adjoin this house, in which the culprits may occasionally work and walk. . . .

Let the various kinds of punishments that are to be inflicted on crimes be defined and fixed by law . . . punishments should always be varied in degree according to the temper of criminals or the progress of their reformation.

Let the duration of punishments for all crimes be limited: but let this limitation be unknown. I conceive this secret to be of the utmost importance in reforming criminals and preventing crimes. . . .

The punishments should consist of bodily pain, labour, watchfulness, solitude and silence. They should all be joined with cleanliness and a simple diet. . . .

To remedy these physical remedies more effectual they should be accompanied by regular instruction in the principles and obligations of religion by persons appointed for that purpose.

Source: Rush, Benjamin. *Essays, Literary, Moral, and Philosophical.* Philadelphia: Thomas and Samuel F. Bradford, 1798, 3–4. 136–160. Found at http://deila.dickinson.edu/theirown words/title/0021.htm.

On the Penitentiary System in the United States (1833)

The creation of the penitentiary in its two models, the Auburn system and the Pennsylvania system, aroused great foreign interest in this radical U.S. development in punishment. Among the visitors from Europe were English novelist Charles Dickens and Frenchmen Beaumont and de Tocqueville, who visited Auburn prison in 1831 and narrated their experience in language that brought to light the rigor of solitary confinement and the rule of silence as well as the differences between the two systems.

[T]he founders of the new penitentiary at Philadelphia, thought it necessary that each prisoner should be secluded in a separate cell during day as well as night.

They have thought that absolute separation of the criminals can alone protect them from mutual pollution, and they have adopted the principle of separation in all its rigor. According to this system, the convict, once thrown into his cell, remains there without interruption, until the expiration of his punishment. He is separated from the whole world; and the penitentiaries, full of malefactors like himself, but every one of them entirely isolated, do not present to him even a society in the prison. If it is true that in establishments of this nature, all evil originates from the intercourse of the prisoners among themselves, we are obliged to acknowledge that nowhere is this vice avoided with greater safety than at Philadelphia, where the prisoners find themselves utterly unable to communicate with each other; and it is incontestable that this perfect isolation secures the prisoner from all fatal contamination.

As solitude is in no other prison more complete than in Philadelphia, nowhere, also, is the necessity of labor more urgent. At the same time, it would be inaccurate to say, that in the Philadelphia penitentiary labor is imposed; we may say with more justice that the favor of labor is granted. When we visited this penitentiary, we successively conversed with all its inmates. There was not a single one among them who did not speak of labor with a kind of gratitude, and who did not express the idea that without the relief of constant occupation, life would be insufferable.

What would become, during the long hours of solitude, without this relief, of the prisoner, given up to himself, a prey to the remorses of his soul and the terrors of his imagination? Labor gives to the solitary cell an interest; it fatigues the body and relieves the soul.

It is highly remarkable, that these men, the greater part of whom have been led to crime by indolence and idleness, should be constrained by the torments of solitude, to find in labor their only comfort. By detesting idleness, they accustom themselves to hate the primary cause of their misfortune; and labor, by comforting them, makes them love the only means, which when again free, will enable them to gain honestly their livelihood. The founders of the Auburn prison acknowledged also the necessity of separating the prisoners, to prevent all intercourse among themselves, and to subject them to the obligation of labor; but they follow a different course in order to arrive at the same end.

In this prison, as well as in those founded upon the same model, the prisoners are locked up in their solitary cells at night only. During day they work together in common workshops, and as they are subjected to the law of rigorous silence, though united, they are yet in fact isolated. Labor in common and in silence forms then the characteristic trait which distinguishes the Auburn system from that of Philadelphia.

Owing to the silence to which the prisoners are condemned, this union of the prisoners, it is asserted, offers no inconvenience, and presents many advantages.

They are united, but no moral connection exists among them. They see without knowing each other. They are in society without any intercourse; there exists among them neither aversion nor sympathy. The criminal, who contemplates a project of escape, or an attempt against the life of his keepers, does not know in which of his companions he may expect to find assistance. Their union is strictly material, or to speak more exactly, their bodies are together, but their souls are separated; and it is not the solitude of the body which is important, but that of the mind. At Pittsburgh, the prisoners, though separated, are not alone, since there exist moral communications among them. At Auburn, they are really isolated, though no wall separates them.

Their union in the workshops has, therefore, nothing dangerous: it has, on the contrary, it is said, an advantage peculiar to it, that of accustoming the prisoners to obedience.

What is the principal object of punishment in relation to him who suffers it? It is to give him the habits of society, and first to teach him to obey. The Auburn prison has, on this point, its advocates say, a manifest advantage over that of Philadelphia.

Perpetual seclusion in a cell, is an irresistible fact which curbs the prisoner without a struggle, and thus deprives altogether his submission of a moral character; locked up in this narrow space, he has not, properly speaking, to observe a discipline; if he works, it is in order to escape the weariness which overwhelms him: in short, he obeys much less the established discipline than the physical impossibility of acting otherwise.

At Auburn, on the contrary, labor instead of being a comfort to the prisoners, is, in their eyes, a painful task, which they would be glad to get rid of. In observing silence, they are incessantly tempted to violate its law. They have some merit in obeying, because their obedience is no actual necessity. It is thus that the Auburn discipline gives to the prisoners the habits of society which they do not obtain in the prisons of Philadelphia.

We see that silence is the principal basis of the Auburn system; it is this silence which establishes that moral separation between all prisoners, that deprives them of all dangerous communications, and only leaves to them those social relations which are inoffensive.

Source: de Beaumont, G. and de Toqueville, A. *On the Penitentiary System in the United States and Its Application in France.* Translated by Francis Lieber. Philadelphia: Carey, Lea & Blanchard, 1833, 23–25.

Female Convicts (1864)

Mary Carpenter was an influential English prison reformer who promoted the idea of constructing reformatories for women offenders where they would live in an environment that closely resembled that of a family. After visiting an Irish prison for women in 1862, and impressed by its potential to rehabilitate women, she began to argue that female offenders could be reformed if they were treated appropriately while incarcerated. In her 1864 book Our Convicts,

Carpenter contended that women should be incarcerated together in a separate facility where a merit system would regulate access to treatment and privileges and where female staff would provide cultural and intellectual support and male guards excluded. Her ideas influenced U.S. women reformers, who applied Carpenter's ideas in establishing the Indiana Reformatory Institution for Women which opened in Indianapolis in 1873 and was the first completely independent women's prison and the first to be operated by entirely female staff.

It is frequently imagined, even publicly asserted, that Convict women are so hopelessly bad that it is useless to attempt any reformation of them. Such an opinion is founded on the knowledge of such cases as those which have been presented at the commencement of this work, and which are frequently occurring in the public prints; on the very painful exhibition of female vice in police-courts among the unhappy women who are lost to all sense of shame; and, not least, from the descriptions of the scenes that occur in the Convict Prisons, which have been given to the public by the Prison Matron. We acknowledge that the reformation of such women is a very difficult work, but at the same time believe that the difficulties are not insurmountable, if a right system is adopted; we believe, too, that the strong impression which prevails as to the impossibility of reforming women who have once entered on a career of crime, arises more from the exhibition to the public of the extraordinary excess of female Convicts who have been forced into an unnatural state of excitement by injudicious treatment, than from the real conviction of experienced persons who have judiciously and perseveringly endeavoured to reform them. . . .

Let us first inquire what is the work which is to be done in the Female Convict Prisons?

The system and arrangements in them must necessarily differ from those for male Convicts, for there is a very great difference between the inmates. Female Convicts are, as a class, even more morally degraded than men. As a general rule, it will be found that women are not brought before a public tribunal except for very aggravated crimes, or for a long course of vice. Wo may attribute this partly to a degree of forbearance which usually exists in the stronger towards the weaker sex; and partly to the fact that they are, when engaging in crime, most commonly the accomplices of their male connections, or shielded by them. From these causes, we learn that in the United States it is rare ever to see women in prison; in our country the proportion of female Convicts to males is usually not one-third of the whole number. But for these very reasons they are especially bad, more deeply hardened than those of the other sex in the same position. They generally, perhaps always, spring from a portion of society more completely cut off from the honest and respectable portion of society, and therefore more lost to shame.

Source: Carpenter, Mary. *Our Convicts. Volume 2.* London: Longman, Green, Longman, Roberts, & Green, 1864, 204–208.

Resolutions of the National Congress on Penitentiary and Reformatory Discipline (1870)

A landmark event in the history of American corrections was the convening of an international conference by U.S. reformers in 1870 in Cincinnati called the Congress of Penitentiary and Reformatory Discipline. Over 250 delegates formulated a set of recommendations that took the form of a declaration. The principles enumerated by the Congress sought to establish new aims and methods of correction and incarceration, and were most publicly translated into practice at the Elmira Reformatory which opened in New York in 1876.

Resolved, That light, diet and discipline are point in prison management of vital importance, and this congress announces as its judgment thereupon the following principles:

I. Light

In the construction of prisons, provision should be made for supplying sunlight to the prison apartments, to the same extent as to apartments occupied by citizens generally. Artificial light for the purposes of study should be furnished at evening, for reasonable hours, to all prisoners who can be induced to use it. A separate light in each room is the best plan.

II. Dietaries

The food for adult prisoners should be of sufficient quantity to maintain satisfactory physical conditions. The demands of prisoners as to quantity and quality should not always govern the supply, for they should be required to use food economically—to waste nothing; and the best criterion of their needs in this particular is not their own notion, but their observed physical condition. Experience teaches that, with improved conditions as to health and mental development, the appetite demands and the system requires a better quality and greater variety of food than is now usually supplied to prisoners. In a graduated series of establishments different dietaries must be introduced, and they may be made a means of reformatory progress among the prisoners.

III. Discipline

The infliction of physical pain upon persons should always be for the purpose of securing obedience in the future, and never to satisfy offended dignity or to mend a broken rule or (except in extraordinary circumstances) to produce an impression upon other prisoners. It should be one privately and deliberately, and with regard to the restoration of the prisoner to right relations, with his self-respect and manhood remaining. The common use of the "dark cell" should be changed by the introduction of light, and by requiring the prisoner to maintain a standing position for a few hours only, when he should be released and taken to the ordinary cell for the night, and returned to the standing position in "solitary" after breakfast each morning, day by day (if he is sane and morally responsible), until he consents heartily to the proper authority of the officers.

... Resolved, That, as the sense of this congress, in the administration of all classes of prisons, the paramount object should be moral and religious improvement, and that this is compatible with industry on the part of the prisoners and economy on the part of its officers; that the desire to make a prison a source of revenue, or even self-sustaining, should never be allowed to supersede those more important and ever-to-be-remembered objects—moral and religious improvement.

Resolved, That each system of juvenile reformatories has its merits, and may be used to advantage, but this congress expresses not preference for either the family or the congregate system; that the important agency for reformation is found in warm-hearted, clear-headed men and women, who, in the spirit of Christ, wield their kind personal influence for this end.

Resolved, That it is the sentiment of this congress that the great principles of Christian love and kindness should be applied to the utmost extent practicable in the management of our prisons and reformatories.

Resolved, That this congress is of the opinion that separate prisons should be established for women, and that neither in city, county nor state prisons should women be incarcerated with men; and further, that women should have charge of the female department in all cases where the sexes are imprisoned within the same inclosure. ...

Source: Wines, E. C. *Transactions of the National Congress on Penitentiary and Reformatory Discipline*, Held at Cincinnati, Ohio, October 12–18, 1870. Albany: Weed, Parsons and Company, Publishers, 1871, 568–570.

Grover Cleveland on Prison Reform (1886)

A federal prison system for those convicted of federal crimes has existed since 1891 following the enactment of the Three Prisons Act in 1890, which authorized the construction of federal prisons at Leavenworth, Atlanta, and McNeil Island, Washington. Before 1890, those sentenced for federal crimes were sent to state prisons under contracts, with the states willing to accommodate them. Between 1890 and 1930 the increase in federal crime convictions resulted in the growth of the federal system to seven prisons. The Federal Bureau of Prisons, responsible for the management of all federal prisons, was finally established in 1930. These facts are illustrated in the message to Congress from President Grover Cleveland, delivered during the time when federal prisoners were accommodated in state prisons.

The conduct of the Department of Justice for the last fiscal year is fully detailed in the report of the Attorney-General, and I invite the earnest attention of the Congress to the same and due consideration of the recommendations therein contained.

In the report submitted by this officer to the last session of the Congress he strongly recommended the erection of a penitentiary for the confinement of prisoners convicted and sentenced in the United States courts, and he repeats the recommendation in his report for the last year.

This is a matter of very great importance and should at once receive Congressional action. United States prisoners are now confined in more than thirty different State prisons and penitentiaries scattered in every part of the country. They are subjected to nearly as many different modes of treatment and discipline and are far too much removed from the control and regulation of the Government. So far as they are entitled to humane treatment and an opportunity for improvement and reformation, the Government is responsible to them and society that these things are forthcoming. But this duty can scarcely be discharged without more absolute control and direction than is possible under the present system.

Many of our good citizens have interested themselves, with the most beneficial results, in the question of prison reform. The General Government should be in a situation, since there must be United States prisoners, to furnish important aid in this movement, and should be able to illustrate what may be practically done in the direction of this reform and to present an example in the treatment and improvement of its prisoners worthy of imitation.

With prisons under its own control the Government could deal with the somewhat vexed question of convict labor, so far as its convicts were concerned, according to a plan of its own adoption, and with due regard to the rights and interests of our laboring citizens, instead of sometimes aiding in the operation of a system which causes among them irritation and discontent.

Upon consideration of this subject it might be thought wise to erect more than one of these institutions, located in such places as would best subserve the purposes of convenience and economy in transportation. The considerable cost of maintaining these convicts as at present, in State institutions, would be saved by the adoption of the plan proposed, and by employing them in the manufacture of such articles as were needed for use by the Government quite a large pecuniary benefit would be realized in partial return for our outlay.

I again urge a change in the Federal judicial system to meet the wants of the people and obviate the delays necessarily attending the present condition of affairs in our courts. All are agreed that something should be done, and much favor is shown by those well able to advise to the plan suggested by the Attorney-General at the last session of the Congress and recommended in my last annual message. This recommendation is here renewed, together with another made at the same time, touching a change in the manner of compensating district attorneys and marshals; and the latter subject is commended to the Congress for its action in the interest of economy to the Government, and humanity, fairness, and justice to our people.

Source: Cleveland, Grover. Second Annual Message, December 6, 1886. In Richardson, James D. *A Compilation of the Messages and Papers of the Presidents, Volume VIII*. Washington, D.C.: Government Printing Office, 1898, 517–518.

Herbert Hoover on Federal Prison Reform (1929)

The federal prison system began its expansion in the 1930s as more federal offenses were created and more offenders were sentenced to imprisonment for committing federal crimes. The first federal prison for women was opened in 1927 at Alderson, West Virginia. President Herbert Hoover, speaking to the press in 1929, explained that the system had already reached overcapacity and that a new prison would be constructed and others expanded. Interestingly, he noted the increase in the prison population was largely the result of sentences for drug offenders. The same situation would be repeated from the 1970s onwards as the federal prison population increased yet again because of drug offenders.

August 6, 1929:

THE PRESIDENT, in response to an inquiry from the press, said:

I have one question this morning that I can comment on. It arises out of the incident at Leavenworth and the situation of the Federal prisons.

I have had an opportunity for lengthy discussions with the Attorney General, and I have the recommendations of Mr. [Sanford] Bates, who is the new Director of Prisons, and I have accepted their view that further Federal accommodations for prisoners cannot be any longer delayed. We will ask Congress at the regular session to give us the necessary authority and appropriations to revise the system.

Atlanta is 120 percent over capacity in inmates at the present time, and Leavenworth 87 percent, all of which is the cause of infinite demoralization and the direct cause of outbreaks and trouble.

Of course, the increased number of prisoners is due to the general increase in crime, the largest item in our Federal prisoners being the violators of the Narcotics Act. They comprise now about 33 percent of the inmates at Leavenworth and Atlanta. Prohibition contributes about 14 percent. The balance is made up of increases all along the line.

Our plans necessitate an expenditure of about $5 million, and will comprise some additions and revisions of the old prisons, and probably a new prison somewhere in the Northeastern States.

It is proposed also to ask authority of Congress to increase the number of probation officers, as Mr. Bates is convinced he can find a larger number of prisoners who merit probation, and not only their own good but the good of the Federal Government will be served by having them out, but we have no staff now adequate to take care of increased probation. So with a new appropriation we hope to get some later.

August 20, 1929:

THROUGH the cooperation of Secretary Good and the Attorney General, I believe we have found temporary solution to the problem of overcrowding in the Federal prisons, especially those at Atlanta and Leavenworth.

The Army has three major prisons—one at Governors Island, one at Leavenworth, and one at Alcatraz.

The Army prison at Leavenworth is a model establishment with a capacity of about 1,600 prisoners. At present there are only 600 Army prisoners in the establishment. At the same time there are many vacancies in both Blackwell's Island and Alcatraz. Also there are vacancies for short time prisoners in some of the Army post prisons. Beyond this again there are a number of men recommended for parole from the Army prisons.

Subject to our being able to overcome any legal difficulties, it is proposed to make the Leavenworth military prison available to the Department of Justice as a temporary measure pending construction of further accommodations by the Department of Justice. This will afford relief to about 1,600 prisoners from the general prisons at Leavenworth and Atlanta.

Source: Public Papers of the Presidents of the United States. Herbert Hoover, 1929. Washington, D.C.: Government Printing Office, 1974, 169–171, 182.

Richard Nixon on Prison Labor (1973)

Prison labor has a long history, starting with the belief that labor in prison would be an essential element in the reform of criminal minds to the development of systems of contract labor and to the convict labor system employed in the South which contributed greatly to economic reconstruction after the Civil War. The early belief in prison labor as a transformational experience was later replaced by the requirement that prison systems earn revenue to cover their costs. Unlike the states, the federal system did not support prison labor, and in 1905 President Roosevelt went so far to prohibit all prisoners, state and federal, from undertaking labor on federal contracts for fear that it would constitute unfair competition between convict and free labor. That position was reversed in to some extent in 1973 by President Nixon, who authorized nonfederal prisons to perform labor on federal contracts subject to safeguards to protect the position of free labor.

The development of the occupational and educational skills of prison inmates is essential to their rehabilitation and to their ability to make an effective return to free society. Meaningful employment serves to develop those skills. It is also true, however, that care must be exercised to avoid either the exploitation of convict labor or any unfair competition between convict labor and free labor in the production of goods and services.

Under section 4082 of title 18 of the United States Code, the Attorney General is empowered to authorize Federal prisoners to work at paid employment in the community during their terms of imprisonment under conditions that protect against both the exploitation of convict labor and unfair competition with free labor.

Several states and other jurisdictions have similar laws or regulations under which individuals confined for violations of the laws of those places may be authorized to work at paid employment in the community.

Executive Order No. 325A, which was originally issued by President Theodore Roosevelt in 1905, prohibits the employment, in the performance of Federal contracts, of any person who is serving a sentence of imprisonment at hard labor imposed by a court of a State, territory, or municipality.

I have now determined that Executive Order No. 325A should be replaced with a new Executive order which would permit the employment of non-Federal prison inmates in the performance of Federal contracts under terms and conditions that are comparable to those now applicable to inmates of Federal prisons.

Now, THEREFORE, pursuant to the authority vested in me as President of the United States, it is hereby ordered as follows:

SECTION 1. (a) All contracts involving the use of appropriated funds which shall hereafter be entered into by any department or agency of the executive branch for performance in any State, the District of Columbia, the Commonwealth of Puerto Rico, the Virgin Islands, Guam, American Samoa, or the Trust Territory of the Pacific Islands shall, unless otherwise provided by law, contain a stipulation forbidding in the performance of such contracts, the employment of persons undergoing sentences of imprisonment which have been imposed by any court of a State. the District of Columbia, the Commonwealth of Puerto Rico, the Virgin Islands, Guam, American Samoa, or the Trust Territory of the Pacific Islands. This limitation, however, shall not prohibit the employment by a contractor in the performance of such contracts of persons on parole or probation to work at paid employment during the term of their sentence or persons who have been pardoned or who have served their terms. Nor shall it prohibit the employment by a contractor in the performance of such contracts of persons confined for violation of the laws of any of the States, the District of Columbia, the Commonwealth of Puerto Rico, the Virgin Islands, Guam, American Samoa, or the Trust

Territory of the Pacific Islands who are authorized to work at paid employment in the community under the laws of such jurisdiction, if

(1) (A) the worker is paid or is in an approved work training program on a voluntary basis;

   (B) representatives of local union central bodies or similar labor union organizations have been consulted;

   (C) such paid employment will not result in the displacement of employed workers, or be applied in skills, crafts, or trades in which there is a surplus of available gainful labor in the locality, or impair existing contracts for services; and

   (D) the rates of pay and other conditions of employment will not be less than those paid or provided for work of a similar nature in the locality in which the work is being performed; and

(2) the Attorney General has certified that the work-release laws or regulations of the jurisdiction involved are in conformity with the requirements of this order.

   (b) After notice and opportunity for hearing, the Attorney General shall revoke any such certification under section 1(a) (2) if he finds that the work-release program of the jurisdiction involved is not being conducted in conformity with the requirements of this order or with its intent or purposes.

SEC. 2. The Federal Procurement Regulations, the Armed Services Procurement Regulations, and to the extent necessary, any supplemental or comparable regulations issued by any agency of the executive branch shall be revised to reflect the policy prescribed by this order.

SEC. 3. Executive Order No. 325A is hereby superseded.

SEC. 4. This order shall be effective as of January 1, 1974.

RICHARD NIXON
The White House,
December 29, 1973.

Source: Executive Order 11755 Relating to Prison Labor. December 29, 1973. 39 FR 779, 3 CFR, 1971–1975 Comp., p. 837.

Barack Obama on Prison Reform (2015)

The creation and enforcement of punishment policies beginning from the 1970s that resulted in mass imprisonment have now caused many to question their utility and especially their cost. Since about 2009, reformist proposals that would reduce the prison population have gained some political and public acceptance. Nevertheless, there remains considerable resistance to any substantial change in current punishment policies. President Barack Obama has been an advocate for reform and in July 2015 became the first U.S. president to visit a federal prison. His statement and responses to questions illustrate many of the themes associated with the issue of reforming punishment and changing the nature of correctional systems.

The President.   Hello, everybody. So I'm just going to make a very quick statement. I want to thank the folks who were involved here in helping to arrange this visit at El Reno, a Federal penitentiary. And this is part of our effort to highlight both the challenges and opportunities that we face with respect to the criminal justice system.

Many of you heard me speak on Tuesday in Philadelphia about the fact that the United States accounts for 5 percent of the world's population; we account for 25 percent of the world's inmates. And that represents a huge surge since 1980. A primary driver of this mass incarceration phenomenon is our drug laws, our mandatory minimum sentencing around drug laws. And we have to consider whether this is the smartest way for us to both control crime and rehabilitate individuals.

This is costing taxpayers across America $80 billion a year. And as I said on Tuesday, there are people who need to be in prison, and I don't have tolerance for violent criminals. Many of them may have made mistakes, but we need to keep our communities safe. On the other hand, when we're looking at nonviolent offenders, most of them growing up in environments in which drug traffic is common, where many of their family members may have been involved in the drug trade, we have to reconsider whether 20-year, 30-year, life sentences for nonviolent crimes is the best way for us to solve these problems.

Here at El Reno, there's some excellent work that's being done inside this facility to provide job training, college degrees, drug counseling. The question is not only how do we make sure that we sustain those programs here in the prison, but how do we make sure that those same kind of institutional supports are there for kids and teenagers before they get into the criminal justice system? And are there ways for us to divert young people who make mistakes early on in life so that they don't get into the system in the first place?

The good news is, is that we've got Demo-
crats and Republicans who I think are starting to work together in Congress and we're
starting to see bipartisan efforts in State legislatures as well to start to reexamine some of
these sentencing laws, to look at what kinds
of work we can do in the community to
keep kids out of the criminal justice system
in the first place, how we can build on the
successes for rehabilitation while individuals
who are incarcerated, and then, what can we
do to improve reentry going forward?

I just had the chance to meet with six
inmates, all of them in for drug offenses.
Many of them here for very long sentences.
And every single one of them emphasized
the fact that they understood they had
done something wrong, they were prepared
to take responsibility for it. But they also
urged us to think about, how could society
have reached them earlier on in life to keep
them out of trouble? They expressed huge
appreciation for the educational opportunities and drug counseling that they get here
in prison, and they expressed some fear and
concern about how difficult the transition
was going to be.

So we've got an opportunity to make a
difference at a time when, overall, violent
crime rates have been dropping at the same
time as incarcerations last year dropped for
the first time in 40 years. My hope is that
if we can keep on looking at the evidence,
keep on looking at the facts, figure out what
works, that we can start making a change
that will save taxpayers money, keep our

streets safe, and perhaps most importantly, keep families intact and break this cycle in which young people—particularly young people of color—are so prone to end up in a criminal justice system that makes it harder for them to ever get a job and ever be effective, full citizens of this country.

So I want to express appreciation to everybody who helped make this happen. I want to give a special shout-out to our prison guards. They've got a really tough job, and most of them are doing it in exemplary fashion. One of the things that we talked about is how we can continue to improve conditions in prisons. This is an outstanding institution within the system, and yet we've—they've got enormous overcrowding issues. I just took a look in a cell where, because of overcrowding, typically, we might have three people housed in a cell that looks to be, what, 15 by—

Correctional Officer Ronald Warlick. Nine by 10.

The President. What?

Officer Warlick. Nine by 10.

The President. Nine by 10. Three, whole-grown men in a 9-by-10 cell. There's been some improvement: Now we have two. But overcrowding like that is something that has to be addressed.

As I said the other day, gang activity, sexual assault inside these prisons—those are all things that have to be addressed. And so we're also going to be consulting with prison guards, wardens, and others to see how we can make some critical reforms.

A lot of this, though, is going to have to happen at the State level. So my goal is that we start seeing some improvements at the Federal level and that we're then able to see States across the country pick up the baton. And there are already some States that are leading the way on both sentencing reform as well as prison reform. We want to make sure that we're seeing what works and build off that.

All right? Thanks, everybody.

The President's Meeting with Inmates/ Criminal Justice Reform

Q.	Mr. President, what struck you most about seeing the prison here today?
The President.	What's that?
Q.	What struck you most about seeing this prison here today?
The President.	Visiting with these six individuals. I've said this before: When they describe their youth and their childhood, these are young people who made mistakes that aren't that different than the mistakes I made and the mistakes that a lot of you guys made. The difference is they did not have the kinds of support structures, the second chances, the resources that would allow them to survive those mistakes.
	And I think we have a tendency sometimes to almost take for granted or think it's normal that so many young people end up in

our criminal justice system. It's not normal. It's not what happens in other countries.

What is normal is teenagers doing stupid things. What is normal is young people making mistakes. And we've got to be able to distinguish between dangerous individuals who need to be incapacitated and incarcerated versus young people who, are in an environment in which they are adapting, but if given different opportunities, a different vision of life, could be thriving the way we are.

That's what strikes me: There but for the grace of God. And that, I think, is something that we all have to think about.

All right? Thank you.

Source: Obama, Barack. Remarks by the President after Visit at El Reno Federal Correctional Institution. July 16, 2015. White House Office of the Press Secretary, https://www.whitehouse .gov/the-press-office/2015/07/16/remarks-president-after-visit-el-reno-federal-correctional-institution.

There is a substantial literature on U.S. prisons, federal and state, and on prison systems. Books and book chapters on prisons range from histories of the creation and growth of the prison, scholarly research on the prison environment, prison culture, and the experience of being a correctional officer to accounts by prisoners and ex-prisoners that offer a first-hand account of prison life, its challenges, and the living conditions. The prison literature includes analyses of topics such as restrictive housing, mental health, and gender differences in the prison environment contained in journal articles. Statistical data on prisons is generated by numerous state and federal government agencies and by private organizations. All these bodies provide analyses of prison population size, rates of increase, characteristics of prisoners, and data on the number and type of prisons and their staffing levels.

Books and Book Chapters

Histories

American Academy of Political and Social Science. Vol 46. March 1913. *The Annals: Prison Labor.* Thousand Oaks, CA: Sage Publications in association with the American Academy of Political and Social Science.

A new inmate housing unit is near completion at the Madera County Jail in California. Counties will get another $270 million for jail construction under the 2016-2017 budget approved by California lawmakers. (AP Photo/Rich Pedroncelli)

Discusses a range of topics associated at that time with prison labor, including the New Penology, convict labor in its various forms, and women and prison labor.

Blomberg, Thomas G. and Lucken, Karol. 2000. *American Penology: A History of Control.* New York: Aldine de Gruyter.
Maps the history of punishment in the United States, including the creation and growth of the prison and accompanying policy changes.

Colvin, Mark. 1997. *Penitentiaries, Reformatories, and Chain Gangs: Social Theory and the History of Punishment in Nineteenth Century America.* New York: St. Martin's Press.
A history of the creation and growth of the prison in the United States.

Crews, Gordon. 2004. Justice and the Origin of Corrections, in Stanko, Stephen, Gillespie, Wayne, and Crews, Gordon A., eds. *Living in Prison: A History of the Correctional System with an Insider's View.* Westport, CT: Greenwood Press, pp. 25–42.
Locates the notion of prison within a historical context.

Freedman, Estelle B. 1984. *Their Sisters' Keepers: Women's Prison Reform in America, 1830–1930.* Ann Arbor: University of Michigan Press.
The first account of the history of women in prison in the United States.

Hindus, Michael Stephen. 1980. *Prison and Plantation: Crime, Justice and Authority in Massachusetts and South Carolina, 1767–1878.* Chapel Hill: University of North Carolina Press.
A historical study of the early development of incarceration in these states.

Hirsch, Adam Jay. 1992. *The Rise of the Penitentiary: Prisons and Punishment in Early America.* New Haven, CT: Yale University Press.

An important study of the rise of the prison with a focus on Massachusetts that locates the origin of the U.S. penitentiary in earlier developments and ideologies in Europe.

Ignatieff, Michael. 1978. *A Just Measure of Pain: The Penitentiary in the Industrial Revolution 1750–1850*. London: Penguin Books.
     A seminal study of the history of the prison and its ideological underpinnings.

Jacobs, James B. 1977. *Stateville: The Penitentiary in Mass Society*. Chicago. The University of Chicago Press.
     A classic study of how Stateville Prison and its governance changed over time as professionalism and bureaucratization replaced autocratic and charismatic rule.

Kahan, Paul. 2008. *Eastern State Penitentiary: A History*. Charleston, SC: The History Press.
     A history of this important early penitentiary and its decline.

Kahan, Paul. 2012. *Seminary of Virtue: The Ideology and Practice of Inmate Reform at Eastern State Penitentiary, 1829–1971*. New York: Peter Lang.
     Explores the history of education for inmates and the specific experience of education programming at this penitentiary.

Kann, Mark E. 2005. *Punishment, Prisons and Patriarchy: Liberty and Power in the Early Republic*. New York: New York University Press.
     Explores the association between the early ideas of liberty and the development of imprisonment as deprivation of liberty.

LeFlouria, Talitha L. 2015. *Chained in Silence: Black Women and Convict Labor in the New South*. Chapel Hill, NC: The University of North Carolina Press.

A detailed history of black women laboring in chain gangs and in institutions in Georgia and how their labor contributed to the reconstruction of the South following the Civil War.

McGowen, Randall. 1995. The Well-Ordered Prison: England 1780–1865, in Morris, Norval and Rothman, David J. *The Oxford History of the Prison: The Practice of Punishment in Western Society*. Oxford: Oxford University Press, pp. 71–99.
Charts the history of the prison during this period in England.

Melossi, Dario and Pavarini Massimo. 1981. *The Prison and the Factory: Origins of the Penitentiary System*. New Jersey: Barnes and Noble.
A Marxist perspective on the creation and development of the prison.

Morris, Norval. 1995. The Contemporary Prison: 1965–Present, in Morris, Norval and Rothman, David J. *The Oxford History of the Prison: The Practice of Punishment in Western Society*. Oxford: Oxford University Press, pp. 202–234.
In this comprehensive and erudite history of the prison, this author discusses the prison between 1965 and the mid-1990s.

Parenti, Christian. 1999. *Lockdown America: Police and Prisons in the Age of Crisis*. New York: Verso.
A nonacademic account of the development of mass incarceration and its adverse effects on minorities and society generally.

Pisciotta, Alexander W. 1994. *Benevolent Repression: Social Control and the American Reformatory—Prison Movement*. New York: New York University Press.
A history and critique of the Reformatory Movement, especially Elmira Reformatory, New York State, and its efforts to reform young criminals and why the movement declined.

Rafter, Nichole Hahn. 1985. *Partial Justice: Women in State Prisons 1800–1935*. Boston, MA: Northeastern University Press.
> A history of women in prison and women's prisons, the first in the field.

Rafter, Nichole Hahn. 1990. *Partial Justice: Women, Prisons and Social Control*. New Brunswick, NJ: Transaction Publishers.
> A follow-up to her 1985 text that continues the narrative of women's prison to 1990.

Rasmussen, Jamie Pamela. 2012. *Missouri State Penitentiary: 170 Years Inside the Walls*. Columbia: University of Missouri Press.
> A history of this penitentiary.

Rothman, David J. 1990. *The Discovery of the Asylum: Social Order and Disorder in the New Republic. New York:* Aldine de Gruyter.
> The seminal study of the creation and development of the prison which the author argues was a means of socially controlling the dangerous classes.

Rothman, David J. 2012. *Conscience and Convenience: The Asylum and Its Alternatives in Progressive America*. New Brunswick, NJ. Transaction Publishers.
> In this classic study, the author asks why in the early nineteenth century a generation of Americans came to conclude that institutional care for its convicts, mentally ill, juvenile delinquents, orphans, and adult poor, was the remedy for social disorder.

Rotman, Edgardo. 1995. *The Failure of Reform: United States, 1865–1965*, in Morris, Norval and Rothman, David J. *The Oxford History of the Prison: The Practice of Punishment in Western Society*. Oxford: Oxford University Press, pp. 151–177.
> A discussion of the Progressive-Era prison reform efforts in the early twentieth century and the ultimate failure of these efforts.

Semple, Janet. 1993. *Bentham's Prison: A Study of the Panopticon Penitentiary*. Oxford: Clarendon Press.
> A study of the ideal prison and why it was never constructed.

Spierenberg, Pieter. 2007. *The Prison Experience: Disciplinary Institutions and Their Inmates in Early Modern Europe*. Amsterdam: Amsterdam University Press.
> A classic study of the origin of the prison in Europe that traces its beginnings to notions of contemplation and solitariness and to the isolation of the monastery.

Textbooks and Reference Books

Bosworth, Mary, ed. 2005. *Encyclopedia of Prisons and Correctional Facilities*, Volumes 1 and II. Thousand Oaks, CA: Sage Publications.
> Contains a range of short essays on most aspects of corrections, including the following:

Bush-Baskette, Stephanie R. War on Drugs, pp. 1028–1031; Steiner, Benjamin. Maximum Security, pp. 576–579; Shelden, Randall G. Prison Industrial Complex, pp. 725–729; and Welch, Michael. Chain Gangs, pp. 108–111.

Finn, Peter. 2009. Correctional Officer Stress: A Cause for Concern and Additional Help, in Tewksbury, Richard and Dabney, Dean, eds. *Prisons and Jails: A Reader*. New York: McGraw Hill, pp. 207–220.
> Discusses the causes, nature, and expression of stress in correctional officers.

Fleisher, Mark and Decker, Scott H. 2009. Gangs Behind Bars: Prevalence, Conduct, and Response, in Tewksbury, Richard and Dabney, Dean, eds. *Prisons and Jails: A Reader*. New York: McGraw Hill, pp. 159–174.
> A study of how prison gangs are formed, sustain themselves, and conduct business in prison systems.

Johnson, Robert. 1996. *Hard Time: Understanding and Reforming the Prison*. Belmont, CA: Wadsworth Publishing.

> As well as a history of the development of the prison, the author provides prisoner accounts of the experience of incarceration.

Leigey, Margaret, E. 2011. Life Sentence, in Chambliss, William J., ed. *Corrections*. Thousand Oaks, CA: Sage Publications, pp. 151–164.

> An account of the history and development of the life sentence and the arguments for and against it.

Leigey, Margaret E., Hodge, Jessica P., and Saum, Christine A. 2009. Kids in the Big House: Juveniles Incarcerated in Adult Facilities, in Ruddell, Rick and Thomas, Matthew O., eds. *Juvenile Corrections*. Richmond, KY: Newgate Press, pp. 113–135.

> An overview of what is known about juveniles serving sentences in adult prisons.

Mays, G. Larry and Winfree, L. Thomas. 2005. *Essentials of Corrections*. Belmont, CA: Wadsworth.

> Discusses the field of corrections as an instructional text.

Pollock, Joycelyn M. 2002. *Women, Prison and Crime*. Belmont, CA: Wadsworth.

> Presents all aspects of women and crime, including the punishment of incarceration.

Pollock, Jocelyn M. 2004. *Prisons and Prison Life: Costs and Consequences*. New York: Oxford University Press.

> An instructional text that reviews all aspects of prison life, inmates and officers, inmate rights, women's prisons, prison programs, and reentry.

Schmid, Thomas J. and Jones, Richard S. 2009. Ambivalent Actions: Prison Adaptation Strategies of First-Time, Short-Term

Inmates, in Tewksbury, Richard and Dabney, Dean, eds. *Prisons and Jails: A Reader*. New York: McGraw Hill, pp. 77–94.

> The authors examine how inmates react to imprisonment and how their strategies change over time as they encounter prison culture.

Vose, Brenda. 2011. Furlough and Work-Release Programs, in Chambliss, William J., ed. *Corrections,* pp. 89–104. Los Angeles; London; New Delhi; Singapore; Washington, DC: Sage Publications.

> The author explains how furloughs and work release programs originated and how they have come to be constrained as they are seen as risks to be managed.

Welch, Michael. 2011. *Corrections: A Critical Approach*. New York: Routledge.

> A leading corrections text for students with a questioning and critical perspective of all aspects of the fields of corrections.

Wolff, Nancy, Blitz, Cynthia L., Shi, Jing, Siegel, Jane, and Bachman, Ronet. 2009. Physical Violence Inside Prisons: Rates of Victimization, in Tewksbury, Richard and Dabney, Dean, eds. *Prisons and Jails: A Reader*. New York: McGraw Hill, pp. 111–120.

> Presents the results of a survey of 13 male and 1 female prisons in a state and estimates the prevalence of inmate-on-inmate and staff-on-inmate violence.

Studies of Aspects of Prisons, Incarceration, and Punishment

Auerhahn, Kathleen. 2003. *Selective Incapacitation and Public Policy: Evaluating California's Imprisonment Crisis*. New York: State University of New York Press.

> Charts the development and impact of policy changes in criminal law in California that resulted in changes in the composition and size of the prison population in the state.

Aviram, Hadar. 2015. *Cheap on Crime: Recession-Era Politics and the Transformation of American Punishment*. Oakland, CA: University of California Press.

> Examines the impact of the 2008 financial crisis on punishment in the United States.

Bishop, D.M. and Frazier, C.E. 2000. Consequences of Transfer, in Fagan, J. and Zimring, F., eds. *The Changing Borders of Criminal Justice: Transfer of Adolescents to the Criminal Court*. Chicago: University of Chicago Press, pp. 227–276.

> Looks at the outcomes for behavior of youth transferred to the adult criminal courts for trial and sentencing.

Blumstein, Alfred and Beck, Allen J. 1999. Population Growth in U.S. Prisons 1980–1996, in Tonry, Michael and Petersilia, Joan, eds. *Prisons: A Review of Research*. Chicago: University of Chicago Press, pp. 17–62.

> A statistical study of the growth of the U.S. prison population during this period.

Britton, Dana M. 2003. *At Work in the Iron Cage: The Prison as a Gendered Organization*. New York: New York University Press.

> A study of gender in correctional systems that examines differences in work practices and attitudes between male and female correctional officers in five prisons.

Cabana, Donald A. 1996. *Death at Midnight: The Confession of an Executioner*. Boston, MA: Northeastern University Press.

> A correctional officer narrates his experience in the prison system, including his involvement in the execution of two inmates.

Caplow, Theodore and Simon, Jonathan. 1999. Understanding Prison Policy and Population Trends, in Tonry, Michael and Petersilia, Joan, eds. *Prisons: A Review of Research*. Chicago: University of Chicago Press, pp. 63–120.

> The authors chart changes in punishment policy and how they impacted the prison population.

Carceral, K.C. 2006. *Prison, Inc: A Convict Exposes Life Inside a Private Prison*. New York: New York University Press.
An inmate's account of his experience serving a sentence in several different prisons.

Castle, Tammy, Hensley, Christopher, and Tewksbury, Richard. 2002. Argot Roles and Prison Sexual Hierarchy, in Hensley, Christopher, ed. *Prison Sex: Practice and Policy*. Boulder, CO: Lynne Rienner, pp. 13–26.
A discussion of sexuality in prison and how inmates react to homosexuality.

Conover, Ted. 2001. *Newjack: Guarding Sing Sing*. New York: Vintage.
Journalist Conover became a correctional officer and narrates his experience at this prison in New York.

Crouch, Ben. 1995. Guard Work in Transition, in Haas, Kenneth C. and Alpert, Geoffrey P., eds. *The Dilemma of Corrections: Multidisciplinary Perspectives*. Prospect Heights, IL: Waveland Press, pp. 183–203.
A discussion of the many elements that comprise the work of a correctional officer and how it has changed over time.

Crouch, Ben and Marquart, J. 1980. On Becoming a Prison Guard, pp. 63–110, in Crouch, Ben, ed. *The Keepers: Prison Guards and Contemporary Corrections*. Springfield, IL: Charles C. Thomas.
Marquart became a prison guard to study inmate and guard cultures and reports on his experiences.

Davis, Angela Y. 2003. *Are Prisons Obsolete?* New York: Seven Stories Press.
In a classic study, Davis presents arguments for limiting the role of incarceration in punishing offenders, critiques the institution of the prison, and suggests alternatives.

Dolovich, Sharon. 2012. Creating the Permanent Prisoner, in Ogletree, Charles J. and Sarat, Austin, eds. *Life without Parole: America's New Death Penalty?* New York: New York University Press, pp. 96–137.
> The author argues that the sentence of life without parole represents a penal strategy designed to maintain a boundary between inmates and the wider society.

Enos, Sandra. 2001. *Mothering from the Inside: Parenting in a Women's Prison.* New York: State University of New York Press.
> A study of the challenges facing incarcerated mothers, including what they must do to retain parental rights over their children.

Fagan, Jeffrey. 2004. Crime, Law and the Community: Dynamics of Incarceration in New York City, in Tonry, Michael, ed. *The Future of Imprisonment.* New York: Oxford University Press, pp. 27–60.
> Examines the links between incarceration and the poorest neighborhoods in New York City.

Garland, David. 2001. *Mass Imprisonment: Social Causes and Consequences.* Thousand Oaks, CA: Sage Publications.
> An edited collection of scholarly analyses of the political, social, and penological causes of mass imprisonment.

George, Erin. 2010. *A Woman Doing Life: Notes from a Prison for Women.* New York: Oxford University Press.
> The author narrates her own experience and that of other female inmates, revealing how women cope with the challenges of prison life.

Gillespie, Wayne. 2004. The Context of Imprisonment, in Stanko, Stephen, Gillespie, Wayne, and Crews, Gordon A., eds. *Living in Prison: A History of the Correctional System with an Insider's View.* Westport, CT: Greenwood Press, pp. 63–88.

Discusses the origin of the notion of imprisonment and the social and political factors in its development.

Gillespie, Wayne. 2004. Crime and Justice in the United States, in Stanko, Stephen, Gillespie, Wayne, and Crews, Gordon A., eds. *Living in Prison: A History of the Correctional System with an Insider's View*. Westport, CT: Greenwood Press, pp. 3–24.
An overview of the U.S. criminal justice system, including corrections.

Girshick, Lori, B. 1999. *No Safe Haven: Stories of Women in Prison*. Boston, MA: Northeastern University Press.
Reviews the life stories of 40 female inmates in a minimum-security prison in North Carolina to reveal how their life experiences brought about their incarceration.

Gottschalk, Marie. 2015. *Caught: The Prison State and the Lockdown of American Politics*. Princeton, NJ: Princeton University Press.
A major study of the growth of mass imprisonment that asks why imprisonment remains the predominant punishment in the United States and what reforms are proposed and why.

Greenwood, Peter, Rydell, C. Peter, Abrahamse, Allan F., Caulkins, Jonathan P., Chiesa, James, Model, Karyn E. and Klein, Stephen P. 1996. Estimated Benefits and Costs of California's New Mandatory-Sentencing Law, in Shichor, David and Sechrest, Dale K., eds. *Three Strikes and You're Out: Vengeance as Public Policy*. Thousand Oaks, CA: Sage Publications, pp. 53–89.
A detailed analysis of the effects of mandatory minimum penalties in California.

Guenther, Lisa. 2013. *Solitary Confinement: Social Death and Its Afterlives*. Minneapolis: University of Minnesota Press.
The author examines the experience of prolonged solitary confinement from its introduction in the early nineteenth century until the supermax prisons of today.

Haney, Craig. 2006. *Reforming Punishment: Psychological Limits to the Pains of Imprisonment.* Washington, D.C.: American Psychological Association.

> Based on many years of interviewing prisoners and drawing on his expertise as a renowned prison psychologist, Haney argues for changes in prison conditions to avoid psychological damage to inmates and adverse outcomes for society generally.

Hassine, Victor. 2011. *Life without Parole: Living and Dying in Prison Today.* New York: Oxford University Press.

> The authors account of his experience as an inmate from 1981 to 2008 when he committed suicide, now in its fifth edition.

Henry, Jessica S. 2012. Death-in-Prison Sentences: Overutilized and Underscrutinized, in Ogletree, Charles J. and Sarat, Austin, eds. *Life without Parole: America's New Death Penalty?* New York: New York University Press, pp. 68–95.

> An examination of the policy that resulted in lengthy sentences without parole and the effects of that sentence.

Hensley, Christopher. 2002. Introduction, in Hensley, Christopher, ed. *Prison Sex: Practice and Policy.* Boulder, CO: Lynne Rienner, pp. 1–13.

> An overview of research on sexuality and sexual practices in prisons.

Hensley, Christopher, Rutland, Sandra, and Gray-Ray, Phyllis. 2002. Conjugal Visitation Programs: The Logical Conclusion, in Hensley, Christopher, ed. *Prison Sex: Practice and Policy.* Boulder, CO: Lynne Rienner, pp. 133–142.

> Looks at conjugal visitation in U.S. prisons and its benefits for inmates and staff.

Irwin, John and Owen, Barbara. 2005. Harm and the Contemporary Prison, in Liebling, Alison and Maruna, Shadd, eds. *The*

Effects of Imprisonment. Cullumpton, Devon: Willan Publishing, pp. 94–117.

> Examines how prisons cause harms to inmates in relation to health, psychological damage, loss of agency, sexuality, family separation, and unfairness in decision making.

Jacobs, James B. 2004. Prison Reform amid the Ruins of Prisoners' Rights, in Tonry, Michael, ed. *The Future of Imprisonment.* New York: Oxford University Press, pp. 179–198.

> Discusses the importance of resources for the improvement of prison conditions and charts the rise and fall of the prisoners' rights movement following the Prison Litigation Reform Act.

Johnson, Robert. 2005. Brave New Prisons: The Growing Social Isolation of Modern Penal Institutions, in Liebling, Alison and Maruna, Shadd, eds. *The Effects of Imprisonment.* Cullumpton, Devon: Willan Publishing, pp. 255–284.

> Discusses amenities in prison, "idle time" and television, and suggests how technology can improve prison conditions.

Kauffman, Kelsey. 1988. *Prison Officers and Their World.* Cambridge, MA: Harvard University Press.

> One of the first studies of the work experience and culture of the correctional officer offers a rich source of information and insights.

King, Roy D. 2005. The Effects of Supermax Custody, in Liebling, Alison and Maruna, Shadd, eds. *The Effects of Imprisonment.* Cullumpton, Devon: Willan Publishing, pp. 118–145.

> A study of the conditions and outcomes of isolation in supermax prisons.

Kunselman, Julie, Tewksbury, Richard, Dumond, Robert W., and Dumond, Doris A. 2002. Nonconsensual Sexual Behavior, in Hensley, Christopher, ed. *Prison Sex: Practice and Policy*. Boulder, CO: Lynne Rienner, pp. 27–48.

> The authors review the limited history of sexual assault research and explore the dynamics and motivations surrounding nonconsensual sexual activity in both male and female correctional facilities.

Kupchik, Aaron. 2006. *Judging Juveniles: Prosecuting Adolescents in Adult and Juvenile Courts*. New York: New York University Press.

> The author compares jurisdictions in two bordering states (three counties in New York and three in New Jersey), imposing different models of justice for juvenile offenders, and explores how juveniles are treated as adults and incarcerated.

Kupers, Terry. 1999. *Prison Madness: The Mental Health Crisis behind Bars and What We Must Do about It*. San Francisco, CA: Jossey-Bass Publishers.

> Explains how many inmates suffer mental health problems, their nature, and the prison response. Following a critical analysis, the author suggests how the status of mentally challenged inmates can be improved.

Liebling, Alison and Maruna, Shadd. 2005. Introduction: The Effects of Imprisonment Revisited, in Liebling, Alison and Maruna, Shadd, eds. *The Effects of Imprisonment*. Cullumpton, Devon: Willan Publishing, pp. 1–32.

> In the introduction to this edited volume, the authors review the research literature, both early and current, on the effects of imprisonment, especially in relation to physical and mental health and the effect on families.

Lin, Ann Chih. 2000. *Reform in the Making: The Implementation of Social Policy in Prison*. Princeton, NJ: Princeton University Press.

In her discussion of rehabilitation programming based on over 350 interviews with staff and prisoners in five medium-security male prisons, the author argues in favor of such programming and identifies programming failures and successes and the challenges of implementation.

Lippke, Richard L. 2007. *Rethinking Imprisonment*. New York: Oxford University Press.
Applies moral theories to the issue of imprisonment as punishment and to the conditions of incarceration.

Logan, Charles. 1990. *Private Prisons: Cons and Pros*. New York: Oxford University Press.
As the title suggests, the author describes private prisons and how they originated and presents the opposing arguments.

Lombardo, Lucien. 1989. *Guards Imprisoned: Correctional Officers at Work* (2nd ed.). Cincinnati, OH: Anderson.
An early study of correctional officers, their culture, and challenges in interactions with inmates.

Lyman, M.D. 1989. *Gangland*. Springfield, IL: Charles C. Thomas.
Addresses the history, structure, and operations (particularly drug trafficking) of various organized crime groups and suggests legal tools and investigative techniques for countering such groups.

Mathiesen, Thomas. 2006. *Prison on Trial*. Winchester, UK: Waterside Press.
This internationally renowned criminologist argues against imprisonment as punishment and suggests alternatives.

Morash, Merry and Schram, Pamela J. 2002. *The Prison Experience: Special Issues of Women in Prison*. Prospect Heights, IL: Waveland Press.

A feminist perspective on the realities of prison life for women.

Owen, Barbara. 1998. *"In the Mix": Struggle and Survival in a Women's Prison*. New York: State University of New York Press.
    Describes the nature of prison culture in a large women's prison in California, interrogating the daily life and emphasizing the gendered nature of its social organization, roles, and normative frameworks.

Petersilia, Joan. 1999. Parole and Prisoner Reentry in the United States, in Tonry, Michael and Petersilia, Joan, eds. *Prisons*. Chicago: University of Chicago Press, pp. 479–529.
    The author explains the current absence of systems of parole and how prisoner reentry is envisioned and operates in practice.

Pollock, Jocelyn. 2010. Afterword, in George, Erin, ed. *A Woman Doing Life: Notes from a Prison for Women*. New York: Oxford University Press, pp. 176–185.
    A short discussion of the author's narrative of her time as an inmate in a women's prison.

Pratt, Travis C. 2009. *Addicted to Incarceration: Corrections Policy and the Politics of Misinformation in the United States*. Thousand Oaks, CA: Sage Publications.
    Argues that the United States has become addicted to the punishment of incarceration because of policies that wrongly represent the crime problem, people's perspectives on crime, and misconceptions about the efficacy of incarceration.

Riveland, Chase. 1999. Prison Management Trends, in Tonry, Michael and Petersilia, Joan, eds. *Prisons: A Review of Research*. Chicago: University of Chicago Press, pp. 163–204.
    The author, a prison administrator, examines and analyses the growth of professionalism in prison systems and

highlights the Attica riots and the prisoner's rights movement as pivotal events in the governance of prisons.

Ross, Jeffrey Ian and Richards, Stephen C. 2002. *Behind Bars: Surviving Prison*. Indianapolis, IN: Alpha Books.
    The authors document the stages from arrest to incarceration and how best to cope with the challenges an offender is likely to face.

Santos, Michael G. 2004. *About Prison*. Belmont, CA: Wadsworth.
    A former inmate narrates his prison experiences, provides profiles of other inmates and correctional officers, and proposes prison reforms.

Shalev, Sharon. 2009. *Supermax: Controlling Risk through Solitary Confinement*. Devon, UK: Willan Publishing.
    A study of all aspects of solitary confinement in the supermax prison.

Shichor, David. 1995. *Punishment for Profit: Private Prisons/Public Concerns*. Thousand Oaks, CA: Sage Publications.
    An analysis of the concerns associated with private prisons and how they compare with public prisons.

Skarbek, David. 2014. *The Social Order of the Underworld: How Prison Gangs Govern the American Penal System*. New York: Oxford University Press.
    Argues that prison gangs fulfill a need within corrections that is unmet by the institutional governance arrangements and that bringing an end of gangs in prisons requires a change in the form of governance.

Spohn, Cassia. 2002. *How Do Judges Decide? The Search for Fairness and Justice in Punishment*. Thousand Oaks, CA: Sage Publications.
    Analyzes aspects of the punishment process, including sentencing, and examines the value of sentencing reforms.

Sykes, Gresham. 1999. *The Society of Captives: A Study of a Maximum Security Prison*. Princeton, NJ: Princeton University Press (original work published in 1958).

A seminal text that was the first to explore and analyze the nature of the prison culture and its origins.

Tonry, Michael. 2004. Has the Prison a Future? in Tonry, Michael, ed. *The Future of Imprisonment*. New York: Oxford University Press, pp. 3–26.

A leading criminologist asks whether incarceration has a future and sets out an agenda of change that locates incarceration as but one element in a system of punishment.

Webb, G.L. and D. Morris. 1980. Prison Guard Conceptions, in Crouch, Ben, ed. *The Keepers: Prison Guards and Contemporary Corrections*. Springfield, IL: Charles C. Thomas, pp. 150–161.

An early exploration of the world and experiences of correctional officers.

Welch, Michael. 2005. *Ironies of Imprisonment*. Thousand Oaks, CA: Sage Publications.

A critical examination of the problems confronting corrections including mass incarceration that links punishment policies to social, economic, and political dimensions.

Zimring, Franklin E. and Hawkins, Gordon. 2004. Democracy and the Limits of Punishment: A Preface to Prisoners' Rights, in Tonry, Michael, ed. *The Future of Imprisonment*. New York. Oxford University Press, pp. 157–178.

Examines the limits to punitiveness and punishment generally in democratic societies by reference to the political, social, and other restraints that circumscribe governmental power.

Zimring, Franklin E., Hawkins, Gordon, and Kamin, Sam. 2001. *Punishment and Democracy: Three Strikes and You're Out in California*. New York: Oxford University Press.

A study and analysis of the origin, impact, and effects of three strikes laws in California.

Journal Articles

There are a number of scholarly journals dealing with corrections, aspects of corrections, and topics such as sentencing. Many of those journals are concerned with criminology and criminal justice and are published regularly, usually four times a year. They present current research findings and significant reports of government agencies. The American Correctional Association also publishes regular reports of topics of concern to correctional professionals. The articles listed here provide a wide range of views and perspectives associated with research findings and observations about the state of corrections in the country.

Armstrong, Gaylene, S., Atkin-Plunk, Cassandra, A., and Wells, Jessica. The Relationship Between Work–Family Conflict, Correctional Officer Job Stress, and Job Satisfaction. *Criminal Justice and Behavior* 42(10): 1066–1082.

Brownlee, Kimberley. 2013. A Human Right against Social Deprivation. *The Philosophical Quarterly* 63(251): 199–222.

Clear, Todd R. 2015. The Criminology of Downsizing. *Victims and Offenders* 10: 358–364.

Crittenden, Courtney A. and Koons-Witt, Barbara A. 2015. Gender and Programming: A Comparison of Program Availability and Participation in U.S. Prisons. *International Journal of Offender Therapy and Comparative Criminology* 5: 1–34.

Eisikovits, Zvi and Baizerman, Michael. 1982. "Doin' Time": Violent Youth in a Juvenile Facility and in an Adult Prison. *Journal of Offender Rehabilitation* 6: 5–20.

Finn, Peter. 1996. No-Frills Prisons and Jails: A Movement in Flux. *Federal Probation* 60(3): 35–44.

Glaser, Daniel and Fry, Lincoln J. 1987. Corruption of Prison Staff in Inmate Discipline. *Journal of Offender Counseling Services Rehabilitation* 12(1): 27–38.

Greer, Kimberly R. The Changing Nature of Interpersonal Relationships in a Women's Prison. *Prison Journal* 80(4): 442–469.

Hensley, Christopher, Koscheski, Mary, and Tewksbury, Richard. 2003. The Impact of Institutional Factors on Officially Reported Sexual Assaults in Prisons. *Sexuality & Culture* 7(4): 16–26.

Hepburn, James. 1985. The Exercise of Power in Coercive Organizations: A Study of Prison Guards. *Criminology* 23(1): 146–164.

Jenness, Valerie and Fenstermaker, Sarah. 2015. Forty Years after Brownmiller: Prisons for Men, Transgender Inmates, and the Rape of the Feminine. *Gender and Society* 20(10): 1–16.

Lenz, Nygel. 2002. "Luxuries" in Prison: The Relationship between Amenity Funding and Public Support. *Crime and Delinquency* 48(4): 499–525.

Levinson, Robert B. and Greene, John J. 1999. New "Boys" on the Block: A Study of Prison Inmates under the Age of 18. *Corrections Today*: 61(1): 60–64.

Light, Stephen C. 1991. Assaults on Prison Officers: Interactional Themes. *Justice Quarterly* 8(2): 242–261.

Mair, Julie Samia, Frattaroli, Shannon, and Teret, Stephen. 2003. New Hope for Victims of Sexual Assault. *Journal of Law: Medicine & Ethics* 31: 602–606.

Marquart, James. 1986. Prison Guards and the Use of Physical Coercion as a Mechanism of Prisoner Control. *Criminology* 24(2): 347–366.

Nader, Christine. 2010. Correctional Facilities. *The Georgetown Journal of Gender and the Law* 11(1): 77–95.

National Institute of Justice. 2006. NIJ's Response to the Prison Rape Elimination Act. *Corrections Today* 68(1): 60–61.

Poole, Eric D. and Regoli, Robert M. 1980. Race, Institutional Rule Breaking, and Disciplinary Response: A Study of Discretionary Decision Making in Prison. *Law and Society Review* 14(4): 931–946.

Reisig, Michael and Pratt, Travis. 2000. The Ethics of Correctional Privatization: A Critical Examination of the Delegation of Coercive Authority. *Prison Journal* 80(2): 210–222.

Riley, J. 2000. Sensemaking in Prison: Inmate Identity as a Working Understanding. *Justice Quarterly* 17(2): 359–376.

Shah, Benish. 2010. Lost in the Gender Maze: Placement of Transgender Inmates in the Prison System. *Journal of Race, Gender and Ethnicity* 5(1): 39–56.

Walker, Jaffrey. 1996. Police and Correctional Use of Force: Legal and Policy Standards and Implications. *Crime and Delinquency* 42(1): 144–156.

Wheeler, S. 1961. Socialization in Correctional Communities. *American Sociological Review* 26: 679–712.

Wozniak, Kevin H. 2014. American Public Opinion about Prisons. *Criminal Justice Review* 39(3): 305–324.

Reports of Federal Agencies

The U.S. Department of Justice is the key federal government agency concerned with criminal justice. Its Bureau of Statistics issues regular reports about corrections, correctional populations, and specific aspects of corrections. Also included here for its comparative value is a U.K. government report on its policy for transsexual prisoners.

Austin, J., Johnson, K.D., and Gregoriou, M. 2000. *Juveniles in Adult Prisons and Jails: A National Assessment.* Washington, D.C.: U.S. Department of Justice.

Beck, Allen J. 2015. *Use of Restrictive Housing in U.S. Prisons and Jails 2011–12.* Washington, D.C.: U.S. Department of Justice, Office of Justice Programs, Bureau of Justice Statistics.

Carson, E. Ann. 2015. *Prisoners in 2014.* Washington, D.C.: U.S. Department of Justice, Office of Justice Programs, Bureau of Justice Statistics.

Ministry of Justice, United Kingdom. 2011, March 2. *The Care and Management of Transsexual Prisoners* (PSI2011-007). London: National Offender Management Service.

Sickmund, Melissa. 2004. *Juveniles in Corrections.* OJJDP. National Report Series Bulletin.

U.S. Bureau of Labor Statistics. Correctional Officers. Washington, D.C.: Bureau of Labor Statistics. Available at http://www.bls.gov/ooh/prtective-service/print/correctional officers.htm, accessed September 4, 2015.

U.S. Department of Justice. June 2015. *PREA Data Collection Activities, 2014.* Washington, D.C.: U.S. Department of Justice, Office of Justice Programs, Bureau of Justice Statistics.

West, Heather C. and Sabol, William J. *Prisons Inmates at Midyear 2008—Statistical Tables.* Department of Justice, Bureau of Justice Statistics.

News Media Reports

Eilperin, Juliet. January 26, 2016. "Obama Bans Solitary Confinement for Juveniles in Federal Prisons." *The Washington Post.* Available at https://www.washingtonpost.com/politics/

obama-bans-solitary-confinement-for-juveniles-in-federal-prisons/2016/01/25/056e14b2-c3a2-11e5-9693-933a4d31bcc8_story.html?utm_term=.fcdf91edca66, accessed March 18, 2016.

Lovett, Ian. September 1, 2015. "California Agrees to Overhaul Use of Solitary Confinement." *The New York Times*. Available at http://www.nytimes.com/2015/09/02/us/solitary-confinement-california-prisons.html accessed September 7, 2015.

The New York Times. April 3, 2015. "Transgender Inmate's Hormone Treatment Lawsuit Gets Justice Dept. Backing." http://www.nytimes.com/2015/04/04/us/ashley-diamond-transgender-hormone-lawsuit.html. Accessed on 17 May 2016.

Obama, Barak. January 25, 2016. "Why We Must Rethink Solitary Confinement." Washington. *The Washington Post*. https://www.washingtonpost.com/opinions/barack-obama-why-we-must-rethink-solitary-confinement/2016/01/25/29a361f2-c384-11e5-8965-0607e0e265ce_story.html?utm_term=.14493eb6b0c5. Accessed on 16 May 2016.

Rodriguez, Sal. January 8, 2016. "California Expects to Save $28 Million by Reducing Solitary Confinement." Solitary Watch. Available at http://solitarywatch.com/2016/01/08/california-expects-to-save-28-million-by-reducing-solitary-confinement/, accessed January 9, 2016.

Schwirtz, Michael and Winerip, Michael. December 16, 2015. "New York State Agrees to Overhaul Solitary Confinement in Prisons." *The New York Times*. Available at http://www.nytimes/2015/12/17/nyregion/new-york-state-agrees-to-overhaul-solitary-confinement-in-prisons.html. accessed December 16, 2015.

Walters, Joanna. December 2, 2015. "Illinois Inmates Increasingly Sued by State to Recoup Incarceration Costs." *The Guardian*. Available at http://www.theguardian.com/us-news/2015/dec/02/illinois-inmates-sued-incarceration-costs, accessed December 3, 2015.

Reports by Private Organizations

Private organizations, such as nonprofit nongovernment organizations, carry out research and advocacy work on aspects of corrections and publish reports of their research.

Human Rights Watch. 2001. *No Escape: Male Rape in U.S. Prisons*. New York: Human Rights Watch.
> The first comprehensive report about rape in male prisons which prompted government action in the form of legislation.

Intersex Society of North America. *"What's the Difference between Being Transgender or Transsexual and Having an Intersex Condition?"* Available at *http://www.isna.org/faq/transgender*, accessed December 15, 2015.
> Explains aspects of being transsexual and the concept of transgender.

National Center for Lesbian Rights. June 2006. "Rights of Transgender Prisoners." Available at www.nclrights.org, accessed August 11, 2011.
> Argues that transgender prisoners have rights and enumerates them.

Stop Prisoner Rape. 2007. *Stories from Inside: Prisoner Rape and the War on Drugs*. Los Angeles: Author. Available at http://www .spr.org, accessed March 23, 2007.
> A report from the organization that first brought prisoner rape to public attention recounting narratives of prison rape.

Nonprint Resources

Visual representations of corrections, including its history, prison overcrowding, prison gangs, past riots, and policy issues such as mass incarceration bring an immediacy to the topic of corrections and associated subjects and issues. Most of the movies listed here can be borrowed through public or college libraries, or they can be purchased where this is indicated.

Against the Wall (1994 TV movie)

Recounts the events leading up to the negotiations following the 1971 Attica riot and the horrific outcome when negotiations ceased. The riot was instrumental in exposing poor management practices and lack of professionalism in prison systems and resulted in major reforms.

Can be purchased on amazon.com.

The American Prison: A Video History (1990 American Correctional Association)

A portrayal of the evolution of the prison in the United States that explores the philosophies and events that have shaped it.

Obtainable from college libraries.

Aryan Terror (2009)

Employing interviews and rare footage, this documentary looks at the Aryan Brotherhood of Texas, the largest prison gang within the Texas Department of Criminal Justice.

Part of a series called "Gangland," this episode can be purchased at http://www.films.com/id/21245.

Burden of Justice: Alternatives to Prison Overcrowding (1991 American Correctional Association)

The film focuses on overcrowding in American prisons, using Alabama prisons as an example, and on the efforts to alleviate the problem through alternative methods of punishment.

Can be obtained from college, community college, and state libraries.

CCI: Case Study of a Southern Prison (1997 Films for the Humanities and Sciences)

Filmed at the Central Correctional Institution in South Carolina, this film examines U.S. correctional methods. Interviews with inmates and staff capture emotions ranging from rage to hopelessness, as they discuss the racism and inherent violence of prison life.

Can be purchased at http://ffh.films.com/id/9099.

Correcting Our Elders (1991 American Correctional Association and U.S. Department of Health and Human Services)

Discussion of the challenges faced by corrections in managing a population of older inmates.

Can be purchased from the American Correctional Association or borrowed from college libraries.

Crime and Punishments (1984 Media and Society Seminars, Columbia Graduate School of Journalism)

Addresses the conflict between the constitutional guarantee against cruel and unusual punishment and the realities of the U.S. prison system. A moderator and a panel that includes former Supreme Court justice Potter Stewart, legislators, government officials, jurists, corrections officers, and the media discuss prison overcrowding, the purpose of punishment, the death penalty, and the role of the media.

Can be borrowed from state and college libraries.

The Execution Protocol (1992 Eye for Justice)

Shot inside a maximum-security prison in southeastern Missouri, the film shows how all of Potosi Correctional Center's inmates face either death or are incarcerated for life without parole. In Potosi, executions are conducted in the prison hospital, using a lethal injection machine. The protocol is devised so that the burden of responsibility spreads across a number of individuals. The executioners speak openly about their role and the condemned men reflect on their lives.

Can be purchased or access paid for streaming at https://www.academicvideostore.com/video/execution-protocol.

The Farm: Life Inside Angola Prison (1998 A & E Home Video)

A film that documents the lives of six men imprisoned in the notoriously harsh conditions of Angola, Louisiana State Penitentiary.

VHS and DVD available at amazon.com and commonly found in state and college libraries.

Incarceration Nation (2013 Bill Moyers)

Moyers speaks with civil rights lawyer and legal scholar Michelle Alexander, whose book *The New Jim Crow: Mass Incarceration in the Age of Colorblindness* became a best seller and spurred a wide conversation about justice and inequality in America.

Watch by segment and read the transcript of the interview at http://billmoyers.com/episode/incarceration-nation/.

Inside Folsom (2002 NBC New Archives)

Goes inside Folsom State Prison, California, showing the antiquated infrastructure, from the general population areas to the dungeon-like Cell Block 5. Conversations with lifers, corrections officers, and warden Diana Butler shed light on Folsom's violent culture and the procedures and programs developed to improve it.

Available through streaming video at college libraries or directly at http://www.films.com/ecStreamingLanding.aspx.

Inside North Carolina's Women's Prison (2006 NBC News Archives)

This documentary goes inside a North Carolina facility containing 1,100 troubled mothers, sisters, aunts, and grandmothers. Warden Annie Harvey conveys the goals and frustrations of her job, while male officers acknowledge an ongoing challenge to maintain professionalism and objectivity. Although sexual relationships among inmates are discouraged, several openly gay prisoners share what life is like for their small community.

Drug addiction and substance abuse are also addressed, along with the daily drudgery and attempts to brighten life inside an eight-by-eight-foot cell.

An NBC documentary can be streamed or purchased at http://www.films.com/producer/1/Films_for_the_Humanities__and__Sciences.

Judgment at Midnight (1996 Films for the Humanities and Sciences)

Shows an inmate waiting to die and a prison preparing to execute him. Takes viewers from the cell block to the execution chamber to preparation of the lethal injection and into the mind of inmate Antonio James as he prepares to pay the ultimate price for his crimes.

Can be obtained from http://www.films.com/ecSearch.aspx?q=judgment+at+midnight through streaming or on DVD.

Legacy (1999 Films for the Humanities and Sciences)

An expose of the story behind the passage of California's stringent "three strikes" law. Key players including judges, legal analysts, and state officials argue both sides of the debate about the law's effectiveness.

Film trailer is available at http://www.pbs.org/pov/thelegacy/video/the-legacy-trailer/ and the complete film from libraries.

Let the Doors Be Made of Iron (1987 Films for the Humanities and Sciences)

Uses old lithographs, photographs, and dramatic reenactments to trace the history of the world's first true penitentiary, the Eastern State Penitentiary, Philadelphia, opened in the early nineteenth century. Events in the history of Eastern include the arrival of the first inmate in 1829. Eastern today is a museum.

Can be purchased at https://www.easternstate.org/shop/dvds/let-doors-be-iron and also through libraries.

Men, Women, and Respect: Stopping Sexual Harassment in Correctional Facilities (1993 American Correctional Association)

Addresses sexual harassment among correctional staff, the nature of that harassment, how it impacts those involved, and why it so often goes unreported. The film also portrays what can be done to stop or prevent sexual harassment, such as the victim's or supervisor's confronting the perpetrator to give a warning that the harassing behavior must stop, mandatory training on the nature of sexual harassment, and development of awareness among employees that certain behaviors or verbal comments may be offensive to other employees. An accompanying study guide presents the main points of the video and provides a review quiz and discussion questions.

A training video from the American Correctional Association is available at www.corrections.com/aca.

New Gulag (1996)

This film argues that building and maintaining prisons has become an industry. Private companies regard profit as more important than the expense of any amenities such as recreation and rehabilitation services. In rural communities, prisons are welcomed for providing jobs and markets for a variety of goods needed inside prison. In a maximum-security prison in Oklahoma, death-row prisoners are kept for years in isolation for 23 hours a day. Alvin Brunstein of the American Civil Liberties Union and Marc Mauer, criminologist, challenge the theory that tougher prisons deter crime.

Available on DVD from Filmakers Library, New York, and from libraries.

Nine Hundred Women (2000 Women Make Movies)

Built in 1970, the Louisiana Correctional Institute is located in the swamps of southern Louisiana in the small town of St. Gabriel. It houses those regarded as the state's most dangerous female prisoners and often exceeds its population capacity of 900. Seventy-five percent of prisoners are mothers, and one-fourth are serving sentences of 15 years or more. This film is a portrait of life in this apparently peaceful environment in which six women, a grandmother, a young high school student, a pregnant woman, a recovering heroin addict, a prison guard, and the only woman on death row, share their frustrations and hopes.

Available for purchase or rental from Women Make Movies at http://www.wmm.com/filmcatalog/pages/c521.shtml.

Prison Crowding (1985 National Institute of Justice)

A moderator and three panelists, including criminologists, discuss some of the factors contributing to the growth of the prison population and approaches being pursued to deal with overcrowding.

Available in college libraries and possibly from the Police Foundation and the National Institute of Justice.

Prison Lullabies (2003 Filmakers Library Winner of Best Documentary Annapolis Film Festival 2005)

The story of four women serving sentences for drug dealing and prostitution, and all arrested while pregnant. All have given birth in prison in the Taconic Correctional Facility in New York State, which is one of only five prisons in the nation that permits mothers to keep their babies for the first 18 months of their lives while the mothers participate in programs ranging from basic child care to anger management and drug counseling.

Available in various versions at http://www.prisonlullabies.com/buy-a-copy.

Prison Tech (2004 Films for the Humanities and Sciences)

Examines the security that prevents escapes and keeps the criminal population in check. Visits low-, medium-, and high-security institutions, where administrators, prison guards, a psychologist, and inmates speak candidly about violence in prisons and the strict security measures designed to control it.

Can be purchased at http://ffh.films.com/id/9099.

Prison Town, USA (2007)

Narrates the story of Susanville, California, a small town that tried to resuscitate its economy by building a prison and the unanticipated consequences.

Available at http://www.pbs.org/pov/prisontown/.

Private Prisons (1986 National Institute of Justice)

A moderated panel discussion of the pros and cons of allowing private enterprise to own and operate prisons systems for states and the federal government.

Available at college and community college libraries.

Quiet Rage: The Stanford Prison Experiment (1992 Stanford University)

The film of the classic social psychology experiment in which 24 male undergraduates at Stanford were asked to role-play as guards and inmates in a mock prison setting. The experiment was terminated after only six days because the situation had become so volatile that the supervising researchers believed they no longer had control over the guards and could not guarantee the safety of their research subjects.

Available for purchase at amazon.com and can be obtained at most college libraries.

The Released (2013)

A film about recidivism—presents the stories of four parolees released with no homes to go to or jobs for support. They ended up in a prisoner reentry facility in New York City known as "The Castle," run by former convicts and established by The Fortune Society.

Can be purchased or viewed at https://www.kanopystream ing.com/product/released-helping-prisoners-re-enter-societ.

Security Levels in Correctional Facilities (1997 American Correctional Association)

Discusses the three security levels—maximum, medium, and minimum security—and how classification assists facilities to meet their goals. Interviews with correctional staff illustrate how the security levels impact daily work and experiences. Perimeter security measures, restrictions on movement, external patrols, and monitoring strategies are also discussed.

Obtainable from American Correctional Association and from college libraries.

Shakedown at Santa Fe (1988 PBS Video)

Explains the mistreatment of inmates that led to a violent riot at the New Mexico State Penitentiary in February 1980. Interviews with inmates who lived through the riot, officers who worked there at the time, and current prisoners kept in segregation add to the narrative.

No longer available at shoppbs.org but obtainable from college libraries.

Three Strikes: Helpful or Hurtful (2004 Films for the Humanities and Sciences)

Questions have been raised about the effectiveness of "three strikes" laws in light of overcrowded prisons, judges with restricted discretion, and the lack of adequate treatment for drug offenders. This program investigates whether these laws are helpful or hurtful by highlighting one woman's case in California, and Alabama's attempt to cope with an escalating prison population.

Obtainable from college libraries.

Torture: America's Brutal Prisons (2005)

Visits correctional institutions in Texas, Florida, and California, uncovering penal systems with cultures of punishment, where prisoners are routinely abused by correctional officers. The film features videos recorded by prison surveillance cameras and by correctional officers themselves, supplemented by interviews with former prisoners, a warden, a prison doctor, inmates' relatives, attorneys and former correction officers who have broken the code of silence.

Available from college libraries. A production of U.K. Channel Four.

Turned Out: Sexual Assault behind Bars (2008)

Looks inside Alabama's Limestone Correctional Facility to uncover the long-term causes and consequences of prison rape. Five inmates reveal the workings of a subculture within the prison where men sell their bodies for bags of coffee or chips, and makeshift families are fabricated.

Can be rented or purchased at https://www.amazon.com/Turned-Out-Sexual-Assault-Behind/dp/B001E39XZA.

Visions of Abolition: From Critical Resistance to a New Way of Life (2012)

The abolition of prison is the focus of this two-part documentary, which gives a critical view of the current prison system from an abolitionist perspective. Breaking Down the Prison Industrial Complex, the first part, examines the racial and gendered violence of the prison system through the voices of two groups: women caught in the criminal justice system and leading scholars of prison abolition. Abolition: Past, Present, and Future, the second part, documents the recent history of the prison abolition movement.

Can be purchased at http://visionsofabolition.org/.

What I Want My Words to Do to You (2003 PBS Home Video)

The story of a writing group led by playwright and activist Eve Ensler at the Bedford Hills Correctional Facility for women in New York State. Ensler's classes have created a writing community in which women from radically different strata of society, all of whom are serving long sentences, help each other tell their stories.

Can be purchased at amazon.com and see the Web site for the film at http://www.pbs.org/pov/whatiwant/.

Women behind Bars: Life and Death in Indiana (2013 Films for the Humanities and Sciences)

The first of a two-part documentary on Indiana Women's Prison and The Indiana Rockville Correctional Facility.

Can be purchased at http://www.films.com/ecTitleDetail .aspx?TitleID=32491.

Young Criminals, Adult Punishment (1996 Films for the Humanities and Sciences)

As crimes committed by youngsters become progressively more violent, the criminal justice system must decide whether harsh sentences given out to adult criminals, including capital punishment, should also apply to violent young offenders. This film examines the issue through the eyes of young criminals; their families; and attorneys, prosecutors, and law enforcement officials.

Can be purchased at http://www.films.com/id/11804.

This chapter gives a chronological overview of major developments and events in the history of prisons in the United States.

1557 The first workhouse or house of correction is established in England in the old royal palace at Bridewell to confine the poor and vagrants but not convicted felons. Labor and discipline are the characteristics of the workhouse. Vagrants could be confined for terms ranging from weeks to years.

1635 The Boston jail opens and becomes the sole place of confinement in that city until 1776.

1713 Legislation in Connecticut calls for the creation of a house of corrections for "persons who wander about."

1726 John Howard, who was to become one of the foremost penal reformers of the age, is born. His survey of prisons in Europe and England, published in 1777, exposes the terror and disease associated with incarceration. Howard greatly influenced American reformers.

1764 Beccaria's *Essay on Crimes and Punishment* is published.

1773 Connecticut enacts a law authorizing the construction of a "Public Gaol or Workhouse" and mandating hard labor there as the sanction for six property crimes, including burglary and robbery.

An inmate at the Madera County Jail in California is taken to an inmate housing unit. (AP Photo/Rich Pedroncelli)

1776   The Constitution of the new state of Pennsylvania requires that corporal punishment be replaced with imprisonment. In England Jonas Hanway publishes *Solitude in Imprisonment*, claiming that solitude is the most humane and effective method of bringing offenders to a "right sense of their condition."

1779   For the first time, the term "penitentiary" appears in the English Penitentiary Act 1779, which mandates hard labor in prison in place of transportation and declares the purpose of punishment to be the reform of prisoners through the transformative power of work and discipline. It provides for the construction of two penitentiaries in London where inmates may be incarcerated for a maximum period of two years. During the day inmates will work in congregate labor and at night be imprisoned in solitary confinement. The act mandates in detail aspects of the penitentiary, including the site location, the nature of the construction, inmate diet and accommodation, work, management, and inspection. The penitentiaries were never built, but the act is seminal in its regulation of the prison.

1785   In New York State a bill applying only to the city of New York is passed, allowing corporal punishment to be replaced with hard labor in the workhouse for up to six months. The law refers to vagrants and "idle persons." In Boston, Castle Island, a fortress guarding Boston Harbor is designated as a place of confinement with hard labor for convicted criminals only, and the Massachusetts legislature revises the criminal code to allow judges to impose the punishment of long-term incarceration as an alternative to public punishments.

1786   Pennsylvania enacts the so-called Wheelbarrow Law, requiring Walnut Street Jail inmates to perform labor in public.

1787   The Philadelphia Society for Alleviating the Miseries of Public Prisons is created on May 8, 1787, with the aim of extending compassion to prisoners and preventing the infliction of illegal punishments. Alternative punishments to prison that would redeem inmates were also to be devised.

1790   The Walnut Street Jail, Philadelphia, built in 1773 as a county jail, is reconfigured as a penitentiary. The prison regime in this jail becomes known as the Pennsylvania system characterized by separate cells and solitary confinement for inmates. By 1815 the jail is overcrowded, and escapes and assaults on guards multiply. Prison reformers Thomas Eddy and John Schuyler of New York inspect the new prison regime and promote legislation to replace corporal punishment with incarceration for noncapital crimes and for the construction of two penitentiaries at Albany and New York City.

1791   Jeremy Bentham, an English prison reformer, publishes *Panopticon*, a term created by Bentham to describe a penitentiary based on the design of a factory built by his brother in Russia. The structural design allows prison guards to keep all prisoners under constant observation. Bentham believed this constant watching of inmates would inculcate the virtues of obedience, industry, and conformity.

1796   Virginia opens a state penitentiary.

1797   Newgate Prison in Greenwich Village, New York City, is constructed, but its small capacity makes it necessary to grant pardons to inmates each year to avoid overcrowding.

1798   Kentucky opens a state penitentiary.

1805   In Massachusetts, modern-style punishment is introduced, with all crimes punishable by fine, imprisonment, or the death penalty. Whipping, branding, and the stock and pillory are abolished. Massachusetts opens a new state prison at Charlestown, with capacity for 300 inmates. Prisoners are isolated at the commencement of sentence and then moved into shared cells. They perform hard labor from dawn to dusk.

1816   Legislation authorizes the construction of a penitentiary at Auburn, New York. The construction allows for congregate accommodation with double cells and rooms that can accommodate 10 or more prisoners. Insanity and sickness multiply among inmates in solitary confinement. This regime becomes known as the Auburn system.

1820   Most states have by now changed their criminal laws to replace the death penalty imposed for numerous crimes with imprisonment.

1823   The Eastern State Penitentiary, Cherry Hill, in Philadelphia, is established. Inmates are isolated and wear hoods when they exit their cells. Hard labor is considered a privilege or reward, and inmates seek any kind of work to replace their otherwise total inactivity.

1826   Western State Penitentiary, Philadelphia, is opened. The Boston Prison Discipline Society is created to promote penal reform in Massachusetts.

1828   A new prison is constructed in New York to replace Newgate Prison. It later becomes known as Sing Sing Prison and applies the Auburn penal regime. The prison cell block is five stories high and contains 1,000 cells only three feet three inches wide and seven feet long. The first warden of Sing Sing is Elam Lynds; he imposes strict discipline generally and orders all prisoners who refuse to work to be whipped.

1829   The Maryland and Massachusetts Penitentiaries are built.

1830   In New Jersey an investigation of state penitentiary conditions reveals that violations of prison rules are punished by strapping inmates to a plank and leaving them in that condition for up to 20 days.

1831   The competing prison regimes of Auburn and Pennsylvania are inspected by de Beaumont and de Tocqueville. They report that the Pennsylvania regime is more expensive to operate but the Auburn scheme is regarded as too difficult to administer. While both regimes achieve reform of inmates, they favor the Auburn model because it is more cost effective. Tennessee and Vermont construct penitentiaries.

1832   Penitentiaries are built in Georgia and New Hampshire.

1835   Legislation provides for construction of the first separate prison for women at Mount Pleasant, Ossining, New York, which begins to take prisoners in 1839.

1839   Missouri adopts the convict lease system: in return for an annual fee, the penitentiary is run by private enterprise, and they may use the convict labor for their private profit. The cost of the first lease is $30,000 for a five-year lease. The lease system ends in 1870 due to complaints that inmates are abused and insufficient revenue.

1842   When Charles Dickens visits Eastern Penitentiary, he writes of his shock of the inhumanity of the prison regime. In London, Pentonville Penitentiary is opened and becomes a model for prison architecture.

1845   The Prison Society of New York is established and advocates the Auburn model prison regime.

1849   In Virginia, the governor announces his opposition to housing black and white races together in the state penitentiary because it "makes the Negro insolent, and debases the white man." The issue is resolved by leasing black inmates to work for employers outside the penitentiary.

1850   By this year the penitentiary has been recognized as a failure because of corruption and debt. In the Southern states of Virginia, Tennessee, and Georgia, where prison industries have proved to be unprofitable, consideration is given to "privatizing" prisons by leasing them to private business.

1858   Virginia leases inmates to railroad and canal companies and sets the pattern for similar convict leasing schemes in the South.

1860   The "Irish" model of incarceration is introduced in the United States. It is regarded as superior to both the Auburn and Pennsylvania models. It reaches its zenith in the Elmira Reformatory.

1865   North and South Carolina finally build penitentiaries having until this time relied on whipping and painful shaming punishments.

1866   Reporting on conditions at the Pennsylvania Western Penitentiary, the Board of Inspectors finds that prisoners kept in solitary confinement and under conditions of total silence exhibit despair, acute loneliness, and depression.

1868   Convict leasing in Alabama results in the deaths of 17 percent of inmates, and by 1870 the rate has risen to 41 percent. By 1883 it is reported that most leased convicts die within three years.

1870   An important meeting of the American Prison Society held in Cincinnati declares that individualized care and scientific treatment based on a medical model will reform prisoners.

1875   Missouri adopts the contract system of labor under which the state contracts out inmate labor to private enterprise for a fee. By 1917 the state has prohibited the use of convict labor for profit by private enterprise.

1876   The Elmira Reformatory opens in New York State, modeled on the Irish system, housing first-time convicted felons aged between 16 and 30. To secure parole, an inmate must advance through ascending grades. Elmira is regarded as the most significant U.S. carceral institution during its "golden age" from 1883 to 1899.

1877   Florida and South Carolina abandon their state penitentiaries and turn to a convict leasing system. Other states expand leasing, leaving their prisons in a state of disrepair and housing a small number of white and black convicts.

1879   Virginia builds a penitentiary modeled on the Panopticon. New inmates undergo a period of solitary confinement of one-twelfth to one-half of their sentence.

1880   With the exception of Virginia, all states in the South are by now leasing out convicts to private enterprises.

1884   Massachusetts enacts the nation's first indeterminate sentencing law.

1890   The decline of the convict leasing system begins, as various factors render leasing convicts less profitable to private enterprises, but only Tennessee, North and South Carolina, and Louisiana abolish convict leasing before 1900.

1897 Construction begins of the first federal prison in Leavenworth, Kentucky, with 1,200 cells. Construction takes 30 years to complete.

1901 Louisiana ends convict leasing and replaces it with putting prisoners to work on state-owned plantations.

1902 A second federal prison is constructed in Atlanta.

1907 Indiana legislates that state prisons must add two surgeons to the prison staff to assess whether any prisoners should undergo forcible sterilization to prevent procreation and the supposed hereditary transmission of criminality.

1909 California legislates for the forcible sterilization of inmates with two convictions for sexual offenses, or three convictions for any crime or are serving a life sentence where there is evidence that the inmate is "a moral and sexual pervert."

1910 At Bedford Hills Reformatory for Women in New York, Katherine Bement Davis creates a program of testing to discover the causes of inmate's criminality. The testing includes comparing their physical characteristics with those of noncriminal women. The first federal Parole Law is enacted.

1913 A Pennsylvania law formally ends the operation of the Pennsylvania system at Eastern State Penitentiary, and inmates cease to be isolated.

1920 By this time only Florida and Alabama continue to lease out convicts, and working inmates on state farms has replaced convict leasing in the South.

1924 In the Nevada State Prison, Gee Jon, a Chinese national, becomes the first prisoner to be executed by lethal gas.

1928 The first federal prison for women is constructed at Alderson, West Virginia, using the cottage plan with no surrounding fence.

1929 The Federal Prisons Bureau is created and declares that rehabilitation is the principal objective of incarceration, putting a new focus on treatment that results in rehabilitation.

1934   The federal prison at Alcatraz is designated a prison of last resort for the most "vicious and irredeemable" convicts who have no hope of rehabilitation. Inmates for Alcatraz are selected from other federal prisons and have virtually no privileges or contact with the outside.

1936   The last public hanging in the United States in Kentucky draws a crowd of 10,000.

1942   The U.S. Supreme Court strikes down legislation that permits the forced sterilization of inmates as a violation of the equal protection clause.

1946   The practice of flogging inmates at the state prison farm at Angola Prison, Louisiana, is revealed, but floggings continue into the 1950s.

1954   The American Prison Association changes its name to the American Correctional Association, proclaims offender rehabilitation its mandate, and asks its members to designate prisons as "correctional institutions."

1960   Chain gangs are no longer to be found in the South.

1963   Alcatraz prison closes. Its replacement as a prison of last resort is the federal prison at Marion, Illinois.

1967   Following the discovery of brutal working conditions in Georgia labor camps where inmates break rocks while chained together and break their own legs to escape the labor, the labor camps are abolished.

1972   The "War on Drugs" begins; over the next 40 years, it is the principal contributor to the prison explosion, prison overcrowding, and the construction of numerous new prisons.

1974   Following the publication of a study of prison rehabilitation programs, some scholars declare that "nothing works" and that with few exceptions efforts to rehabilitate have had no appreciable effect on recidivism.

1975   States move from indeterminate sentencing with parole to determinate sentencing.

1976   After striking down death penalty laws in 1972 in *Furman v. Georgia*, the U.S. Supreme Court in *Gregg v. Georgia* now determines that several recent death statutes meet constitutional requirements.

1986 The American Bar Association declares that private prisons are inconsistent with the Constitution on the basis that incarcerating persons is a function of the government and should not be transferred to private enterprise.

1989 By this time privatization of prisons has become an established policy in many states.

1995 Alabama announces that it will reintroduce chain gangs; this is challenged in court and after one year the state ends the practice.

1996 By this time the war on drugs has fueled an increase in the prison population: in 1985 drug offenders made up 34.3 percent of the federal prison population, but by 1995 this has increased to 60.8 percent and by 1996 to 72 percent. The No Frills Prison Act is passed, banning televisions, certain movies, and weightlifting equipment in the cells in federal prisons.

1997 By this time about half the states and the federal government have enacted mandatory minimum penalty laws.

1998 After a court case against New York State that lasted 26 years, Frank Smith, one of the leaders of the Attica Prison uprising in 1971, is awarded $4 million compensation by a federal jury based on claims that he was beaten and tortured by prison guards and state police even after the riot was brought under control.

1999 The number of female prisoners increases by 4.4 percent compared with an increase of 3.3 percent for male prisoners. At midyear 1.2 million inmates are being held in state and federal prisons. Twenty-nine state and federal prisons are built in this year.

2000 In February, a conflict at Pelican Bay supermax prison in California between 200 black and Latino inmates results in a hail of gunfire, with guards killing 1 inmate and wounding 16 others. A further 32 inmates have stab and slash wounds. Guards found

88 weapons that include knives manufactured out of pieces of metal and a toothbrush that had been sharpened.

2001   Because of a shortage of correctional officers, Kansas reduces the age requirement for recruits from 21 to 19 years, and Alabama reduces its age requirement to 20 years. Oklahoma considers an age reduction to 18 years after losing 57 percent of its recruits from year 2000.

2002   In an attempt to limit rising HIV and hepatitis C infection rates and to reduce recidivism, federal prisons commence offering methadone maintenance treatment to any prisoner with an opiate addiction.

2003   At year-end, 1.47 million persons are incarcerated in state and federal prisons. About 1 in every 109 men and 1 in every 1,613 women are sentenced prisoners. The Prison Rape Elimination Act provides for the analysis of the incidence and effects of prison rape, and for information, resources, recommendations, and funding to protect individuals from prison rape.

2004   In this year 1.8 percent of inmates are found to be HIV positive, more than four times the estimated rate in the general population. In January inmates in a northern Oklahoma prison are locked down in their cells after complaining about a new low-fat healthy menu by boycotting the cafeteria.

2006   A report commissioned by the U.S. Department of Justice concerning the effectiveness of federal supermax prisons finds that while such prisons address a need for the effective and safe management of prison populations, their effectiveness is problematic and that empirical research is greatly needed, along with rigorous benefit–cost studies that include reasonable estimates of both benefits and costs.

2007   A survey of tobacco use in prisons finds that 60 percent of corrections systems imposed total tobacco bans, with the others imposing an indoor ban. No prisons distribute free tobacco, but bans resulted in tobacco becoming a major item of contraband.

2008   A report by the Pew Charitable Trusts finds that over the previous 20 years in the Northeast, spending on corrections increased by 61 percent and spending on higher education dropped by 6 percent. In the West, spending on prisons increased by 205 percent and higher education spending rose by 28 percent.

2009   In August a federal court orders California to reduce its prison population to no more than 137.5 percent of the design capacity in prisons operated in the state. The court finds that overcrowding was the principal cause of the state being unable to provide prisoners with adequate health care as required by the Constitution. The U.S. Supreme Court later upholds this decision.

2013   At year-end 2013 about 1.5 million persons are being held in custody in state and federal prisons, giving an incarceration rate of 478 per 100,000. Private prisons hold about 8 percent of the total prison population, with the Federal Bureau of Prisons accounting for 31 percent of all inmates housed in private prisons at this time. Almost 3 percent of black males are imprisoned at year-end compared to 0.5 percent of white males.

2014   On December 31, 2014, 131,261 inmates are held in private prisons making up 8.4 percent of the total inmate population in the country, and about 40,000 of those prisoners are serving sentences for federal crimes comprising 19 percent of federal prisoners.

Administrative segregation   The conditions of confinement, including isolation, of prisoners categorized by a prison administration as escape risks, gang members, predators, high risk, and terrorists.

Auburn system   A type of prison regime that lasted from about 1830 to 1870 that featured a rule of silence, inmates occupying individual cells, and prisoners working together, again in total silence, in what came to be known as the congregate system. The Auburn system was less expensive to operate than the competing Pennsylvania system and was therefore adopted by most states.

Cell extraction   The forcible and often violent removal of an inmate from his or her cell when the inmate has refused to exit the cell when required to do so. Officers are trained to conduct extractions in teams wearing protective clothing.

Conjugal visits   Conjugal or family visits are a privilege afforded to inmates in the low-risk category in only a few states. They are justified as a means of reducing tension and violence in prisons but are opposed by some as granting a privilege that is inconsistent with the punishment of incarceration. Generally, families are allowed to be with the inmates for several days and nights in accommodation separate from the actual prison but within its perimeter. Some correctional systems supply condoms, while others require that a spouse provide them on each visit.

Determinate sentence   A sentence of imprisonment imposed for a fixed period of time so that a prisoner always knows his or her release date.

Deterrence   The theory that punishments should aim to prevent a criminal from reoffending (individual deterrence) and prevent others from engaging in criminal acts (general deterrence).

Eugenics movement   A social movement that began in the 1870s and ended about 1925 that argued criminality was associated with inferior genes and therefore criminality could best be reduced by not allowing criminals to reproduce. The theory was especially influential in women's reformatories where it was used to justify extended sentences so that women would not be able to reproduce.

Incapacitation   The theory that offenders should be physically removed from society through incarceration for lengthy periods of time as a punishment for an offense so that they cannot commit further offenses. The theory disregards rehabilitation and takes no account of the need to reduce or prevent recidivism.

Indeterminate sentence   The opposite of a determinate sentence. Under this sentencing model a prisoner is sentenced to a minimum and maximum period of incarceration and does not know his or her release date which is determined by a parole board.

Panopticon   Describes a model of the "ideal prison" designed by Englishman Jeremy Bentham in which all inmates in that prison would be under constant surveillance but could not observe those guarding them.

Parole   Originated in combination with indeterminate sentencing and provided for a prisoner serving such a sentence to be released on parole when a parole board considered the prisoner had been rehabilitated and could show a history of good behavior in prison. Release under parole is conditional because the released person has to comply with parole conditions and can be returned to prison if those conditions are violated.

Penitentiary   Drawn from the British Penitentiary Act 1779, this term describes a specific type of prison characterized by high forbidding walls of stone, very strict discipline, and a rigorous regime of incarceration.

Pennsylvania system   The competing prison regime to the Auburn system that also enforced a rule of silence but allowed prisoners to work only in their cells and therefore kept them totally isolated from other inmates. This required high expenditure on cells which had to be larger and have their own attached exercise yards.

Principle of less eligibility   A principle first expounded in England in the 1834 Poor Law that a person in a workhouse who was receiving government aid because of poverty should not enjoy conditions of living that were more attractive than the poorest laborer outside the workhouse. As now applied to prisons, the principle has been used to deny certain benefits to inmates such as weightlifting equipment, televisions, coffeepots, and hot plates in the cells of federal prisoners. It also prohibits computers, electronic instruments, and certain movies rated above PG under the federal No Frills Prison Act 1996.

Prisonization   A term used to describe the impact and effect of incarceration on an inmate.

Recidivism   The return to criminality of an offender following his or her conviction and punishment for a criminal offense. Recidivism is estimated to be between 40 percent and 80 percent of released offenders. Most recently, more attention has been given to recidivism as correctional systems have adopted "reentry programs" that try to prevent its occurrence by offering programs to inmates close to release.

Retribution   The theory that offenders deserve to be punished. Retributionists regard punishment as justified because it imposes accountability and responsibility for criminal acts that have violated societal rules.

Shank   A prison-made weapon that functions as a knife. It may include a cloth strap, enabling the shank to be wrapped around the wrist so it cannot be taken away when used for attacking or defending oneself.

Shot-caller   A term used by inmates to describe an inmate who is a member of a prison gang who is appointed by the gang to manage its business interests within the prison and to meet with new incoming inmates to identify their background and probable gang affiliation.

Supermax (super-maximum security prison)   A federal or state prison or prison unit with the highest-security classification intended to accommodate "the worst of the worst." Such prisons isolate inmates in extreme conditions that include being locked down in a cell for 23 hours a day with little or no human contact and no congregate activity. Supermax prisons may be separate institutions or units within regular prisons described as control units, administrative maximum prisons or penitentiaries, intensive housing units, intensive management units, maxi–maxi units, maximum control facilities, restrictive housing units, secured housing units, or special housing units.

About the Author

Cyndi Banks is associate vice president of Student Success at Capilano University in Vancouver Canada and emeritus professor of criminology and criminal justice. She was previously dean of University College at Northern Arizona University and chair of the Department of Criminology and Criminal Justice at Northern Arizona University. She is internationally recognized for her work as a criminologist in the Asia/Pacific region, Bangladesh, Myanmar, Iraq, Sudan, East Timor, and Iraqi Kurdistan in international children's rights, juvenile justice reform, and rule of law policy. She has published widely on international, comparative and cultural criminology, international children's rights, women in prison, punishment in America, indigenous incarceration, and criminal justice ethics. She has authored nine books including *Criminal Justice Ethics*, 4th edition (Sage); *Youth, Crime and Justice* (Routledge); and, with co-author James Baker, *Comparative, International and Global Justice: Perspectives from Criminology and Criminal Justice* (Sage).